ROSS PAUL BRUNER is a managing director at the Istituto Mobiliarc Italiano (IMI) Group. Previously, he was a vice president of global equity strategy at ABN AMRO Hoare Govet and a portfolio strategist at Dean Witter Reynolds. He holds a B.A. in history from Rutgers College and an M.S. in investment management from the Lubin School of Business. Mr. Bruner is a Greenwich- and Extel-rated strategist and was contributing author of *Quantitative Investing for the Global Markets*. He is registered as a supervisory analyst with the New York Stock Exchange and as a principal with the National Association of Securities Dealers

ADVANCED APPROACHES TO STOCK SELECTION

Edited by
Ross Paul Bruner

VISION BOOKS
(Incorporating Orient Paperbacks)
New Delhi • Mumbai • Hyderabad

ISBN 81-7094-572-0

This Indian Sub-continent Edition Published in agreement with
The Glenlake Publishing Company Ltd., USA
by
Vision Books Pvt. Ltd.
24 Feroze Gandhi Road, Lajpat Nagar III,
New Delhi-110024 (India)
Phone: (+91-11) 2983 6470
Fax: (+91-11) 2983 6490
E-mail: visionbk@vsnl.com

Printed at
Rashtra Rachna Printers
C-88, Ganesh Nagar, Pandav Nagar Complex,
Delhi-110092 (India).

For Alexandra,
my partner and friend.

CONTENTS

Contributors ix

Preface xv

1. Growth-at-a-Reasonable-Price 1
   Ross Paul Bruner

2. Investing in the 21st Century 27
   Stephen R. Waite

3. Economic Value Added (EVA) 43
   Vincent van Doorn

4. Enterprise Value/Sales Beats Price/Sales and Price/Earnings in a Three-Way Model Race 53
   Melissa R. Brown

5. Normalized Value 75
   Ross Paul Bruner

6. Sector and Style Rotation: A Valuation Approach 107
   Michael F. Wilcox and Dan Fox

7. Enhanced Index Portfolio Construction Using Full Covariance Optimization for a Small-Capitalization Portfolio 125
   Bernard V. Tew

8. Multifactor Equity Models 139
   Herbert Blank

Index 161

CONTRIBUTORS

Herbert Blank

Herbert Blank is a quantitative Consultant for Worldscope. Previously, he served as the Chief Investment Officer and Senior Portfolio Manager of the CountryBaskets Index Fund, Inc. In addition to managing all CountryBaskets portfolios, Mr. Blank directed all research and development activities and served as Chairman of the CountryBaskets Research Round Table. In that capacity, he also served as a Director of Deutsche Morgan Grenfell, the global investment arm of Deutsche Bank. Mr. Blank frequently writes articles for national publications and speaks at conferences on his areas of expertise. These include global asset allocation, indexation, and quantitative analysis.

Mr. Blank has 16 years of experience in quantitative research and investment management. Prior to joining Deutsche Morgan Grenfell in 1994, he served as Value Line's Director of Quantitative Research and Asset Management for five years. He also worked alongside Dr. Stephen Ross to create the first APT-based asset management product. He holds an MBA in finance from NYU Stern School of Business and a B.A. in Mathematics from the University of Pennsylvania.

Melissa R. Brown

Melissa Brown is a Managing Director and the Director of Quantitative Research for Prudential Securities in New York. She has been with the firm since 1982 and has held various positions within the quantitative research and investment strategy departments. Since 1985, her primary function has been to research, develop, and deliver stock valuation analysis and ratings, as well as to provide an overall quantitative market perspective. A member of the firm's Investment Policy Committee, Ms. Brown has appeared on *Institutional Investor* Magazine's "All-Star" list each year since 1988.

Outside of Prudential Securities, Ms. Brown is a former sub-chairperson of the Institute of Chartered Financial Analysts' Candidate Curriculum Committee and is currently a member of the Chicago

Quantitative Alliance. She has appeared on *Wall Street Week* and *The Nightly Business Report,* and is a frequent guest on CNBC and CNN. And, outside of the financial world, she is an avid scuba diver and underwater photographer.

Prior to joining Prudential Securities, Ms. Brown was a financial analyst with Nabisco Brands in 1981 and 1982, and a technical consultant for Interactive Data Corp. from 1979 to 1981. A Chartered Financial Analyst (1987), she received a B.S. in Economics from the Wharton School of the University of Pennsylvania in 1979 and an M.B.A. in Finance from New York University in 1984.

Ross Paul Bruner

Ross Paul Bruner is a managing director at the Istituto Mobiliare Italiano (IMI) Group. Previously, he was a vice president of global equity strategy at ABN AMRO Hoare Govett and a portfolio strategist at Dean Witter Reynolds. He holds a B.A. in history from Rutgers College and an M.S. in investment management from the Lubin School of Business. Mr. Bruner is a Greenwich- and Extel-rated strategist and was contributing author of "Quantitative Investing for the Global Markets" (Glenlake Publishing). He is registered as a supervisory analyst with the New York Stock Exchange and as a principal with the National Association of Securities Dealers.

Dan Fox

Dan Fox is currently a member of the asset management division of Morgan Stanley. His responsibilities there include the management and trading of global equity portfolios. Prior to joining the asset management group, he worked on the brokerage side of the house, providing analytical support for the trading desks. His research experience encompasses such topics as hedging techniques and asset valuation.

Before joining Morgan Stanley in 1985, Mr. Fox worked for TIAA/CREF in the equity department. His duties there involved developing models to analyze and execute trading and portfolio management strategies in both active and passive funds. He was the portfolio manager for small-cap equity funds.

Mr. Fox's previous experience ranged from econometric model building at Wharton Econometrics to owning and managing small businesses in California and Alaska. He was educated at the Wharton School of the University of Pennsylvania, where he received an M.B.A. in 1982. His studies were concentrated in the Ph.D. curriculum in econometrics. He received his undergraduate degree from the University of California at Berkeley in 1972 and is a graduate of the Choate School.

Bernard V. Tew

Dr. Bernard Tew is a Founding Principal and Chairman of Q.E.D. Investments, LLC. He has developed a wide range of mathematically based quantitative equity products designed to outperform passive equity benchmarks, such as the S&P 500 or the RUSSELL2000 indices. Dr. Tew's expertise is in portfolio theory and applications, linear and nonlinear mathematical programming applications, Baysian statistical implementations, and general operations research modeling. He earned a B.S. in general science and business from Purdue University in 1975, an M.B.A. from Indiana University in 1978, and a Ph.D. in applied economics from the University of Georgia in 1984. Prior to the formation of Q.E.D., Dr. Tew was a principal of Weiss, Peck, and Greer LLC. from July 1991 through March 1997. He was a founding member of the Quantitative Equity Division of that firm, where he was responsible for the design, formation, and management of the quantitative equity portfolios. During his tenure, assets under management grew from zero to more than $1.3 billion. Dr. Tew also has held positions as the Co-Director of Research, Eden Financial Corp., and as a faculty member in the departments of finance and economics at the University of Kentucky and Colorado State University. Dr. Tew is a member of the American Economic Association, the American Finance Association, the Eastern, Midwest, and Southern Finance Associations, and several Operations Research Associations. He has published several articles in national and international finance and economic journals.

Vincent Frank van Doorn

Vincent Frank van Doorn earned a M.B.A. at the school of organization at the University of Groningen in The Netherlands. After earning his

M.B.A., he worked for Anderson Consulting in The Hague as a management consultant for two and half years before joining ABN AMRO Hoare Govett as a sales and research account manager. He works currently at Paribas in New York in the same capacity. Mr. van Doorn enjoys ocean sailing and racing J-24 in the New York Harbor.

Stephen Waite

Stephen Waite is a portfolio manager and global strategist with BEA Associates in New York. He shares responsibility for stock selection, asset allocation, and quantitative analysis. Prior to joining BEA, he was Vice President and Senior European Economist for Merrill Lynch & Co. in London, with responsibility for the firm's European economic and financial market research and forecasts. Before joining Merrill Lynch in May 1992, Mr. Waite was an economic consultant to Capital Group in Los Angeles and a Vice President with the International Capital Access Group.

Mr. Waite began his career on Wall Street in 1986 as an economist with Morgan Stanley & Co., after working as Associate Economist at Comerica Bank, Inc., in Detroit. He is the author of several published studies on corporate finance and financial markets. Mr. Waite earned a M.A. in Economics from Pennsylvania State University, and a B.S. in Economics from Central Michigan University.

Michael F. Wilcox

Michael F. Wilcox, CFA, founder and CEO of Alford Associates, has more than 25 years of investment management experience. During that time, he has developed investment research and management solutions for major institutions in Harford, New York, and Boston. Immediately before founding Alford Associates in 1992, he was an International Equity Portfolio Manager and the head of Global Asset Allocation at State Street Global Advisers in Boston. Prior to that, he spent 10 years in the Wall Street environment, the last five as head of Quantitative Research in the Equity Research Department at Morgan Stanley. Wilcox holds a M.S. degree in Economics from Trinity College in Hartford. He became a CFA in 1981 and a registered securities agent in 1982.

Mr. Wilcox is an active member of several professional groups, including two popular monthly discussion groups established in Boston and New York. He has served as an advisor to the Board of Directors of INQUIRE Europe and as a member of its program committee. He is an internationally recognized authority on quantitative investment methods and speaks frequently at international investment conferences. Mr. Wilcox is a specialist in the areas of asset allocation and currency management, and has broad experience in the valuation and trading of all types of securities and derivatives.

Mr. Wilcox is also editor of a publication of the Center for Retirement Research called *Thrift Savings Investment Quarterly*. This newsletter, oriented toward federal employees who are members of the federal government's Thrift Savings Plan, offers advice on financial planning for retirement and on proper fund allocation.

PREFACE

"Analytical Approaches To Stock Selection" provides practical illustrations for enhancing the selection process through the use of quantitative management tools. Fundamentally based investment strategies organized around growth, value, size and sector rotation are examined from a number of different perspectives by the contributors. Price-momentum strategies such as covariance and factor analysis are also explored, illustrating the view that outperformance comes from a variety of different approaches. It turns out that having a framework is as important as the focus of the framework itself; consistency adds value almost by definition, but not all strategies are created equal. This research breaks new ground in thinking about the selection process in more robust ways and from a number of different perspectives.

The book begins by thinking about growth in the context of cost (Growth-at-a-Reasonable-Price), using a low-P/E-to-consistent-growth-rate strategy on a contemporaneous selection universe of American shares over the last 26 years. In essence, it represents an effort to bring the principles of value investing to the process of selecting growth stocks; the strategy adds value in part by reducing the dividend yield shortfall typical of high-growth investment strategies. The second chapter, by Steve Waite of BEA Associates, focuses on the differences between investing in the machine age compared with the information age and the implications for Investing in the 21st Century. Some of the key differences include: zero sum versus positive sum, physical capital versus human capital, and diminishing returns versus increasing returns. In chapter three, Vincent van Doorn, of Paribas Capital Markets, begins the coverage of value strategies by examining an Economic Value Added (EVA) discounted cash flow valuation of Heineken NV. Next, Melissa Brown, of Prudential Securities, develops a broader study of value strategies focusing on enterprise value-to-sales, price-to-sales and price-to-earnings. Over the period 1978-1996, her study of the 1,000 largest stocks in America indicates that enterprise value-to-sales is the best measure of value; debt-adjusted market capitalization penalizes companies that use leverage without generating commensurate increases in unit volume to warrant the extra risk. In chapter five, quality is put in the context of cost (return on equity / price-to-book), effectively normalizing value for companies which produce high returns at the expense of stockholders' equity. Next, Rosemary Macedo, of Bailard, Biehl & Kaiser, looks at continental European small stocks with a view toward understanding whether small stocks outperform large stocks, and if there are beneficial effects in terms of diversification or active stock selection. Next, Michael Wilcox and Dan Fox, of Alford Associates, examine valuation tools such as price-to-earnings and price-to-book for sector and style rotation, respectively, and conclude that it is possible to add value across each dimension. In chapter eight, Bernard Tew, of QED Investments, describes his portfolio construction techniques using full covariance optimization for a small-capitalization portfolio. Dr. Tew's real results since 1993 illustrate that purely price-based statistical construction techniques also add value over time, in much the same way as more fundamentally-oriented approaches. In conclusion, Herbert Blank, of QED International, describes different kinds of multifactor equity models, beginning with simple scoring systems, continuing on to fundamental factor regression, and concluding with a discussion of orthogonal factors and risk management systems.

Finally, I would like express my gratitude to Carlo Corradini, Benedetto Marti, and Stefano Mazzola from the IMI Group for their continuing support of the Global Strategy & Management product, and for the invaluable assistance provided by Barbara Craig, Robert Klein, and Janet Sullivan that made this book possible.

Growth-at-a-Reasonable-Price

Ross Paul Bruner
Managing Director
Istituto Mobiliare Italiano (IMI) Group

Overview

Find Value in Growth

Growth-at-a-reasonable-price (GARP) is based on the notion that cost is as important as quality in selecting individual shares. In essence, it represents an effort to bring the principles of value investing to the process of selecting growth stocks. Given the historical total return shortfall of growth investing since 1970 (-11%), we think such an approach is not only helpful but essential to consistently outperform market benchmarks such as the S&P 500 (see Figure 1.1). In this chapter, we focus on P/E-to-growth (price-to-earnings/consistent earnings growth) as one measure of identifying undervalued growth stocks. As with value strategies in general, extreme valuation can often be a proxy for risk.

Growth Underperforms in the Long Term

The total return underperformance ot growth over the 70s, 80s, and first half of the 90s is striking, given the significant outperformance in capital appreciation over the same period (see Figure 1.2). Over our 26-year contemporaneous study, growth underperformed the market by 11% in total

Figure 1.1

Figure 1.2

return, but outperformed the S&P 500 by 23% in terms of capital appreciation. We think this suggests that growth investing is not appropriate for a purely passive implementation. In our view, this return disparity validates one of the fundamental principles of value investing; i.e., that cost and quality both matter. Value (measured by price-to-book ratio), by contrast, outperformed the market by 144% in total return over the whole period and by 42% in terms of capital appreciation (see Figures 1.3 and 1.4). Most of the outperformance, however, was generated during 1974-1976 and 1981-1983, which we think implies some difficulty with respect

Figure 1.3

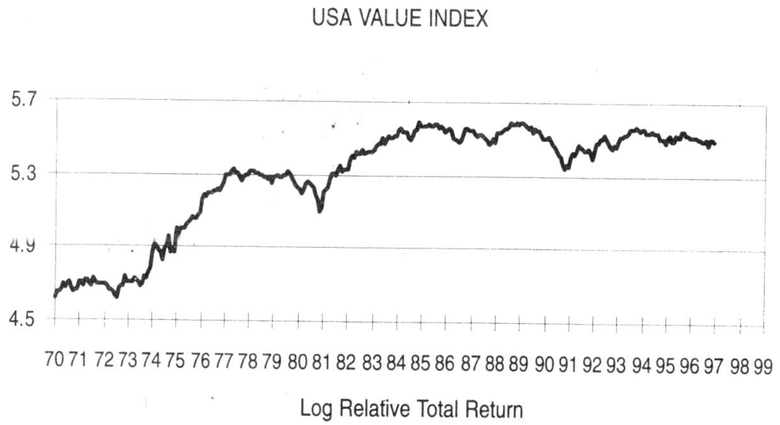

Figure 1.4

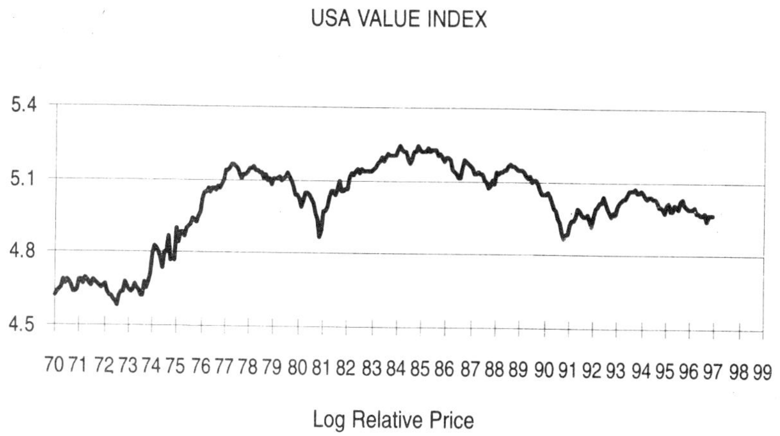

to a purely value-based approach as well. Our equal-weighted low-P/E-to-growth strategy outperformed our value strategy by 244% in relative total return over the period 1970-1996 (see Figure 1.5).

Figure 1.5

P/E-To-Growth Adds Value

Over the 26 years of our study, P/E-to-growth added value in four out of five quintiles (all except the high-P/E-to-growth quintile) on an equal- and capitalization-weighted basis (see Figures 1.6 through 1.14). We ranked a contemporaneous universe of growth stocks by trailing P/E multiple divided by EPS (earnings per share) growth in order to evaluate cost relative to growth. We believe the equal- and cap-weighted excess relative total returns across quintiles two through five demonstrate the effectiveness of P/E-to-growth and suggest that, as with value strategies in general, extreme valuation is often a proxy for risk. In other words, stocks that trade at extremely high valuations to EPS growth are inherently riskier investments, although extreme undervaluation can also be associated with higher risk. For this reason, we use quantitative tools to support an active management process.

Figure 1.6

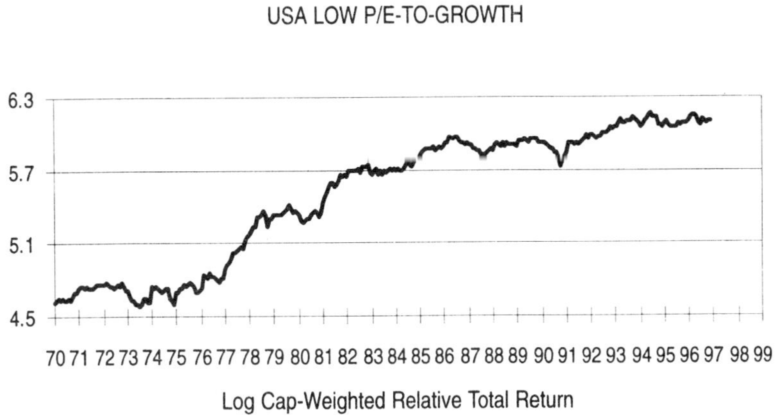

Figure 1.7

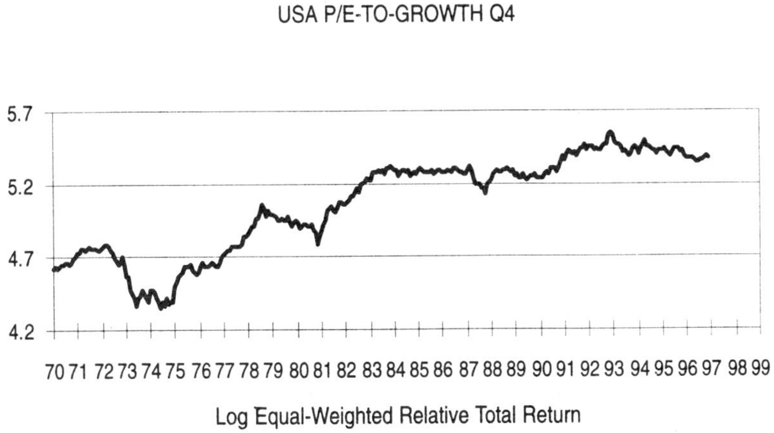

Figure 1.8

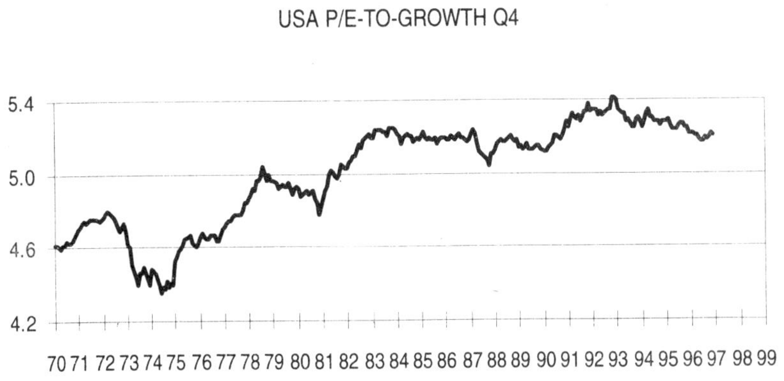

Log Cap-Weighted Relative Total Return

Figure 1.9

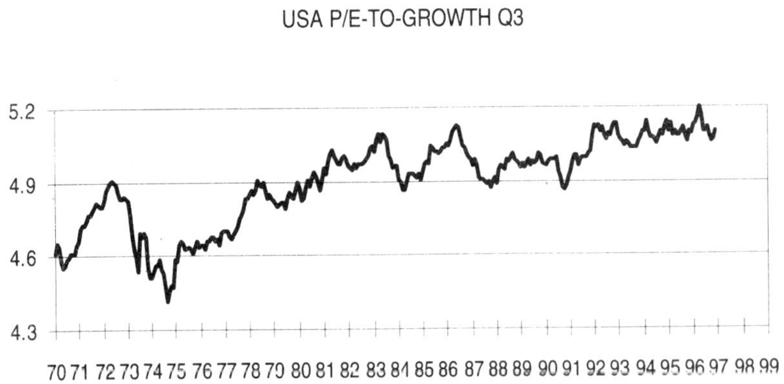

Log Equal-Weighted Relative Total Return

Figure 1.10

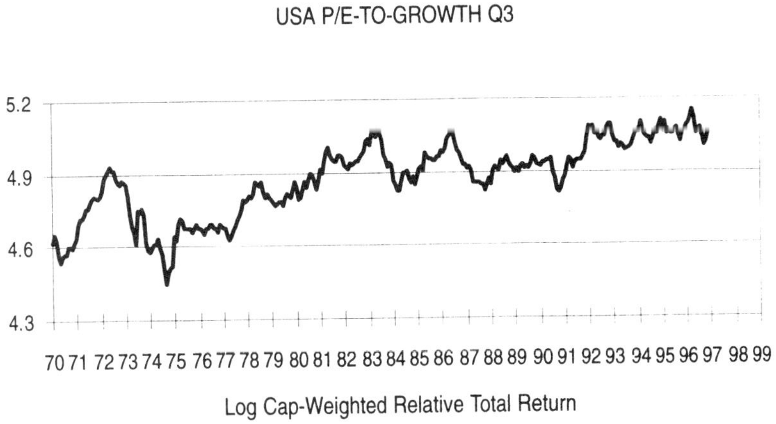

Figure 1.11

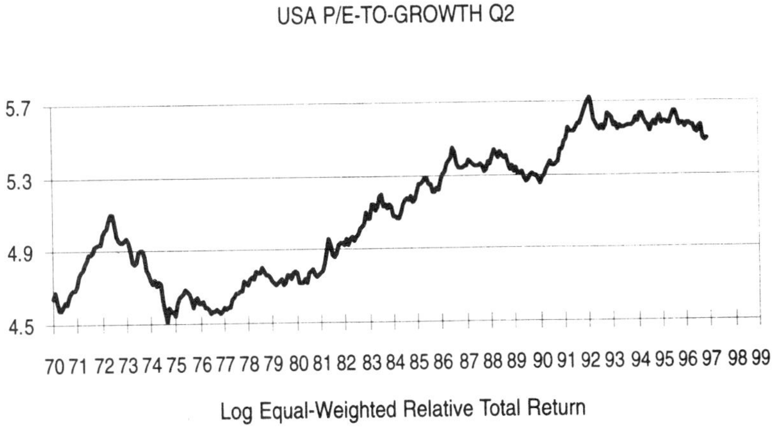

Figure 1.12

Figure 1.13

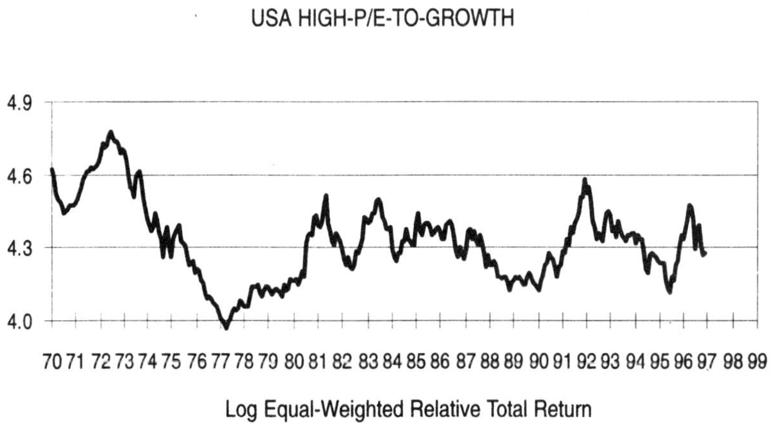

Figure 1.14

Methodology

P/E-to-Consistent-EPS-Growth

We rank our consistent-growth universe of 100 stocks by trailing P/E ratio divided by three-year consistent EPS growth. We adjust for consistency by dividing by the standard deviation in order to purge cyclical companies from the composition of our growth universe. Dividing the EPS growth rate by the standard deviation reduces the consistent growth rate for cyclical shares across the EPS cycle. It also reflects the fact that investors value consistency.

Controlling Turnover

We control turnover by using an annual selection process that results in turnover ranging from 60% to 90%. Because we define growth in terms of financial characteristics, the natural rate of turnover is slower than for value strategies, which we define in terms of price. Growth is, at best, a quarterly strategy, while value strategies can be run as frequently as daily. Our value benchmarks are created from an annual price-to-book ranking of the largest 500 companies on a contemporaneous basis. P/E-to-growth extends the frequency of growth investing to a monthly or even daily basis.

Dividends Matter Over Time

The underperformance of growth in total return (-11%) compared with outperformance in capital appreciation (23%) illustrates the fact that dividends matter over time. A dividend stream is far less volatile than a capital-appreciation stream and thus benefits from the effect of consistency on the compounding process. This is not to say that investors should avoid high-growth, high-P/E, and zero-yield shares, but rather that buying growth stocks successfully over time requires some of the same skills as value investing. Often stocks that score well on a P/E-to-growth basis pay dividends but are not necessarily the highest growth stories in the market. In fact, our low-P/E-to-growth strategy typically pays 95% (see Figure 1.15) of the market dividend yield (3.6% versus 3.8% over the last 26 years). We believe this is the reason why P/E-to-growth investing adds value over time.

Figure 1.15

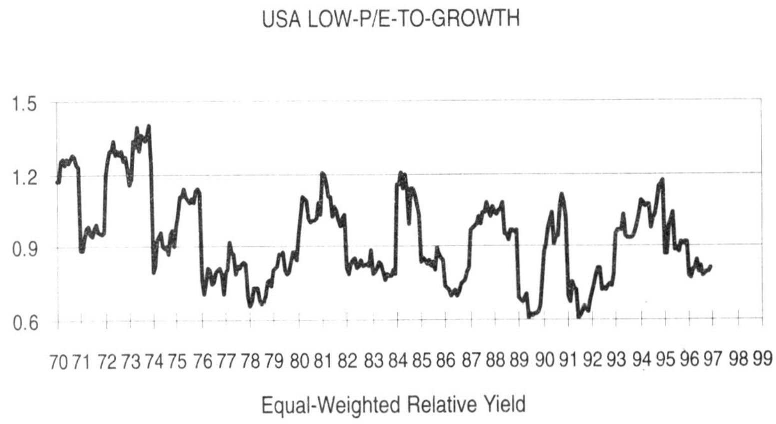

Small-Capitalization Effects

The process of equal-weighting positions introduces a small-capitalization bias into portfolio returns. In our view, the small-capitalization effect exists because there are structural limits to growth. Truly superior growth does not continue forever, largely because at some point a stock becomes the whole sector, market or economy. By putting the growth rate in context of cost (expressed by the P/E multiple), P/E-to-growth strategies can take advantage of larger and more mature shares, which often pay significant dividends.

Construction

Equal- Versus Capitalization-Weighting

Equal-weighting company exposure reduces company-specific risk and introduces a small-capitalization effect into portfolio returns. The results of our P/E-to-growth study confirm our previous experience that equal-weighted strategies outperform capitalization-weighted strategies. Equal-weighting exposure, however, implies that a portfolio overweight with respect to sectors can be constructed only if there are a large number of companies available to choose from. We integrate risk management into the construction process by controlling company-specific risk through an equal-weighting discipline. Equal-weighting company exposure ensures that one position does not determine the performance of the entire portfolio. It also reduces the upside benefit from a single decision. As long-term investors, we are comfortable with the implications of such an approach.

Contemporaneous Selection

Our 26-year growth, P/E-to-growth, and value strategies are each developed from a contemporaneous selection universe, which means that we focus on what a fund manager could have owned rather than on companies that have survived over time. We believe this to be an effective way of dealing with the issue of "survivor bias," although it has been our experience that current composition strategies can yield largely the same results and have a compelling rationale as well. For example, a fund manager implementing a strategy today is more concerned with today's selection possibilities than those of the past. In essence, the fact that some companies survive over time is just as significant to a fund manager as the fact that others do not. When we find strategies that work under a variety of different scenarios or methods, we feel more comfortable with the effectiveness of the process.

Annual Recomposition

We recalculate the composition of our growth, P/E-to-growth, and value strategies on an annual basis with the information that was available at the time of selection. Annual rebalancing using lagged data ensures that performance results are achievable (i.e., relatively low turnover) and fair given the information that was available at the time. In practice, we use the preceding year's financial data so that the portfolio simulation is inherently a process that can be replicated going forward. It is our experience that increasing the rebalancing frequency to a monthly basis produces approximately the same rate of turnover per month and does not work particularly well outside the American equity market.

Total Return Versus Price Change

We think the return shortfall of growth (-11%) measured by relative total return makes a strong case for putting growth in the context of cost (measured by the P/E ratio). Stocks trading at a significant discount to consistent growth often pay a significant dividend. In fact, our P/E-to-growth strategy typically yields 69% more than growth stocks in general. We believe the total return shortfall of growth results from the fact that the highest-growth companies pay little or no dividend, which puts a "pure" growth manager at a significant disadvantage over time. In short, to capture the price-appreciation potential of growth stocks in portfolio total returns, a growth manager must seek out dividend yield.

Results

Performance, Valuation, and Composition

Stocks at the top of our P/E-to-growth ranking are trading at extreme valuations relative to growth and have already been "discovered." High-P/E-to-growth shares underperformed significantly on an equal- and capitalization-weighted basis (-28% and -21%, respectively). The second-quintile results were very strong, however, outperforming the market on an equal- and capitalization-weighted basis (142% and 140%, respectively). Third-quintile results were also strong on an equal- and capitalization-weighted basis (65% and 57%, respectively). Fourth-quintile performance was a bit better than the third on an equal- and capitalization-weighted basis (117% and 82%, respectively). The results for the second, third, and fourth quintiles are consistent with dozens of value studies we have developed across markets where extremely high valuation is often a proxy for risk. In other words, we view this nonlinear return distribution as a kind of "sweet spot" that begins at the second quintile and extends to the low-P/E-to-growth quintile. As we expected, the fifth-quintile results were significantly better than the other groups on an equal- and capitalization-weighted basis (379% and 350%, respectively).

The foregoing performance results illustrate the effect of dividends on total return over time. Over the 26 years in our study, the high P/E-to-growth quintile averaged a 1.0% dividend yield, compared with 1.6% for second quintile, 2.1% for the third quintile, 2.9% for the fourth quintile, 3.6% for the low P/E-to-growth quintile, and 3.8% for the S&P 500 (see Figures 1.16 through 1.19 on pages 14 and 15). We believe this is why the low-P/E-to-growth strategy outperformed the market and the high-P/E-to-growth strategy did not. Currently, the high-P/E-to-growth quintile has a dividend yield of 0.3%, compared with 0.8% for the second quintile, 0.9% for the third, 1.9% for the fourth, 1.7% for the low-P/E-to-growth quintile, and 2.0% for the S&P 500. In short: reduce the yield differential versus the market and then enhance the relative growth of the portfolio.

Figure 1.16

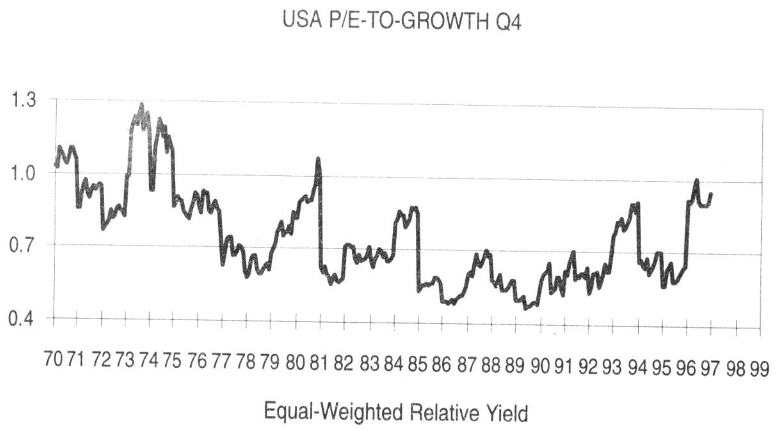

Figure 1.17

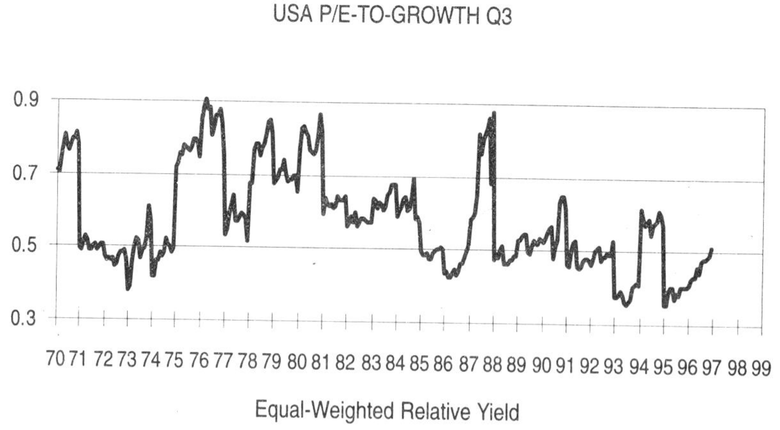

Figure 1.18

Figure 1.19

The composition of our high-P/E-to-growth and low-P/E-to-growth strategies illustrates the fact that we placed no size restriction on the selection process. The impact of size has very little effect on the efficacy of our P/E-to-growth strategy, which is evidenced not only in the congruence between the equal- and cap-weighted results but also in the pattern of the excess return. In other words, because the cap-weighted total returns confirm the equal-weighted results and value can be added in quintiles two through five, the strategy can be employed on a portfolio of any size. For example, in 1970, Mobil ($4,669 million), Amoco ($3,320 million), USX-Marathon ($1,076 million), American Electric Power ($1,792 million), and Occidental Petroleum ($1,255 million) were the five largest stocks in the low-P/E-to-growth quintile (see Table 1.1 on pages 18 and 19). In 1980, Boeing ($3,249 million), TRW ($1,136 million), Providian ($560 million), US LIFE ($515 million), and Overseas Shipbuilding ($447 million) were the largest names in the low-P/E-to-growth quintile (see Table 1.2 on pages 20 and 21). In 1990, American Home Products ($16,799 million), McDonalds ($12,489 million), Emerson Electric ($8,697 million), Raytheon ($4,561 million), Mercantile Bankshares ($1,479 million), and Hubbell ($1,225 million) were the largest stocks (see Table 1.3 on pages 22 and 23). In 1995, Schering-Plough ($13,765 million), AFLAC ($3,188 million), Fifth Third Bancorp ($3,106 million), Jefferson Pilot ($2,513 million), and Republic New York ($2,381 million) were the largest shares in our low-P/E-to-growth strategy (see Table 1.4 on pages 24 and 25).

Conclusion

P/E-to-Growth Reflects Risk

The results of our 26-year study illustrate the relationship between P/E-to-consistent-growth and risk. The high P/E-to-growth quintile trades at a 20% discount to growth and underperformed significantly on an equal- and capitalization-weighted basis (-28% and -21%, respectively). The second quintile trades at a 50% discount to growth but outperformed significantly on an equal- and capitalization-weighted basis (142% and 140%, respectively), illustrating our concept of a "sweet spot" beginning at the second quintile and moving through to the low-P/E-to-growth quintile. Remember, we adjust EPS growth for consistency, which has the effect of raising growth rates for companies with consistently high growth. We have seen this nonlinear return distribution in dozens of other value strategies we have developed across markets. The third quintile trades at a 60% discount to consistent growth and outperformed on an equal- and capitalization-weighted basis (65% and 57%, respectively). The fourth quintile trades at a 70% discount and also outperformed on an equal- and capitalization-weighted basis (117% and 82%, respectively). The fifth quintile trades at an 80% discount to consistent growth and outperformed on an equal- and capitalization-weighted basis (379% and 350%, respectively). In short, avoid only the most highly valued shares relative to growth and search for dividend yield within the "sweet spot."

Table 1.1 USA P/E-to-Growth 1970

		Market Cap $	1-Year % Chg	1-Year Return	P/E LTM	P/B LTM	DY LTM	EPS CGR	P/E / CGR
	HIGH-P/E-TO-GROWTH								
BCR	BARD (C.R.) INC	210	-14.9	-14.4	57.3	6.6	0.5	18.5	309.8
JNJ	JOHNSON & JOHNSON	3,288	-5.0	-4.4	47.2	8.5	0.5	20.2	234.1
NLC	NALCO CHEMICAL CO	647	-34.8	-33.7	43.0	8.7	1.1	19.1	225.6
AUD	AUTOMATIC DATA PROCESSING	197	8.8	8.8	na	na	0.0	39.8	191.2
MXM2	MAXXAM GROUP INC	384	12.2	13.3	41.5	8.5	0.9	22.5	184.4
BDX	BECTON DICKINSON & CO	928	-34.0	-33.5	57.4	7.7	0.5	31.8	180.6
HMT	HOST MARRIOTT CORP	458	-20.5	-20.5	46.8	5.9	0.0	26.6	176.0
AVP	AVON PRODUCTS	4,936	3.2	4.7	58.5	na	1.0	33.9	172.5
ABT	ABBOTT LABORATORIES	1,032	-1.3	0.3	29.7	4.7	1.4	18.2	162.9
PKN	PERKIN-ELMER CORP	29[illegible]	-31.5	-31.3	39.0	4.7	0.0	24.4	159.8
LZ	LUBRIZOL CORP	624	20.6	21.9	34.9	6.7	1.0	22.2	157.1
DNB	DUN & BRADSTREET CORP	61	-10.5	-7.9	28.5	6.0	2.3	18.2	156.9
XRX	XEROX CORP	8,23[illegible]	-18.2	-17.6	50.8	10.8	0.6	33.7	150.7
BAX	BAXTER INTERNATIONAL INC	804	-12.7	-12.3	59.3	7.8	0.3	39.7	149.2
UIS	UNISYS CORP	2,712	-30.6	-30.2	47.4	6.5	0.4	31.8	148.9
BMY	BRISTOL MYERS SQUIBB	2,184	-14.7	-12.9	34.1	8.1	1.6	23.2	146.7
IBM	INTL BUSINESS MACHINES CORP	41,450	-12.8	-11.4	44.4	7.9	1.1	30.7	144.7
KM	K MART CORP	1,886	6.7	7.6	34.2	6.7	0.7	25.2	135.5
ROL	ROLLINS INC	307	-28.9	-28.4	33.3	12.5	0.5	24.7	134.9
3RNGR	RANGER INDUSTRIES	64	14.2	14.8	30.9	7.4	0.4	23.0	134.1
	AVERAGE	3,56[illegible]	-10.2	-9.3	43.1	7.5	0.7	26.4	172.8

continued on next page

		Market Cap $	1-Year % Chg	1-Year Return	P/E LTM	P/B LTM	DY LTM	EPS CGR	P/E / CGR
	LOW-P/E-TO-GROWTH								
ATE	ATLANTIC ENERGY INC	180	8.7	15.6	11.7	1.6	6.2	29.5	39.9
NSC1	NORFOLK SOUTHERN RAILWAY VA	316	35.6	44.3	7.3	0.4	6.5	18.8	39.0
MAYS	MAYS (J.W.) INC	45	5.6	8.4	12.9	2.6	2.2	33.1	38.9
K	KELLOGG CO	737	17.1	22.4	16.6	3.3	3.9	43.0	38.6
NSI	NATIONAL SERVICE INDS INC	227	23.8	28.2	15.2	2.7	3.3	39.5	38.4
FSR	FIRSTAR CORP	129	8.7	13.8	8.9	1.1	4.8	24.9	35.6
PSD	PUGET SOUND ENERGY INC	126	0.9	7.5	11.1	1.0	6.1	31.2	35.6
OXY	OCCIDENTAL PETROLEUM CORP	1,255	-23.3	-19.0	8.1	4.6	4.1	24.2	33.5
AEP	AMERICAN ELECTRIC POWER	1,792	-5.4	0.4	13.7	2.0	5.4	42.0	32.6
AOS	SMITH (A O) CORP	109	8.0	12.3	7.5	0.8	3.2	25.2	29.9
NVP	NEVADA POWER CO	81	4.3	7.8	14.5	1.8	2.9	49.4	29.5
MRO	USX-MARATHON GROUP	1,076	1.0	6.7	12.0	1.5	4.5	44.6	26.9
RGS	ROCHESTER GAS & ELECTRIC	191	3.5	8.8	10.7	1.3	4.6	40.1	26.7
AN	AMOCO CORP	3,320	9.6	15.6	10.6	1.0	4.8	41.2	25.7
MOB	MOBIL CORP	4,669	25.0	31.9	10.2	1.1	4.8	39.9	25.6
CCK	CROWN CORK & SEAL CO INC	354	5.8	5.8	15.4	2.1	0.0	61.6	25.0
3EPIHQ	EAGLE-PICHER INDS	115	-2.9	0.7	11.0	1.6	3.1	47.0	23.3
NOC	NORTHROP GRUMMAN CORP	169	-33.8	-30.9	9.1	1.3	2.8	40.9	22.2
CX	CENTERIOR ENERGY CORP	442	20.5	28.8	11.1	1.6	3.3	59.7	18.6
CX2	CLEVELAND ELECTRIC ILLUM	442	20.5	28.8	11.1	1.6	3.3	59.7	18.6
	AVERAGE	789	6.7	11.9	11.4	1.7	4.3	39.8	30.2

Source: Compustat & IMI estimates

Table 1.2 USA P/E-to-Growth 1980

		Market Cap $	1-Year % Chg	1-Year Return	P/E LTM	P/B LTM	DY LTM	EPS CGR	P/E / CGR
	HIGH-P/E-TO-GROWTH								
SFA	SCIENTIFIC-ATLANTA INC	186	106.2	107.2	17.5	3.2	0.5	44.2	39.7
BEC	BECKMAN INSTRUMENTS INC	572	26.1	27.5	16.2	2.8	1.1	42.2	38.3
WANG	WANG LABS INC	350	143.9	144.8	22.8	6.9	0.5	60.3	37.8
EGG	EG&G INC	323	78.5	80.8	15.6	3.1	1.2	42.7	36.5
CVN	COMPUTERVISION CORP	287	273.1	273.1	17.3	6.5	0.0	47.8	36.1
ADI	ANALOG DEVICES	111	100.3	100.3	15.7	3.3	0.0	44.3	35.5
DPT	DATAPOINT CORP	430	129.3	129.3	16.4	3.3	0.0	46.8	35.0
EDS	ELECTRONIC DATA SYSTEMS COR	368	22.0	26.8	13.9	3.0	3.7	42.2	32.8
DNB	DUN & BRADSTREET CORP	1 216	29.9	35.3	13.8	3.6	4.0	43.2	31.8
VIA.B	VIACOM INC -CL B	148	45.7	46.9	15.2	2.5	0.8	48.9	31.2
SLB	SCHLUMBERGER LTD	11 916	87.2	89.2	18.1	5.0	1.2	58.2	31.1
WMT	WAL-MART STORES	525	74.1	75.8	14.9	5.2	0.9	49.4	30.1
PLL	PALL CORP	259	100.0	102.3	16.4	4.7	1.2	56.6	29.0
JNJ	JOHNSON & JOHNSON	4 851	25.9	29.4	13.8	2.4	2.5	47.5	29.0
FLK	FLUKE CORP	126	20.9	20.9	13.1	2.9	0.0	45.4	28.9
THY	TRANSITIONAL HOSPITALS CP	91	56.6	59.5	14.4	3.4	2.0	50.2	28.7
DIS	DISNEY (WALT) COMPANY	1 450	14.2	16.1	12.0	1.5	1.6	42.1	28.5
AMP	AMP INC	1 448	28.9	32.0	12.0	3.0	1.9	42.7	28.1
TFX	TELEFLEX INC	43	46.9	49.1	11.7	2.2	1.3	41.8	28.0
IFF	INTL FLAVORS & FRAGRANCES	719	15.9	20.9	11.7	2.5	4.1	43.3	27.0
	AVERAGE	1 296	71.3	73.4	15.1	3.6	1.4	47.0	32.2

continued on next page

		Market Cap $	1-Year % Chg	1-Year Return	P/E LTM	P/B LTM	DY LTM	EPS CGR	P/E / CGR
	LOW-P/E-TO-GROWTH								
BA	BOEING CO	3,249	30.7	35.7	6.4	1.8	4.7	52.9	12.1
FDO	FAMILY DOLLAR STORES	51	21.6	25.7	6.5	1.6	3.1	53.8	12.1
CCK	CROWN CORK & SEAL CO INC	437	-2.6	-2.6	6.3	0.9	0.0	52.3	12.0
BOR	BORG-WARNER SECURITY CP	747	19.2	26.9	4.9	0.7	6.4	42.4	11.7
PVN	PROVIDIAN CORP	560	-10.1	-4.6	6.7	0.9	4.7	57.6	11.6
CSL	CARLISLE COS INC	109	246.4	256.2	5.9	1.3	3.7	52.6	11.3
HMX	HARTMARX CORP	100	20.0	29.3	4.8	0.5	7.4	43.8	11.1
RIGS	RIGGS NATL CORP WASH D C	109	32.9	42.7	5.0	0.7	7.7	45.5	11.0
SMI	SPRINGS INDUSTRIES -CL A	163	-7.3	-0.1	4.7	0.5	6.4	42.9	11.0
FLT	FLEET FINANCIAL GROUP INC	107	12.1	22.5	4.5	0.7	9.1	42.1	10.7
OSG	OVERSEAS SHIPHOLDING GROUP	447	63.0	65.8	6.8	1.3	1.3	64.2	10.6
BZ	BAIRNCO CORP	55	14.5	18.0	5.4	0.8	3.2	52.3	10.3
STB	STAR BANC CORP	126	-15.2	-7.4	5.6	0.8	7.1	54.7	10.2
USH	USLIFE CORP	515	4.8	8.4	6.2	0.9	2.9	61.4	10.0
FTU	FIRST UNION CORP (N C)	98	22.1	30.3	4.2	0.6	6.8	41.7	10.0
ONE	BANC ONE CORP	173	30.0	38.2	5.8	0.9	6.0	58.3	9.9
TRW	TRW INC	1,136	58.0	65.5	6.3	1.2	5.2	63.8	9.9
3FMDB	FIRST MARYLAND BANCORP	91	1.8	9.0	4.9	0.8	5.8	52.2	9.4
RGBK	REGIONS FINL CORP	108	35.5	44.6	4.8	0.8	6.9	53.7	9.0
ABM	ABM INDUSTRIES INC	30	7.8	13.4	6.5	0.8	4.8	72.1	9.0
	AVERAGE	421	29.3	35.9	5.6	0.9	5.2	53.0	10.6

Source: Compustat & IMI estimates

Table 1.3 USA P/E-to-Growth 1990

		Market Cap $	1-Year % Chg	1-Year Return	P/E LTM	P/B LTM	DY LTM	EPS CGR	P/E / CGR
	HIGH-P/E-TO-GROWTH								
TSS	TOTAL SYSTEM SERVICES INC	429	20.4	21.4	38.0	8.4	1.0	42.2	90.1
CDN	CADENCE DESIGN SYS INC	608	12.4	12.4	25.0	5.4	0.0	37.6	66.5
FRX	FOREST LABORATORIES -CL A	804	18.8	18.8	30.6	3.8	0.0	46.2	66.1
MSFT	MICROSOFT CORP	4,844	73.0	73.0	23.8	6.6	0.0	36.7	64.7
DP	DIAGNOSTIC PRODUCTS CORP	403	-0.7	0.0	28.1	5.7	0.7	43.6	64.5
FDLNA	FOOD LION INC -CL A	3,502	20.7	22.0	25.3	6.5	0.9	41.8	60.5
HACH	HACH CO	120	-19.4	-18.7	24.4	3.7	0.6	42.4	57.5
AIR	AAR CORP	578	-68.1	-67.2	21.6	3.2	1.3	38.1	56.6
SIAL	SIGMA-ALDRICH	1,430	1.7	2.4	22.3	4.8	0.7	39.4	56.5
BLUD	IMMUCOR INC	39	87.5	87.5	22.7	1.8	0.0	41.6	54.6
WMT	WAL-MART STORES	25,398	34.8	35.5	26.1	7.1	0.5	48.8	53.4
SNDT	SUNGARD DATA SYSTEMS INC	324	-52.6	-52.6	19.5	2.8	0.0	38.1	51.1
SJM.A	SMUCKER (JM) CO -CL A	536	27.3	29.4	18.4	3.4	1.4	36.1	51.0
STJ	ST JUDE MEDICAL INC	1,127	43.0	43.0	22.5	6.1	0.0	44.6	50.5
GKSRA	G&K SERVICES INC -CL A	181	-18.5	-17.8	19.4	2.8	0.7	40.1	48.3
TMO	THERMO ELECTRON CORP	600	-5.7	-5.7	23.0	2.7	0.0	48.3	47.6
ACN	ACUSON CORP	731	27.7	27.7	20.0	5.0	0.0	43.0	46.6
INTV	INTERVOICE INC	149	-71.8	-71.8	20.6	2.9	0.0	44.9	46.0
BMET	BIOMET INC	764	37.3	37.3	29.9	6.9	0.0	65.1	45.9
NLC	NALCO CHEMICAL CO	1,787	14.1	17.5	16.4	4.0	3.0	35.9	45.8
	AVERAGE	2,218	9.1	9.7	23.9	4.7	0.6	42.7	56.2

continued on next page

	LOW-P/E-TO-GROWTH	Market Cap $	1-Year % Chg	1-Year Return	P/E LTM	P/B LTM	DY LTM	EPS CGR	P/E / CGR
PMS	POLICY MANAGEMENT SYSTEMS C	656	22.1	22.1	21.3	2.3	0.0	77.3	27.5
MCD	MCDONALDS CORP	12,489	-15.6	-14.6	17.7	3.5	0.9	65.7	26.9
AHP	AMERICAN HOME PRODUCTS CORP	16,799	-2.1	2.2	15.2	8.5	3.6	57.0	26.7
TFX	TELEFLEX INC	339	4.8	6.6	12.8	2.1	1.5	48.2	26.6
SGC	SUPERIOR SURGICAL MFG	68	32.1	34.8	9.7	1.5	2.0	37.6	25.9
MRBK	MERCANTILE BANKSHARES CORP	1,479	-19.0	-15.5	11.1	3.4	3.2	43.1	25.7
EMR	EMERSON ELECTRIC CO	8,697	-3.2	0.8	14.7	2.8	3.2	58.2	25.2
HUB.B	HUBBELL INC -CL B	1,225	1.8	5.4	15.7	2.9	3.0	62.3	25.1
WILM	WILMINGTON TRUST CORP	671	6.0	10.2	11.3	2.6	3.3	47.2	23.9
CNK	CROMPTON & KNOWLES CORP	36	11.4	13.8	15.4	3.7	2.0	64.2	23.9
RTN	RAYTHEON CO	4,561	0.9	4.6	8.7	1.9	3.2	36.9	23.5
RXL	REXEL INC	222	-56.2	-55.6	12.5	2.0	0.6	53.6	23.3
IFSIA	INTERFACE INC -CL A	305	45.1	-44.1	12.4	1.9	1.4	53.3	23.3
DAPN	DAUPHIN DEPOSIT CORP	40	13.9	-9.6	9.2	1.4	4.5	44.3	20.8
SOTR	SOUTHTRUST CORP	617	29.7	-25.4	8.3	1.2	4.2	46.7	17.9
SRCE	1ST SOURCE CORP	79	-13.1	-10.8	7.6	1.0	2.1	44.1	17.3
CFBS	CENTRAL FIDELITY BANKS INC	475	-13.8	-9.0	8.7	1.3	4.0	51.4	17.0
HIB	HIBERNIA CORP -CL A	598	-69.9	-67.7	9.6	1.5	4.2	59.4	16.1
PCH	POTLATCH CORP	1,061	-21.1	-18.3	7.7	1.3	3.3	48.8	15.7
KBH	KAUFMAN & BROAD HOME	377	-32.1	-29.8	5.6	2.0	2.2	50.7	11.0
	AVERAGE	2,575	-14.6	-11.5	10.9	2.4	2.9	50.0	21.6

Source: Compustat & IMI estimates

Table 1.4 USA P/E-to-Growth 1995

		Market Cap $	1-Year % Chg	1-Year Return	P/E LTM	P/B LTM	DY LTM	EPS CGR	P/E / CGR
	IGH-P/E-TO-GROWTH								
ESRX	EXPRESS SCRIPTS INC -CL A	542	38.8	38.8	43.8	10.3	0.0	41.1	106.3
FAST	FASTENAL CO	775	106.7	106.9	41.7	11.5	0.1	45.4	91.9
MEDA	MEDAPHIS CORP	698	59.1	59.1	43.5	3.1	0.0	47.5	91.4
TSS	TOTAL SYSTEM SERVICES INC	1,707	78.1	78.9	48.9	9.0	0.5	57.0	85.8
HD	HOME DEPOT INC	20,[illegible]01	3.8	4.3	36.8	6.3	0.3	50.7	72.6
OXHP	OXFORD HEALTH PLANS INC	1,262	86.4	86.4	49.5	9.9	0.0	70.9	69.8
PMTC	PARAMETRIC TECHNOLOGY CORP	1,976	92.8	92.8	28.8	7.4	0.0	43.3	66.3
HS	HEALTHSOURCE INC	1,279	76.1	76.1	33.0	4.0	0.0	49.9	66.0
CVTY	COVENTRY CORPORATION	695	-15.8	-15.8	26.3	5.3	0.0	42.1	62.5
DG	DOLLAR GENERAL	1,598	-13.5	-12.9	26.1	5.6	0.7	43.6	59.9
PAYX	PAYCHEX INC	1,212	84.7	86.2	36.5	9.9	0.9	64.7	56.4
ROTC	ROTECH MEDICAL CORP	275	-3.5	-3.5	26.9	3.1	0.0	48.6	55.3
MCRS	MICROS SYSTEMS INC	296	30.5	30.5	28.0	6.4	0.0	51.2	54.6
PHSYB	PACIFICARE HEALTH SYS -CL	1,321	31.8	31.8	20.6	4.2	0.0	41.0	50.2
TMO	THERMO ELECTRON CORP	2,288	73.8	73.8	22.1	2.3	0.0	44.2	50.0
UNH	UNITED HEALTHCARE CORP	7,799	44.9	45.0	27.5	2.8	0.1	57.0	48.3
CRVL	CORVEL CORP	117	37.4	37.4	22.6	3.5	0.0	46.9	48.1
SYY	SYSCO CORP	4,699	26.2	28.1	20.0	3.6	1.4	41.6	48.0
SMED	SHARED MEDICAL SYSTEMS CORP	751	66.0	69.4	21.7	3.4	2.6	45.5	47.7
FDC	FIRST DATA CORP	5,100	41.2	41.4	25.3	5.0	0.3	53.8	47.1
	AVERAGE	2,755	47.3	47.7	31.5	5.8	0.3	49.3	63.9

continued on next page

		Market Cap $	1-Year % Chg	1-Year Return	P/E LTM	P/B LTM	DY LTM	EPS CGR	P/E / CGR
	LOW-P/E-TO-GROWTH								
SGP	SCHERING-PLOUGH	13,765	48.0	51.7	15.3	8.7	2.8	62.1	24.6
MFN	MERCURY FINANCE CO	1,485	52.9	55.8	17.6	6.5	2.5	71.6	24.5
RLC	ROLLINS TRUCK LEASING	544	-6.3	-4.9	13.2	2.1	1.3	54.5	24.2
JP	JEFFERSON-PILOT CORP	2,513	34.5	38.7	11.0	1.5	3.3	46.9	23.4
AHL	AMERICAN HERITAGE LIFE INVS	265	19.6	23.9	11.2	1.5	3.5	48.3	23.2
SAI	SUNAMERICA INC	1,311	96.6	99.0	9.8	2.2	1.7	42.6	23.0
NCBC	NATIONAL COMM BANCORP/TN	558	15.4	18.6	12.9	2.5	3.0	57.2	22.5
CBSH	COMMERCE BANCSHARES INC	906	48.7	51.9	9.5	1.2	2.4	43.0	22.1
WEN	WENDY'S INTERNATIONAL INC	1,463	47.8	49.8	15.5	2.1	1.7	70.1	22.0
NTRS	NORTHERN TRUST CORP	1,893	60.0	64.0	11.0	1.7	3.0	51.4	21.5
MTG	MGIC INVESTMENT CORP/WI	1,934	63.8	64.3	12.3	2.3	0.5	57.5	21.3
FMBC	FIRST MICHIGAN BANK CORP	405	24.0	27.8	12.7	1.9	3.2	65.4	19.4
STB	STAR BANC CORP	1,084	63.6	68.9	9.4	1.5	3.8	48.4	19.3
BGG	BRIGGS & STRATTON	947	32.4	46.0	8.4	2.2	3.1	44.2	19.0
FITB	FIFTH THIRD BANCORP	3,106	52.6	56.4	12.6	2.2	2.6	66.4	19.0
CBSS	COMPASS BANCSHARES INC	834	50.0	55.8	8.3	1.4	4.2	46.1	18.0
AFL	AFLAC INC	3,188	35.9	37.6	11.3	1.8	1.4	63.2	17.8
PHH	PHH CORP	595	34.5	37.6	9.0	1.1	3.7	55.0	16.4
SOTR	SOUTHTRUST CORP	1,466	42.4	47.4	8.4	1.3	3.8	51.2	16.3
RNB	REPUBLIC NEW YORK CORP	2,381	37.3	40.9	7.8	1.2	2.9	52.4	14.9
	AVERAGE	2,032	42.7	46.6	11.3	2.4	2.7	54.9	20.6

Source: Compustat & IMI estimates

CHAPTER 2

Investing in the 21st Century

Stephen R. Waite*
Vice President
BEA Associates

"Many a false step is made by standing still."

Chinese Proverb

The tools and techniques used by today's active equity portfolio managers vary widely depending on the process or discipline employed. These tools and techniques range from qualitative assessments of corporate management to quantitative techniques that incorporate the latest advances in the field of artificial intelligence.

Despite the proliferation of valuation tools and techniques over the past 100 years, many active equity managers apparently are still struggling to justify their *raison d'être*. Witness the numerous articles in the popular financial press trumpeting the merits of passive or indexed-based investing. The case for passive investing in the United States has gained credence over the past two years, as a majority (approximately 80%) of equity managers underperformed the S&P 500 index during the 1995-96 period. This has been true overseas as well. U.K. portfolio managers, for example, have underperformed their respective benchmarks by an average of 30 basis points per year—a margin that roughly reflects the costs of active management.

What accounts for the recent disappointing performance of active managers? There are several possible explanations. Some analysts believe that the extraordinarily high, risk-adjusted excess returns on the S&P 500 index over the past two years are the root cause of underperfor-

*The author would like to thank James Abate, Ross Bruner and Steve Gibson for their helpful comments.

mance. These analysts argue that it is difficult for active managers to beat the market when the returns on the benchmark are far above normal. Others, mainly proponents of passive investing, believe that the high level of efficiency in developed equity markets is the primary reason for this underperformance—a rationale consistent with modern portfolio theory.

Whatever the reason, it is intriguing to note that the disappointing performance record of active managers coincides with the growing importance of the information technology sector in the global economy and the lack of credible valuation tools and techniques that can help active managers capture the high returns associated with this sector. During the 1995-96 period, many U.S. equity fund managers underweighted technology stocks, citing "high" valuations, only to see the market capitalizations of several prominent information technology companies soar amid explosive growth in global demand for information technology.[1]

The high excess returns on the S&P 500 index in recent years is associated in part with the returns on several large information technology stocks that are pioneers in their respective sectors. Consider the fact that over the period 1995-96, the price returns on three such pioneering companies—Microsoft, Intel, and Cisco Systems—were 171%, 309%, and 262%, respectively, relative to the 61% gain on the S&P 500 index. Of course, passive managers automatically retained a neutral weighting in these information technology stocks.[2] In hindsight, this put them at an advantage over active managers who underweighted these stocks in their portfolios. Some may argue that 1995-96 was an unusual period. This is not the case. Over the period 1990-95, three of the top five value-creating industries were in the information technology sector—computer software and services ($61 billion), semiconductors ($31 billion), and electronics ($29 billion).[3]

It can be argued that the rapid pace of change in the global economy and the concomitant rise of information technology's importance in the global economy are creating new market inefficiencies. The lack of cred-

---

[1] As was well documented in the financial press, the nation's biggest fund, Fidelity Magellan, sold a big share of its technology stocks during 1995. Other active managers apparently followed a similar strategy.

[2] Currently, Microsoft, Intel, and Cisco Systems collectively account for 4.6% of the total market capitalization of the S&P 500.

[3] Value created or market value added (MVA), as it is commonly known, is the difference between market capitalization and invested capital. See Steven Milunovich and Albert Tsuei, "EVA in the Computer Industry," Journal of Applied Corporate Finance, Spring 1996, pp. 106-7.

ible valuation tools and techniques to gauge valuations in the information technology sector—not to mention a fundamental lack of understanding of the evolving new technologies—are sources of market inefficiency. Active portfolio managers who develop better tools and techniques to capture the high returns associated with technology stocks can exploit these market inefficiencies.

Portfolio Management in the Information Age

Information technology is one of the most dynamic and fastest-growing sectors in the United States and global economies. As Figure 2.1 shows, the share of spending on information technology relative to spending on all producers' durable equipment has risen dramatically over the past 25 years. Today, spending on information technology represents over 40% of all durable equipment spending, up from just over 5% in 1970 (note that these figures do not include spending on software). The technology sector today comprises nearly 15% of the S&P 500 index—a figure that is almost certainly destined to rise in the years ahead, along with the evolution of the Internet and the World Wide Web. According to a recent survey, the number of hosts connected to the Internet rose 70% in 1996 to 16.1 million, far above the roughly 5% per annum growth rate in U.S. nominal GDP.[4]

Figure 2.1 US Information Technology Spending ($ billions)

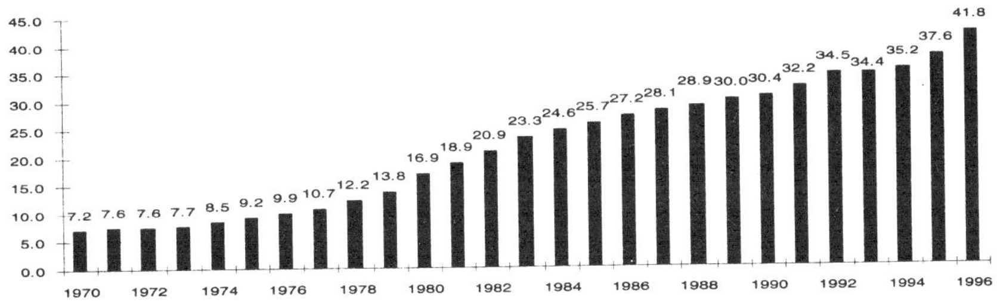

Source: WEFA

[4] See the Network Wizards home page at http://www.nw.com for more information including historical statistics on the growth of the Internet. For a wide range of thoughts on the future of the computer in the 21st century, see: Peter Denning and Robert Metcalfe. 1997. Beyond Calculation: The Next Fifty Years of Computing, Springer-Verlag, New York.

As we approach the 21st century, active portfolio managers may also want to keep a close eye on developments in the emerging biotechnology sector—an industry that is likely to grow rapidly in the next millennium. The advances in the field of biotechnology today are breathtaking and are being driven in part by the proliferation of new information technologies. Consider the emerging biochip industry. Biochips allow medical researchers to analyze genes in a manner heretofore unthinkable.[5] The implications of such advances for medicine and healthcare are staggering. Moreover, these advances are occurring at a point in time when the demographics of the developed world are pointing toward explosive growth in the demand for healthcare in the early part of the 21st century. There are many similarities between information- and bio-technology companies—similarities explored in more detail below.

Technology and healthcare currently account for 25%—one-quarter—of the total capitalization of the S&P 500. It is likely that these sectors will grow in importance in the 21st century, not only in the United States but globally as well. Clearly, the consequences of not understanding the evolving structure of the global economy and the investment environment are enormous.

It is our ignorance about the future that lies at the heart of the debate over active versus passive fund management. Unfortunately, portfolio managers today may not be well equipped to make informed, sound investment decisions regarding companies in the information- and biotechnology sectors. Curiously, many active portfolio managers today appear to use the same valuation yardsticks to analyze companies in the information technology sector as they do companies in traditional manufacturing or service industries. This may be misguided. The economics of these industries are fundamentally different in many respects relative to the industries that have dominated the U.S. and global economies over the past century.

To the extent the information- and bio-technology sectors capture a large and growing share of the S&P 500 index or some other benchmark index in the future, active portfolio managers should have the appropriate tools and techniques to gauge valuation in these sectors. In sum, new valuation tools and techniques are needed, befitting the Information Age as opposed to the Machine Age.[6]

---

[5] See, for example, David Stipp, "Gene Chip Breakthrough," Fortune, March 31, 1997, pp. 56-73.

[6] The term "Information Age" encompasses both information- and bio-technology. While there may be a more appropriate description of the 21st century (e.g., the "Cyber Age"), the term is used here merely to distinguish the next century from the 20th-century "Machine Age" or "Industrial Age."

New Concepts for the 21st Century Investor

As the 20th century gives way to a new millennium, portfolio managers and investors are confronted with new and/or unfamiliar concepts that are closely associated with the transition from the Machine Age to the Information Age. These new concepts will replace or augment existing concepts that are widely accepted by portfolio managers today (see Figure 2.2). It should be noted that the list of concepts featured in Figure 2.2 is incomplete, but it does capture some of the more important shifts in thinking that are underway today.

Figure 2.2 New Concepts for the Information Age Investor

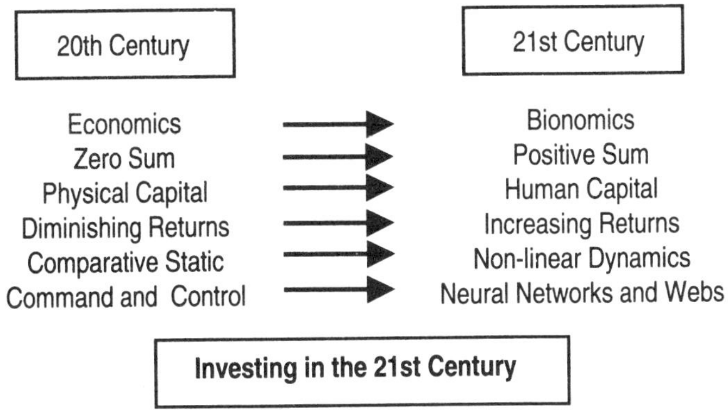

It is conventional today to view the economy or a corporation as a machine, cast in a Newtonian framework. Nowhere is this better illustrated than on Wall Street. A casual perusal of the financial press reveals comments such as, "the Fed may need to raise interest rates to prevent the economy from overheating," or "the Fed must step on the brakes soon to slow the economy." Machine-age metaphors are widely disseminated in today's financial press, and many economists and portfolio managers embrace them without thinking about the consequences of viewing the economy or a corporation as a machine.

As the economy evolves from the Industrial Age to the Information Age, machine-age thinking and metaphors will only serve to undermine an understanding of the new economic and financial landscape. For active portfolio managers, the consequences could be dire, because a lack of understanding could lay the foundation for persistent underperformance.

The study of bionomics, as opposed to economics, may be more appropriate for understanding and analyzing the evolving Information Age. Unlike conventional economics, which views the economy as a machine, bionomics views the economy as an ecosystem. Conventional economic analysis holds technology constant. In bionomics, technology holds center stage in the economy. Bionomics argues that biologic and economic life are organized and operate in much the same way. As the leading proponent of bionomics, author and entrepreneur Michael Rothschild states, "history has demonstrated that no economy behaves like a simple, cyclical machine. Like ecosystems, economies are spectacularly complex and endlessly adaptable."[7] Rothschild argues persuasively that bionomics—which studies economic relations among organisms and their environments—offers the best vantage point for a total rethinking of the received economic wisdom as the economy makes the transition from the Industrial Age to the Information Age.

As we enter the 21st century, investors and portfolio managers are likely to hear much more about positive feedback as opposed to negative feedback or zero-sum games. This will be accompanied by more discussion and analysis about the importance of human capital as opposed to physical capital. Increasing returns may come to dominate current thought over diminishing returns. Nonlinear dynamics and neural network models will become important methods of analysis used to study economies and markets, augmenting or replacing comparative static analysis and command and control models.[8]

As economist Brian Arthur of Stanford University and the Santa Fe Institute points out:

> Conventional economic theory is built on the assumption of diminishing returns. Economic actions engender a negative feedback that leads to a predictable equilibrium for prices and market shares. Such feedback tends to stabilize the economy because any major changes will be offset by the very reactions they generate. According to conventional theory, the equilibrium marks the

---

[7] See Michael Rothschild, Bionomics: Economy as Ecosystem, Henry Holt and Company, 1990.

[8] See John L. Casti, Would-Be Worlds: How Simulation Is Changing the Frontiers of Science, New York: John Wiley & Sons, 1997. Also see: Joshua Epstein and Robert Axtell, Growing Artificial Societies, Brookings Institution Press, 1996; Mitchel Resnick, Turtles, Termites, and Traffic Jams, MIT Press, 1995; John H. Holland, Hidden Order, Addison-Wesley Publishing Company, Inc., 1995; Richard Day and Ping Chen, Nonlinear Dynamics & Evolutionary Economics, Oxford University Press, 1993.

> "best" outcome possible under the circumstances; the most efficient use and allocation of resources. Such an agreeable picture often does violence to reality. In many parts of the economy, stabilizing forces appear not to operate. Instead positive feedback magnifies the effects of small economic shifts; the economic models that describe such effects differ vastly from the conventional ones. Diminishing returns imply a single equilibrium point for the economy, but positive feedback—increasing returns—makes for many possible equilibrium points. There is no guarantee that the particular economic outcome selected from among the many alternatives will be the "best" one. If one product or nation in a competitive marketplace gets ahead by "chance," it tends to stay ahead and even increase its lead.[9]

Arthur notes that technological conventions or standards, as well as particular technologies, tend to become locked in by positive feedback. Although a standard itself may not improve with time, widespread adoption makes it advantageous for newcomers to a field—who must exchange information or products with those already working there—to fall in with the standard, be it the English language, a computer operating system, a screw thread, or a typewriter keyboard. Standards that are established early can be hard to dislodge, no matter how superior would-be successors may be. Certainly, one can point to many examples today of positive feedback in the information- and bio-technology sectors.

As portfolio managers begin embracing the concepts in Figure 2.2, it will fundamentally change the way they think about the economy, markets, businesses, products, margins, and returns. At the beginning of this century, industrial economies were based largely on the physical capital and land. As we enter the 21st century, these economies are increasingly based on the processing of knowledge and human capital. As Arthur notes, "The increasing-returns world is characterized by observation, positioning, flattened organizations, missions, teams, and cunning. It is a world of psychology, of cognition, of adaptation."[10]

---

9 See W. Brian Arthur, Increasing Returns and Path Dependence in the Economy, The University of Michigan Press, 1994.

10 See W. Brian Arthur, "Increasing Returns and the New World of Business," *The Harvard Business Review,* July-August 1996, p 108.

A majority of portfolio managers may be uncomfortable with this world, but positive feedback and increasing returns are concepts Microsoft CEO Bill Gates and Intel CEO Andy Grove know an awful lot about. Active portfolio managers who analyze information technology companies in conventional ways may have difficulty investing in companies such as Microsoft and Intel. As Arthur points out, "many [business] managers have some intuitive grasp of this new increasing-returns world. Few understand it thoroughly." The same thing can probably be said of portfolio managers.

Inadequacies of Machine-Age Valuation Tools

Understanding thoroughly these new, unfamiliar concepts could enhance a portfolio manager's ability to analyze and assess companies in the information- and bio-technology industries. At the moment, many portfolio managers and Wall Street strategists view these sectors through the same lens as they view other sectors.

Figure 2.3 lists several conventional valuation tools that are widely used by fund managers today. Obviously, there are more than three valuation yardsticks, but we have listed three of the more popular in use today: price-to-book value, price-to-earnings, and enterprise value-to-replacement cost. The one common thread among all three of these conventional valuation parameters is that they came to prominence in the Machine Age.

Price-to-book value is the pre-eminent machine-age valuation yardstick, as it captures the original cost of physical assets such as plant, equipment, and land. This measure is appropriate for trying to assess the value of a steel or property company. But consider the meaning of book value for companies such as Intel, Oracle, Amgen, or Gilead Sciences. In the case of companies such as these, book value is largely meaningless and irrelevant given that their most important asset—human or intellectual capital—does not even appear on the balance sheet.

Figure 2.3

Traditional Machine Age Valuation Tools

- Stock Price Relative to Book Value
- Price Per Share Relative to Earnings Per Share
- Enterprise Value Relative to Replacement Cost

Investing in the 21st Century

Is it any wonder that some Wall Street analysts with a machine-age mindset look with incredulity upon the high price-to-book ratios for human-capital-intensive companies? Indeed, as the economy makes the transition from the Machine Age to the Information Age, book value as conventionally measured will become even less relevant to portfolio managers and investors as a valuation yardstick.

Enterprise value-to-replacement cost in its current definition is also perfectly suited to gauge the value of machine-age firms. It is relatively easy for accountants to tell traditional manufacturers the replacement cost of a piece of capital equipment or the cost of a parcel of land. But what is the replacement cost of Andy Grove's paranoia? What is the replacement cost of Bill Gates' business acumen? What is the replacement cost of Amgen's research and development staff?

Currently, attempts are being made by companies to address the issue of how to capture the value of human capital at firms where human capital accounts for the lion's share of assets. This topic is bound to grow in importance as we enter the 21st century, and new methods of accounting may be developed to help address this important issue.[11] Suffice it to say

---

[11] Interested readers might find the following book of interest: Leif Edvinsson and Michael S. Malone, Intellectual Capital, HarperBusiness, 1996. Also see "Is Intellectual Capital the New Wealth or the Latest Consulting Wank?," *Forbes* ASAP, April 7, 1997.

the enterprise value-to-replacement cost ratios are largely meaningless for information- and bio-technology companies.

Of the three yardsticks, the price/earnings ratio is probably the least biased measure of value in terms of being a representative yardstick for a machine-age or information-age firm. Yet conventional accounting distorts the use of this measure in the information- and bio-technology sectors because of the way research and development spending is treated. Accountants treat R&D spending as an expense that is incurred in the current time period. As such, it reduces stated corporate earnings.

This is an important issue for information- and bio-technology companies precisely because they spend huge sums of money on R&D. In 1996, research and development spending was 5% of total sales for the broadly defined, global, information technology sector and 7.5% of total sales for the global healthcare sector. Combined R&D spending for these two sectors was 12.5% of sales relative to an average of only 0.85% for all other global sectors (see Figure 2.4). These statistics clearly illustrate the importance of R&D to information- and bio-technology companies.

Figure 2.4 Global R&D Spending by Sector

Industry	R&D 1996	Sales 1996	R&D % Of Sales
Basic Material	23.13	1,293	1.8
Consumer Durable	53.45	1,749	3.1
Consumer Merchandise	0.04	1,264	0.0
Consumer Non-Durable	7.29	1,047	0.7
Consumer Service	1.03	584	0.2
Energy	5.52	1,027	0.5
Financial	0.03	2,728	0.0
Health Care	32.85	442	7.4
Industrial	18.49	3,026	0.6
Technology	82.86	1,613	5.1
Utility	8.21	1,212	0.7
Total	232.90	15,984	1.5

Source: FactSet

At the heart of bionomics is the notion that growth and corporate profitability are functions of organizational learning. Put simply, the higher the level of organizational learning, the higher the level of corporate profitability and growth. Investment in R&D is an admittedly crude proxy for learning, but it is probably the best available measure of a company's commitment to learning. Research and development spending is as important to information- and bio-technology companies as spending on property, plant, and equipment is for traditional manufacturing firms. In 1996, Microsoft spent a reported $1.7 billion on R&D and only $500 million on capital expenditures. Amgen spent $500 million on R&D in 1996, twice the firm's outlays on capital expenditures.[12] Contrast these examples with General Motors—the perennial machine-age firm—which in 1995 spent $19.2 billion on capital expenditures compared with $7 billion on R&D.

To illustrate the differences between machine-age firms and information- and bio- technology companies, Figure 4.5 compares and contrasts various valuation yardsticks of several technology companies with General Motors. Note the dramatic difference in price-to-book value ratios for the information-age firms relative to General Motors. So-called value managers accustomed to searching for relatively low price-to-book value stocks would undoubtedly pass over such stocks as Microsoft, Intel, Cisco, and Amgen. The same can be said of price-to-earnings valuations. Note the relatively high P/E ratios among the group of information-age firms relative to General Motors. We have also listed each firms' R&D-to-Sales and Capital Expenditure-to-Sales ratios for comparison.

Some analysts argue that the valuation ratios associated with information-age companies are unsustainable in the long run. That may or may not be true. The main point is that there are fundamental differences between information-age firms and machine-age firms that may help to explain discrepancies in valuations. Understanding these discrepancies may lead active portfolio managers to develop new tools and techniques to find value in information-age stocks, rather than simply dismissing the valuations of such stocks out of hand.

---

12 High R&D outlays help explain why information- and bio-technology companies often have high price-earnings ratios relative to Machine Age firms.

Figure 4.5 Machine-Age vs. Information-Age Valuation Comparisons

	Price-to-Book Value	Price-to-Earnings	R&D-to-Sales	Cap Ex.-to-Sales
Microsoft	10	40	18.4%	5.4%
Intel	5	19	8.6%	16.9%
Cisco Systems	13	44	14.1%	6.8%
Amgen	9	26	23.5%	10.3%
General Motors	2	6	4.4%	18.1%

Note: Microsoft data as of 12/96; Intel data as of 9/96; Cisco data as of 1/97; Amgen data as of 9/96; General Motors data as of 9/95.
Source: Factset

Given the rising importance of research and development in the U.S. and global economies, it will become increasingly important for analysts and portfolio managers to look beyond conventional accounting measures to better measure the value of such activity. There is some evidence that the market does attempt to place a more realistic value on R&D spending. A number of studies have shown that companies' stock prices tend to increase when they announce increases in their overall R&D spending. There is also evidence that the stock market views R&D expenditures not as an immediate expense (as accountants treat it), but rather as a long-lived asset that should instead be capitalized and amortized.[13] Nevertheless, there may still be large inefficiencies in the way R&D is valued in the markets today. A more appropriate accounting treatment of this important activity is warranted in the transition from the industrial age to the information age.

In Search of Valuation Tools and Techniques for Information Age Companies

Consider the following quote, taken from the popular financial press in 1996. The quote was from a prominent fund manager at one of the largest mutual fund companies in the world.

---

[13] See George Pinches, V.K. Narayanan, and Kathryn Kelm, "How The Market Values the Different Stages of Corporate R&D," Journal of Applied Corporate Finance, Spring 1996, pp. 60-69.

> "By sticking to our discipline, we generally can't buy those high-tech stocks. But I'm not saying people can't make money on them."

This quote illustrates well the problems and challenges many portfolio managers face today. The valuation tools and screens that have traditionally been used to analyze machine-age companies are not very useful for information-age firms. That is not to say that managers who do not invest in information- or bio-technology companies will not consistently beat their respective benchmarks. On the contrary, there are active money managers who have consistently outperformed their respective benchmarks based on machine-age valuation tools and techniques. However, it is eminently sensible to assert that a comprehensive portfolio management process in the 21st century would incorporate tools and screens that would allow an active equity portfolio manager to recognize value in every sector, including information- and bio-technology.

There are a few portfolio managers today who are developing new tools and techniques to analyze information- and bio-technology companies. Some interesting work, for example, is being done by Michael Murphy, founder and editor of the *California Stock Technology Letter*. Murphy argues persuasively that investors who can buy into innovative, R&D-intensive companies at an attractive price will reap high profits over the long run."[14]

Murphy's valuation framework incorporates a number of variables, such as R&D spending, sales growth, pre-tax earnings, and return on equity. Murphy's main valuation tool is "price-to-growth flow," which is simply the price per share of a company's stock divided by the sum of its earnings per share (EPS) and R&D spending per share (RDS). In equation form, Murphy's yardstick for valuing information- and bio-technology companies is:

$$\text{Price-to-Growth Flow Ratio} = \text{Stock Price Per Share} / (\text{EPS} + \text{RDS})$$

---

14 See Michael Murphy, "Growth Flow Investing," 1996.

Note that the growth flow concept incorporates the machine-age valuation yardstick price-to-earnings per share. Importantly, the growth flow concept explicitly attempts to value R&D spending, which the accountants treat as an expense and hence, a deduction from earnings. According to Murphy, a company that meets a number of qualifications, including having a price-to-growth flow ratio of less than 4.0, is attractively valued.

There are several variations one could employ to broaden the growth flow concept to attempt to enhance its usefulness as a valuation tool. For instance, one could use cash flow per share (i.e., EBIT or EBITDA) instead of earnings per share to overcome the fact that many information- and bio-technology companies have no reported earnings but some level of cash flow. One could also use revenues instead of cash flow and get a modified price-to-sales ratio that adjusted for R&D spending.

To illustrate the potential usefulness of the growth flow valuation tool, we developed a stock screen that selected at the beginning of each year since 1985 those information technology companies that had a price-to-growth flow ratio (using cash flow instead of earnings) of less than 4.0 (note: to simplify, we did not include biotechnology companies in this screen). The portfolio was rebalanced once a year, and no trading costs were deducted from the returns of the portfolio.[15]

Figure 2.6 shows the results of this screen, which is measured against the performance of the S&P 500 index. As can be seen from the results, the growth flow valuation screen produced a return far in excess of the return on the S&P 500. The average annual price return on the growth flow portfolio over the period 1985-1995 was 31%, versus 15% on the S&P 500. In 1995, the screening process uncovered many stocks that performed extremely well in the subsequent 12 months. For example, stocks with a price-to-growth cash flow ratio of less than 4.0 included Seagate Technology, Sun Microsystems, and Xerox, to name just a few.

Of course, not all stocks in the 1995 growth flow screen results performed well. For example, AST Research screened in the top quartile but fell nearly 50% in the 12-month period. Needless to say, any quantitative

---

[15] I am indebted to Ross Bruner for his able assistance developing this quantitative screen.

Figure 2.6 Growth Flow Screen Results

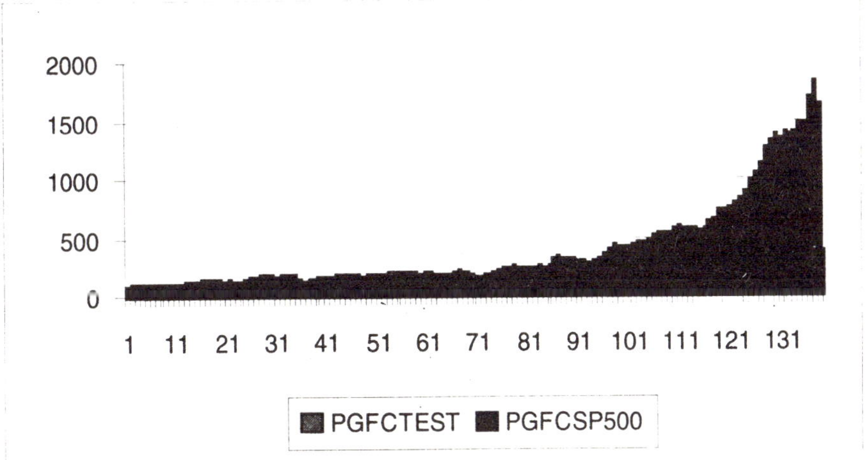

screening process must be accompanied by comprehensive top-down and bottom-up qualitative and quantitative analysis to enhance the success of the portfolio-management process. Admittedly, the screen developed here is simple, but the results are impressive when viewed against the performance of the S&P 500. Of course, we could develop more sophisticated quantitative and qualitative screens that include more parameters and constraints. This would certainly seem to be a fruitful area of future research.

"All Are Information Technology Companies Today"

The above quote, taken from Percy Barnevik, Chairman of ABB in Switzerland, is extremely perceptive and testifies to the changing nature of the global economy. Information technology is altering the very fabric of the global economy in ways that are not well understood today. In the 21st century, biotechnology may combine with information technology to emerge as a powerful force of change and evolution in the global economy.

It is crucial that active equity portfolio managers have the necessary tools, techniques, and framework to assess and analyze value in all sectors of the global economy, including information-and bio-technology. We have attempted to address several issues that may be hampering the ability of active managers to outperform their respective benchmarks. It is important for active managers to develop a rigorous discipline or process that can be efficiently and effectively employed and adhered to. Quantitative screens that help managers uncover value in the information- and bio-technology sectors are destined to become more valuable in the next millennium.

We are likely at the early stages of an evolution (revolution may be a better word) in the development of new valuation tools and techniques that can be applied to companies in the information- and bio-technology sectors. Whether active managers will be able to improve their performance with the development of new valuation tools and techniques is an empirical question that will be answered in time. One conclusion seems quite clear: active U.S. and global equity managers need to re-orient and supplement their valuation tools and techniques to thrive in the information age. Failure to do so may only strengthen the case for passive management in the 21st century.

Economic Value Added (EVA)

Vincent van Doorn
European Research Sales
Paribas Corporation

Introduction

On a recent business trip in Europe, visiting different companies over several days, I encountered many managers talking about shareholder value. Besides being a nice topic to talk about with portfolio managers and company managers alike, it appeared to me that shareholder value, as interpreted by company managers, is a concept that has wide semantic scope. One company raved about a changing shareholder structure being shareholder value enhancing. Another company, in a notorious cyclical business, thought it would enhance its shareholder value by diversifying into non-cyclical businesses.

The clever reader understands immediately that this creates undefined possibilities to enhance the intrinsic value of the funds under management by either going short or long these interpretations. In this chapter I will try to explain a framework of shareholder value as a function of capital employed, the cost of capital and the return on capital employed. This framework gives you an ample tool to calculate and evaluate a company's performance over its total capital. This means, regardless of the capital structure, a company's performance can be measured and evaluated periodically. However, I leave it up to you to determine and discuss the different definitions of shareholder value that companies use in their drive for enhancing their share price performance.

The Merchant of Venice, EVA and DCF

A pound of flesh. No more, no less...There are many books and methods that describe in more or less detail what I am about to explain here. All require a detailed understanding of balance sheet items and lines in the profit and loss statements invented mainly for tax reduction purposes. Apparent and of pivotal importance is to understand that a firm's value is derived from cash from operations discounted over the life of a company. I would like to highlight two books that stand alone in taking this concept one step further: "The Quest for Value," by G. Bennett Stewart III and "Valuation" by Mckinsey & Company. Both books point to the intellectual fathers of the value approach and the concept of cash flow and its present value method, namely professors Merton Miller and Franco Modigliani.

Bennett Stewart shows us a method measuring the value of a company in any given year with a concept he calls Economic Value Added or EVA. EVA is basically the difference between the operating profit and the cost of capital employed. Any year that a company is in business and generates more operating profit than its capital charge, it is creating economic value. By discounting this spread, taking the present values of all future EVAs at the rate of the cost of capital employed, you get the cumulative present value of all future EVAs. Add this to the current capital and you derive the value of a company.

Again it should not be surprising to the alert reader that this EVA method will come to the same valuation as would be achieved through discounting all future cash flows. This is correct and hence, a pound of flesh can equal only a pound of flesh. However, the beauty of EVA is that it is more than calculating the value of a company. EVA incorporates a thinking about financial structures that also facilitates a better understanding of the mechanics in a balance sheet and P&L. Pure cash flow analysis will miss crucial opportunities by disregarding companies with negative cash flows. Most importantly, EVA gives you a very handy set of tools to understand and question management's actions and value its progress year by year.

Capital Employed

Except for a happy few in this world, we would not be living in our owned pieces of real estate without the ability to leverage ourselves. Most banks are more than eager to help you fulfill your dream, however at a cost. In order to calculate a cash return, subtract from your sale price all the cash that has been borrowed plus the down payment plus cash payments for home improvements. All cash left is profit before taxes. In other words, to define a return, the total amount of cash invested in a particular venture must be added up. Capital employed is defined as all cash invested in a company during its lifetime. For our purpose this means all cash invested in going-concern business activities in order to produce an operating return.

Whether this cash is equity or debt does not concern us at this stage. All the extra investment for home improvement is cash invested and thus capital employed to make your stay a little more pleasant. A prudent home owner has kept meticulous records of all the cash invested over time, both for tax purposes and for calculating the value in lieu of a transaction. This was the easy part. Now try to find capital employed in an average company annual report, good luck!

What concerns us is to define the total cash amount invested over time in a company. Admittedly this is almost impossible to find due to a lack of published historical figures. But as usual it is better to be approximately right than precisely wrong. A good starting point is an examination of the net assets in the balance sheet: begin by looking three or four years back in history in order to adjust figures and cumulate them to the future. In order to determine all the cash that has been provided to the company, the net assets should be adjusted for.

Marketable securities: subtract these because this is capital most likely used for other than going-concern business activities, ergo non-operational. Cash-rich companies, such as Novartis and Roche, both pharmaceutical companies, can undermine their total return on all capital when their return on liquidities is underperforming vis a vis their return on operating capital. Do the calculations for Novartis or Roche and you will see this is currently the case!

The present value of non-capitalized leases should be added to fixed assets (this is capital locked up in the company). These items are mostly off balance, but mentioned in the footnotes. This is capital locked up unless a company is able to sell the leases to third parties or break a lease without penalty, which is most likely the case only with A-location retail property leases.

Cumulative goodwill amortization and cumulative exceptional losses or gains should be added back to net assets as well. According to Dutch accounting standards a company has to book all its goodwill at once against its equity. When Wolters Kluwer, a Dutch publisher, acquired CCH, it had to change its accounting method. The goodwill of CCH was greater than Wolters Kluwer's equity. This would have given a nice return on negative equity (ROE). I rest my case...

Writing down assets because of lower valuations is prudent. But for our purpose, to find a return on all cash invested, it is not helpful. Therefore written-off assets should be added back. Assets that were too expensive do not give you cash back or result in a store credit of any kind. This method, practiced by Alcatel Alsthom, a French conglomerate, makes for a nice increase in ROE but does not tell us what the real performance is off *all* the cash that was invested in the past.

You can make a case to capitalize cumulative cash that has been spent as R&D. I am in favor of doing this as I am in favor of capitalizing all cash investments made to build and strengthen brands. In the case of the former you can argue that this will smooth the cost of huge R&D projects over the economic life of a project. Current shareholders are punished unfairly in the short term if a large cash outlay in R&D depresses the snapshot value of a company due to low or even negative cash flows and returns in the year under review.

In case of the latter, I see brands as an asset and therefore cash outflows to build and strengthen brands as cash investments and not as costs.

Without going into an academic exercise, which we could easily do, I would like to stress the fact that it is imperative to use a consistent capital base method in order to judge a company's progress. Companies that employ an increasing pool of operating capital need to make a return that is higher than the cost of that capital. The difference between success and failure is the difference between capital destruction and capital creation. This brings us to the next subject: how to measure a return on capital employed.

Return on Capital Employed

As I wrote earlier, capital and returns can be calculated in many ways using different capital bases. Return on equity, total assets, investment and maybe someone will try to calculate the return on debt one day! All of the above can give you false indications of how the underlying businesses are performing. The same counts for profitability. Net profits,

EBIT, and EBITDA are all meaningful in one way or another. However, as investors, we are looking for the true yield on all cash invested. In other words the amount of profit that is available to return to all capital providers of a company. Whether the tax authorities enjoy a larger or smaller piece of that yield does concern us. Whether credit institutions demand higher interest rates for their capital does concern us because of the tax implications. We are looking for the cash return that can be distributed to all capital providers. Therefore any other yardstick is less meaningful and a derivative from the true yardstick: return on capital employed.

In order to come to a true economic return, a few adjustments should be made to net profits. Net profits are a good starting point and must be adjusted for operating and financing distortions. These distortions were made either to facilitate tax reductions or to smooth net earnings. After the adjustments we will have a cleaner figure that represents a true economic profit.

Operating distortions are amortization of goodwill, which should be added back, fluctuations in tax reserves, fluctuations in other reserves/provisions, unusual gains/losses and increases in LIFO reserves. Remember we are not questioning these items in the P&L or passing judgment on them; all we want to know is what the true economic return is on all cash invested in a company.

Financing distortions are after-tax interest charges that are added back to eliminate the effects of capital structure. The debt/equity ratio is covered by the average cost of capital which we will discuss later. We want to find a measure that gives us an operating performance over total capital. With this in mind we can also use this measure to test performance against similar companies disregarding their mix of debt to equity.

The times when companies blatantly used provisions to smooth their net income streams are gone. But, as we can see in every reporting season, the quality of net earnings is more often dubious than not. Unfortunately the truth can only be found in the footnotes of an annual report. So, unless a company releases a detailed half-year report, you have to wait for the current annual to be published to evaluate a company's performance.

A word of caution. Before you start a meticulous quest for distortions, remember the following. Time has a cash value for most of us who work, so be reasonable and look for the distortions that make up 80% of what you are looking for. Be sure that for every adjustment to net profits you make an adjustment to net assets as well. Different businesses demand different priorities of adjustments: you are looking for good or bad performing capital, not a Ph.D. in Finance.

Cost of Capital

Cost of capital, the last of the three musketeers. Providers of capital demand a reward for their capital. That reward equals the cost of capital, or capital charge, of a company. The cost of capital varies with the mix of debt to equity and its perceived business risk, beta. Beta is a measure of the company's stock price volatility versus the overall market. Volatility lessens with increased predictability of a company's cash flow stream and vice versa.

It is widely known that a risk-free reward equals the long-term yield of a government bond (there is ample academic proof for this). Measured over a long period, the risk-free rate equals roughly 6%. Also widely known is the typical risk premium for equity, which equals 6%. Therefore an all-equity-financed company with a beta of one generates a cost of capital of 12%.

A different way of calculating the cost of capital can be done only if the information in the annual report is detailed. Line by line you can figure out what the different interest rates of debt classes demand. Since total capital changes during the year, a weighted average cost of capital (WACC) should be calculated.

Last but not least you can take the interest charge as your starting point and take this over total debt to come to an average cost of debt.

Where the Former Three Meet, Value Begins

Capital employed, return on capital employed and cost of capital are the three main pillars to measure a firm's ability to create economic value. This economic value will sooner or later be translated into an increased intrinsic value, but more importantly, an increased market value, which you as a shareholder would very much appreciate. If the cost of capital is deducted from its return we have a spread that, when multiplied by capital employed, gives us EVA or economic value added.

> (Return of capital - Cost of capital) * Capital employed at beginning of year = EVA

By calculating the present value of all future EVAs and adding these to the enterprise value plus any surplus cash, we arrive at a company's total value. The companies that over time will create the most economic value are the companies that have the largest spread between return and cost of capital and the largest increase of capital employed over time! Companies with negative EVAs are busy destroying economic value, which results in a lower intrinsic value per share and ultimately in a lower share price. The managements of these companies better have good restructuring stories to tell unless their businesses are going through the bottom of a performance cycle. Otherwise it is probably wiser to buy that risk-free government bond.

Heineken, a Detailed Example

What follows is a detailed example of international beer company Heineken. According to this analysis Heineken's value is close to Dfl 380.00 per share. The stock current price stands at Dfl 330.00. The market will ultimately be the judge of Heineken's value.

Table 3.1 Determination Of Operating Capital Employed

	Equity And Equivalents	1997e	1996	1995	1994	1993	1992	1991	1990
1	Equity	4,900,000	4,514,008	4,734,058	4,353,957	3,972,778	3,650,473	3,366,651	3,146,143
2	Plus Preferred Stock	0	0	0	0	0	0	0	0
3	Plus Minority Interests	450,000	410,039	346,182	353,856	239,499	278,828	353,295	353,549
4	Plus Deferred Tax Reserve	635,000	635,449	575,000	581,809	584,303	566,100	599,264	592,702
6	Plus Cumulative Goodwill Paid	900,000	839,208	515,159	442,917	315,430	295,165	174,236	0
8	Plus Other Reserves (Excluding Taxes)	1,000,000	982,757	800,000	780,489	696,827	583,669	600,433	530,294
9	Plus Invest. Equalization/Received Subsidies	99,000	99,700	119,392	119,242	130,122	146,887	173,752	186,767
10	Plus Cumulative Unusual Gains(-)/Losses(+)	(58,636)	(58,636)	(58,636)	(58,636)	0	0	0	0
11	Total Equity & Equivalents	7,925,364	7,422,525	7,031,155	6,573,634	5,938,959	5,521,122	5,267,631	4,809,455
	Debt And Equivalents								

12	Plus Short Term Debt	700,000	774,159	300,000	327,487	218,961	380,733	544,826	397,879
13	Plus Current Portion Of Long Term Debt	0	0	65,000	105,727	260,140	89,992	89,639	224,216
14	Plus Senior Long Term Debt	800,000	792,400	450,000	503,357	462,057	576,464	643,115	674,507
15	Plus Capitalized Lease Obl.	28	110	105	97	45	46	43	28
16	Total Debt And Equivalents	1,500,028	1,566,669	815,105	936,668	941,203	1,047,235	1,277,623	1,296,630
17	Liquidities	1,800,000	1,628,344	2,155,000	1,740,000	1,566,000	1,162,000	687,000	1,005,000
18	Net Debt(+)/Net Cash(-)	(299,972)	(61,675)	(1,339,895)	(803,332)	(624,797)	(114,765)	590,623	291,630

19	Operating Capital Employed	7,625,392	7,360,850	5,691,260	5,770,302	5,314,162	5,406,357	5,858,254	5,101,085
20	Capital Investment During Year N	264,542	1,669,590	(79,042)	456,140	(92,195)	(451,897)	757,169	0
	Determination Of Net Operating Profit After Taxes (NOPAT)								
21	Net Profit	720,000	655,351	664,417	662,091	518,746	564,263	442,934	365708
	Operating Distortions								
22	Plus Amortization Of Goodwill	0	0	0	0	0	0	0	0
23	Plus Increase/Minus Decrease Tax Reserve	(449)	60,449	(6,809)	(2,494)	18,203	(33,164)	6,562	592,702
24	Plus Inc./Minus Dec. In Capitalized Intangibles	0	0	0	0	0	0	0	0
25	Plus Unusual Losses/Minus Unusual Gains	0	0	(101,650)	0	(58,636)	0	0	0
26	Plus Inc./Dec. Other Reserves(Ex-Taxes Res)	17,243	182,757	19,511	83,662	113,158	(16,764)	70,139	530,294
27	Plus Increase/Decrease Investment Equalization	(700)	(19,692)	150	(10,880)	(16,765)	(26,865)	(13,015)	186,767
	Financing Distortions								
29	Minority Interest	40,000	38,000	31,000	28,000	27,000	25,000	22,000	29
30	Preferred Dividend	0	0	0	0	0	0	0	30
31	Interest Exp.(+)/Gain(-) After Taxes (Intr.*0.65)	(24,700)	(4)	(15,600)	(1,040)	(975)	(13,000)	(19,500)	31
32	Interest Exp. Av.Capitalized Lease Obl.(Am*.0.65)	1	6	5	5	2	2	2	32
33	NOPAT	751,395	916,867	591,024	759,344	600,733	499,472	509,122	33
	Analysis Of Results								
	===================	1997e	1996	1995	1994	1993	1992	1991	1990
34	NOPAT/Beginning Operating Capital Employed	10.21%	16.11%	10.24%	14.29%	11.11%	8.87%	9.29%	0.00%
37	Operating Margin (NOPBT/Sales)	8.40%	10.02%	8.63%	10.36%	9.54%	9.68%	10.15%	37
38	Sales/Capital Employed	1.77	1.66	1.83	1.73	1.70	1.65	1.48	0.00
39	Total Operating Return Per Year	14.87%	16.59%	15.84%	17.91%	16.25%	16.01%	15.07%	0.03%
40	Sales	13,500,000	12,188,823	10,443,000	9,974,000	9,049,000	8,944,000	8,696,000	40
41	Reported Taxes	400,000	368,592	384,000	319,869	318,354	340,000	380,000	41
42	Change In Tax Reserve	(449)	60,449	(6,809)	(2,494)	18,203	(33,164)	6,562	42
43	Adjustment For Taxes On Excess Liquidities	17,998	3,701	80,394	48,200	37,488	6,886	0	43
44	Cash Operating Taxes	382,451	304,443	310,415	274,163	262,663	366,278	373,438	44
45	Net Operating Profit Before Taxes (NOPBT)	1,133,846	1,221,309	901,440	1,033,507	863,397	865,750	882,560	45
	Effective Cash Tax Rate	33.73%	24.93%	34.44%	26.53%	30.42%	42.31%	42.31%	
46	Number Of Shares	50,174	50,174	50,174	40,139	40,139	40,139	50,174	46
		Bonus Share Issue 1:4		Bonus Share Issue (1 For 4)					

Table 3.1 Determination Of Operating Capital Employed, *Cont'd from page 50*

	Economic Value Added (EVA)								
	====================								
50	Return On Capital(R)	10.21%	16.11%	10.24%	14.29%	11.11%	8.87%	9.29%	50
51	Cost Of Capital(C)	9.61%	9.55%	9.80%	9.73%	9.68%	9.62%	9.53%	51
52	(R-C)*Capital (EVA)	45,640	482,788	25,032	262,859	76,064	(40,675)	(14,127)	52
58	R/C	1.06	1.69	1.04	1.47	1.15	0.92	0.97	58
	Market Value Added (MVA)								
	==================								
53	Market Value Common Stock End Of Year	17,059,160	15,303,070	14,249,416	8,389,051	7,505,993	#Value!	#Value!	53
54	Minus Capital (Employed + Net Cash)	9,425,392	8,989,194	7,846,260	7,510,302	624,797	114,765	0	54
58	Market Value Added (MVA)	7633768	6313876	6403156	878749	6881196	0.92	0.97	58
60	Adjusted Book Value	157.96	147.94	140.14	163.77	147.96	#Value!	#Value!	60
	MVA Per Share	152.15	125.84	127.62	21.89	171.43			
	Premium To Book	2.15	2.06	2.03	1.28	1.26			
49	Share Price (End Of Year Quote)	340.00	305.00	284.00	209.00	187.00	#Value!	#Value!	49
	Input:								
67	Business Risk Index	0.72							
68	Risk Free Rate	6.00%							
69	Risk Premium	6.00%							
70	Tax Rate	35.00%							

Table 3.2 Heineken's Value

Discount rate	9.67%		EVA growth is a function of capital growth accumulated at the r-c spread
Growth rate first 10 years EVA	15.00%		Discount rate is C, the average cost of capital over last 4 years
Growth rate last 5 years EVA	5.00%		

	YEAR 1	YEAR 2	YEAR 3	YEAR 4	YEAR 5	YEAR 6	YEAR 7	YEAR 8	YEAR 9	YEAR 10
EVA (average past 4 years)	204,080	$234,691.88	$269,895.67	$310,380.02	$356,937.02	$410,477.57	$472,049.21	$542,856.59	$624,285.08	$717,927.84
Growth rate EVA flow	15%	15%	15%	15%	15%	15%	15%	15%	15%	15%
EVA flow year n+1	234692	269896	310380	356937	410478	472049	542857	624285	717928	825617
Discount factor	0.911790925	0.83136269	0.758028956	0.691163923	0.630196992	0.574607898	0.523922267	0.477707568	0.435569425	0.397148249
Discounted value per annum	$213,989.93	$224,381.19	$235,277.04	$246,701.99	$258,681.73	$271,243.20	$284,414.66	$298,225.71	$312,707.42	$327,892.35

Cumulative present value future EVAs		3481939
Residual value		
EVA in year 10	825617	
Growth rate last five yrs	5%	
EVA in year 11	866898	
Capitalization rate	5%	
Value at end year 10	18546184	
Discoutn factor yr 10	0.397148249	
Present value residual		7365584
Cash		1800000
Capital Employed 1997		7625392
Market value		20272916
Shares outstanding		50180
Value per share		404.00
Quoted market price (April 1997)		345.00
Value premium to market quote		17%

Enterprise Value/Sales Beats Price/Sales And Price/Earnings In a Three-Way Model Race

Melissa R. Brown, CFA
Managing Director
Prudential Securities

The search for a simple way to evaluate the investment prospects of a group of stocks is a never-ending process. Some ratios have turned out to be effective tools as predictors of future performance, and although they may not be the end of the search, they certainly can be a good starting point. Sales, earnings, and capitalization data are readily available and relatively easy to use.

We have evaluated price/sales, enterprise value/sales (which takes debt into account), and the old standby, price/earnings. We believe that enterprise value/sales is a somewhat better measure than price/sales because companies that use heavy debt end up understating the capitalization required to support a level of sales, and they therefore look better on a price/sales ratio (PSR) than they perhaps should. Earnings can be manipulated more easily than other financial statement items, and therefore P/E may not be what it appears.

We tested a model that examined the quintiles of P/E, PSR, and ESR among the biggest 1,000 stocks from 1978 to 1996, rebalancing the universe and the two models quarterly. We calculated average returns both unweighted and weighted by market cap.

We also looked at performance by sector to determine whether this would be a particularly good construction for certain areas of the economy.

A Look at the Results

We found that over this 19-year period, stocks in the top quintile of PSR returned on average 18.8% annually, compared with a bottom-quintile average of 14.9% and a universe return of 16.8% (this was a particularly good period for stocks in general). The average spread between top- and bottom-quintile returns was 3.4% (Table 4.1).

Table 4.1 Price/Sales Ratio Does Work as a Stock-Selection Tool

	Average Annual Return Price/Sales Ratio Quintile							
	Q1	Q2	Q3	Q4	Q5	Universe	Q1/Q5 Spread	Information Coefficient
Largest 1,000 Companies								
Unweighted	18.8	17.6	17.3	14.6	14.9	16.8	3.4	0.025
Capitalization Weighted	17.2	17.4	16.1	14.2	15.3	16.1	1.6	0.025
Unweighted for P/E Model	20.5	17.1	16.2	14.5	15.5	16.9	4.4	
Percent Of Companies Beating Universe								
All Markets	50.7	48.0	50.7	48.0	46.7	48.8	*	*
Up Markets	52.6	54.4	52.6	52.6	59.6	54.4	*	*
Down Markets	44.4	27.8	44.4	33.3	5.6	31.1	*	*
Average Beta	1.18	1.11	1.03	1.04	1.31	1.13	*	*
Returns For Macroeconomic Sectors								
Basic Industry	15.8	17.2	15.0	14.9	12.6	15.3	2.8	0.023
Business Services	16.6	17.9	14.8	16.5	14.1	16.5	2.2	0.019
Capital Spending	18.5	12.5	14.5	10.7	11.9	14.0	5.9	0.032
Consumer Cyclical	13.5	17.0	16.6	10.9	9.2	14.0	3.9	0.024
Consumer Services	21.5	16.4	16.9	19.5	15.9	18.3	4.8	0.013
Consumer Staples	23.8	21.2	20.9	17.7	17.0	20.4	5.8	0.051
Energy	18.7	15.2	13.4	9.1	8.4	13.3	9.5	0.072
Financial Services	17.3	18.6	21.5	16.4	17.1	18.4	0.2	0.023
Health Care	19.1	19.8	20.6	19.2	13.6	19.1	4.9	0.025
Technology	20.8	13.9	14.2	15.7	16.3	16.7	3.9	0.003
Utilities	15.3	15.2	14.9	13.6	13.0	14.5	2.0	0.038

Note: Results are for the largest 1,000 companies and for the price/sales ratio unless otherwise noted. Returns are in percent, and based on quarterly rebalancing from the second quarter of 1978 through the fourth quarter of 1996.

Source: Prudential Securities Inc.

Returns by PSR decile show the best performance occurred in Decile 2, and the worst in Decile 8.

Weighted by market value, the results look somewhat less potent, with an average spread of 1.6%.

The spread between the top- and bottom-quintile returns was positive, on average, for all sectors, although just barely so for financial services.

The top PSR quintile in consumer cyclical and financial services lagged other stocks in the sector and equaled the universe's return for health care.

In every sector, the bottom quintile lagged the rest of the group, but just barely for technology (in which the second quintile had the worst return).

The sectors for which returns decrease more or less monotonically by quintile—in other words, where the model works the best—are basic industry, consumer staples, energy, and utilities.

PSR: A Good Defensive Strategy

The PSR model appeared to work better in down markets, during which only about 31% of companies beat the S&P Composite overall. When stocks were down, an average of 44% of Quintile 1 companies and only 5.6% of Quintile 5 companies beat the market. In up markets, the statistics reversed, and more Q5 than Q1 names outpaced the S&P.

However, the results looked much better when capitalization took debt into account.

From 1978 through 1996, the top quintile of enterprise value/sales returned 19.9% (an unweighted average) for the largest 1,000 companies, compared with 16.8% for the universe and 14.4% for the bottom quintile (Table 4.2). The average information coefficient was 0.027.

Table 4.2 Enterprise Value/Sales Has Been an Effective Stock-Picking Model

	Average Annual Return*							
	Enterprise Value/Sales Ration Quintile							
	Q1	Q2	Q3	Q4	Q5	Universe	Q1/Q5 Spread	Information Coefficient
Largest 1,000 Companies								
Unweighted	19.9	17.0	15.6	16.4	14.4	16.8	4.8	0.027
Capitalization Weighted	18.2	16.9	14.3	16.5	14.0	16.0	3.7	—
Largest 50 Companies								
Unweighted	17.4	16.0	15.9	16.2	16.6	16.7	0.7	—
Percent Of Companies Beating Universe								
All Markets	61.3	52.0	40.0	48.0	41.3	48.5	—	—
Up Markets	61.4	54.4	47.4	54.4	52.6	54.0	—	—
Down Markets	61.1	44.4	16.7	27.8	5.6	31.1	—	—
Average Beta	1.10	1.12	1.13	1.06	1.23	1.13	—	—
Returns For Macroeconomic Sectors								
Basic Industry	16.9	16.9	15.4	12.9	13.4	15.3	3.1	0.034
Business Services	16.9	18.3	16.1	16.0	12.8	16.6	3.7	0.030
Capital Spending	18.2	14.6	13.6	10.9	11.1	14.0	6.4	0.042
Consumer Cyclical	18.1	15.8	15.5	11.4	7.1	14.1	10.3	0.057
Consumer Services	23.5	16.3	15.1	17.6	17.8	18.3	4.9	0.017
Consumer Staples	23.4	23.8	18.8	16.6	18.1	20.4	4.5	0.051
Energy	20.0	15.1	12.3	11.5	5.6	13.3	13.6	0.081
Financial Services	19.0	17.6	18.8	17.1	18.3	18.3	0.6	0.021
Health Care	17.4	20.8	20.6	20.7	13.2	19.1	3.7	0.016
Technology	22.0	14.8	13.4	13.2	17.4	16.7	3.9	0.013
Utilities	16.7	16.2	12.9	13.8	12.2	14.5	4.1	0.045

*Returns are for the largest 1,000 companies unless otherwise noted. Returns are in percent and are based on quarterly rebalancing from the second quarter of 1978 through the fourth quarter of 1996.

Source: Prudential Securities, Inc.

The ESR Model Works Slightly Better on the Sell Side

The bottom quintile lagged the overall universe in 12 of 19 years, whereas the top quintile beat the universe in 11 of them. Q1 beat Q5 in 12 of the years as well. An average of 48.5% of the companies in the overall universe outpaced the S&P Composite; 54.0% did so in up markets, and 31.1%, in down markets. Stocks in the top quintile beat the S&P Composite 61% of the time or more, no matter what the market did, and just 41% of Q5 stocks fared better than the S&P. In down markets, however, this model really shone on the sell side—only 5.6% of the Q5 constituents beat the market in those periods.

Results were not quite as good when returns were weighted by capitalization, but they were better than "plain" PSR's weighted statistics. The top quintile gained 18.2% per year, and the bottom quintile was up 14.0%, with an average spread of 3.7%. The universe had an average annual return of 16.0%.

Table 4.3 Most Years, When One Works, They All Work, But the Degree of Success Varies

	Rolling 3-Year Annualized Returns*								
	Price/Sales Ratio			Enterprise Value/Sales			P/E (Trailing Earnings)		
			Q1/Q5			Q1/Q5			Q1/Q5
3 Years Ended	Q1	Q5	Spread	Q1	Q5	Spread	Q1	Q5	Spread
1980	21.1	36.0	-11.0	19.4	26.3	-5.4	24.3	37.5	-9.6
1981	21.7	25.4	-3.0	22.9	22.4	0.4	26.6	25.6	0.8
1982	21.6	17.5	3.5	23.5	18.4	4.3	21.8	21.0	0.7
1983	25.9	5.0	20.8	27.9	7.9	18.5	21.2	10.0	10.3
1984	26.0	3.9	21.3	26.5	5.8	19.6	21.6	8.5	12.1
1985	26.1	7.1	17.8	20.5	7.0	10.1	28.8	7.4	20.0
1986	18.5	9.3	8.4	21.3	11.0	9.3	28.5	5.1	22.3
1987	13.8	15.5	-1.5	16.4	13.7	2.3	19.6	13.1	5.8
1988	14.2	10.2	3.7	15.1	9.9	4.7	14.4	9.1	4.9
1989	14.8	15.3	-0.5	16.9	15.0	1.7	13.2	14.1	-0.8
1990	8.5	11.1	-2.3	11.8	11.8	0.0	7.4	8.1	-0.6
1991	9.9	22.6	-10.4	13.4	22.6	-7.5	16.7	18.0	-1.1
1992	11.6	11.0	0.5	14.2	11.2	2.7	17.7	13.3	3.9
1993	28.1	18.9	7.7	26.8	20.3	5.4	29.4	26.7	2.2
1994	14.9	2.4	12.1	15.2	1.2	13.8	10.7	9.5	1.1
1995	17.2	12.6	4.1	18.1	10.4	7.0	15.0	13.1	1.7
1996	18.5	12.1	5.8	20.1	10.5	8.7	19.7	9.2	9.7

*Returns are for the largest 1,000 companies and are based on quarterly rebalancing.

Source: Prudential Securities

Comparing the P/E Model with PSR and ESR

We also compared the popular P/E model with PSR and ESR. None was perfect (obviously no model is)—they weren't even models one should scrutinize (defined as models with returns decreasing monotonically or where Q1 beats the other quintiles and Q5 lags in most years). No model clearly beat the other two, either, but in our estimation ESR came out the best. P/E worked the best of the three as a buy recommendation, ESR's sell recommendations worked better than those of the other two, and so the spread between Q1 and Q5 was highest for ESR. P/E did have a slightly higher correlation coefficient, however.

The test results of P/E over the same period looked better than for PSR, especially on the buy side. The lowest-P/E quintile returned 20.5%, 1.7 percentage points more than the lowest PSR quintile, but just slightly ahead of ESR's 19.9% return. From beginning to end, the highest-P/E quintile (or sell ideas), however, had a higher average return (15.5%) than the highest-PSR quintile. ESR came out ahead of PSR, with the lowest Q5 return, 14.4%. The average annual spread for P/E is 4.4%, one percentage point higher than for PSR, but lower than ESR's average 4.8% spread. The top quintile beat the bottom one for both the PSR and P/E models in 41 of the 75 quarters tested, whereas the spread was positive in 43 quarters for ESR.

The lowest-P/E companies had a much higher likelihood of beating the market than did the lowest-PSR ones (64.0% versus 50.7%); ESR's "hit ratio" was 61.3%. Higher-P/E stocks were also less likely to outpace the market (44.0% versus 46.7%), but high-ESR stocks were the most likely to lag—only 41.3% beat the market on average.

PSR and ESR shine on the sell side in down markets, when less than 6% of the highest-quintile names beat the S&P compared with 11.1% of the highest-P/E names.

The Models Didn't Always Correlate

Although the models' performance is highly correlated, there were a few years when one or two worked and the others didn't (Figures 4.1 through 4.3).

For example, 1982 and 1993 were good years for the sales-based models, but not for P/E. In 1986 and 1991, P/E fared well, whereas PSR and ESR did poorly. In 1995 P/E did well, ESR did marginally well, and PSR had a negative spread between top- and bottom-quintile returns.

We also looked at the returns for three-year rolling periods, since the effectiveness of a model (or its user) is likely to be brought into question if returns fall short for lengthy periods. In general, since all the models have a value orientation, when one worked over three years they all worked, although this was not true for every three-year period (Table 4.3).

On a three-year rolling basis, the spread for ESR was positive in all but two periods: right at the beginning of the test (1978-80) and in 1989-91 (when most measures of value fared poorly).

PSR showed a negative spread (albeit sometimes only slightly) in those years but also in the four years ended 1981, 1987, 1989, and 1990.

P/E showed a much less negative spread in 1991 but was also slightly negative (although insignificantly so) in the three years ended 1989 and 1990. Of the 17 three-year periods in the study, P/E had the highest spread in 8, ESR in 6, and PSR in 3.

For one-year periods, ESR came out slightly ahead: It had the best spread in 8 years, followed by P/E in 7, and PSR in 4 of the 19 years.

Figures 4.1 through 4.3

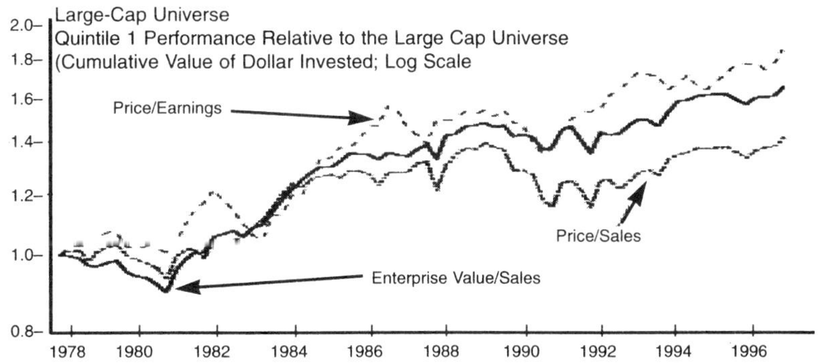

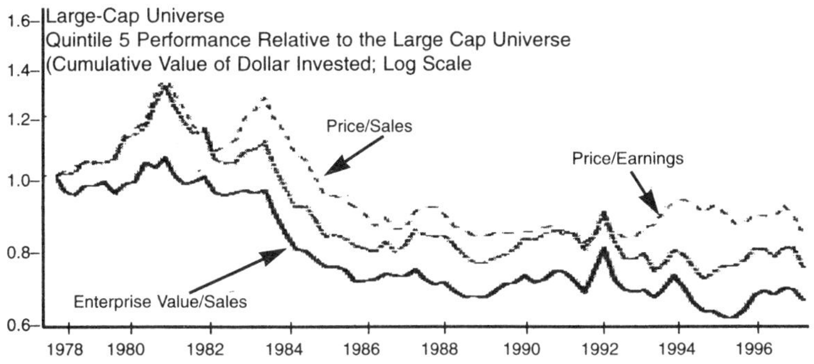

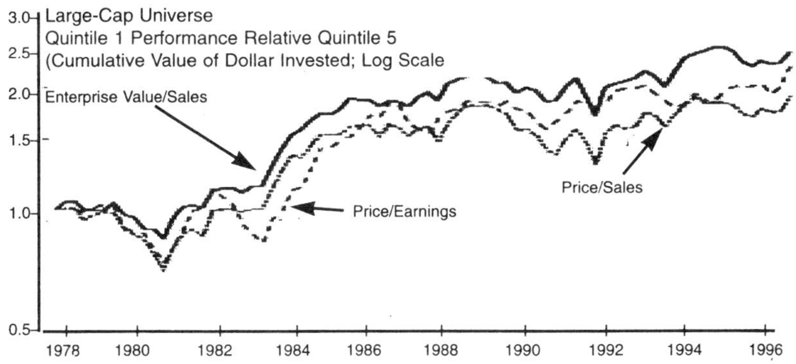

Sector Composition

These various models produce such different results at least in part because of the sector weightings they suggest. We found that buying the most attractive stocks according to each of these models would yield extremely different sector weightings. In addition, these sector weightings could change quite a bit through time. These differences came about because of changes in the overall composition of the large-cap universe we tested, as well as the idiosyncrasies of each sectors' valuations. The percent of the biggest 1000 companies in financial services, for example, ranged from 9.7% in 1980 to about 19.5% in 1992. In 1980, the top quintile of PSR was just under the universe's weighting in the group, whereas both ESR and P/E showed a big overweighting (Tables 4.4 and 4.5).

Table 4.4 Q1 Beat Q5 More Than Half the Quarters for All Sectors

	Percent of Years			Percent Of Companies Beating S&P Composite		
	Q1 Beat Sector	Q5 Lagged Sector	Q1 Beat Q5	All	Q1	Q5
Basic Industry	47.4	63.2	57.9	46.9	52.0	41.3
Business Services	63.2	63.2	63.2	49.6	52.0	42.7
Capital Spending	68.4	47.4	63.2	45.3	48.0	44.0
Consumer Cyclical	52.6	73.7	63.2	44.5	52.0	40.0
Consumer Services	63.2	57.9	57.9	53.9	56.0	54.7
Consumer Staples	57.9	57.9	68.4	56.5	62.7	50.7
Energy	73.7	84.2	78.9	49.1	60.0	40.0
Financial Services	[illegible]	[illegible]	57.9	50.0	53.3	58.7
Health Care	36.8	73.7	57.9	52.8	48.0	46.7
Technology	57.9	57.9	57.9	46.9	50.7	50.7
Utilities	68.4	63.2	68.4	46.1	50.7	45.3
Large-Cap Universe	57.9	63.2	63.2	48.5	61.3	41.3

Model is enterprise value/sales.

Source: Prudential Securities Inc.

Table 4.5 Top Quintile (Most Attractive): Percent of Companies in Economic Sectors

Economic Sector	1980 PSR	1980 WSR	1980 PE	1980 Universe	1984 PSR	1984 WSR	1984 PE	1984 Universe
Basic Industry	16.7	6.0	17.3	19.4	15.0	5.7	14.6	15.8
Business Services	1.3	0.9	1.9	4.2	1.8	0.7	0.5	4.3
Capital Spending	1.3	2.6	1.2	7.2	3.5	2.1	3.8	5.2
Conglomerates	3.8	1.7	1.2	1.3	2.7	1.4	0.9	1.6
Consumer Cyclical	10.3	8.6	6.8	4.1	7.1	5.7	4.7	4.1
Consumer Services	35.9	23.3	9.3	11.6	23.0	22.9	3.8	14.8
Consumer Staples	10.3	6.0	4.9	6.4	3.5	4.3	1.4	5.8
Energy	5.1	3.4	3.1	13.7	11.5	5.0	12.3	8.6
Financial Services	7.7	40.5	33.3	9.7	15.0	37.9	23.1	14.2
Health Care	2.6	3.4	1.9	3.7	4.4	3.6	0.9	4.8
Technology	3.8	3.4	0.6	9.0	3.5	5.0	2.8	9.9
Utilities	1.3	0.0	18.5	9.5	8.8	5.7	31.1	10.7

Economic Sector	1988 PSR	1988 WSR	1988 PE	1988 Universe	1992 PSR	1992 WSR	1992 PE	1992 Universe	1996 PSR	1996 WSR	1996 PE	1996 Universe
Basic Industry	4.7	7.3	21.1	15.6	10.6	6.8	14.5	13.6	17.2	8.1	18.7	12.2
Business Services	0.0	0.8	1.2	4.6	1.1	1.0	4.3	4.4	2.2	4.7	4.2	5.4
Capital Spending	3.5	2.4	2.5	4.7	3.2	2.9	2.7	4.3	2.2	3.5	4.2	3.6
Conglomerates	0.0	0.0	2.5	1.5	1.1	1.9	0.5	1.0	1.1	2.3	0.6	0.9
Consumer Cyclical	5.8	5.6	3.3	3.3	4.3	1.0	2.7	2.9	7.5	4.7	3.6	2.4
Consumer Services	16.3	14.5	9.5	13.3	21.3	14.6	9.7	13.9	25.8	30.2	10.2	13.5
Consumer Staples	5.8	5.6	0.8	5.8	3.2	1.0	2.7	5.8	1.1	2.3	0.6	4.8
Energy	3.5	0.8	6.6	6.7	7.4	3.9	8.1	6.5	5.4	5.8	6.0	8.4
Financial Services	47.7	49.2	36.4	19.8	38.3	47.6	34.9	19.5	16.1	17.4	22.3	17.8
Health Care	5.8	5.6	2.5	4.9	3.2	3.9	6.5	7.7	9.7	11.6	4.8	7.6
Technology	7.0	8.1	5.8	8.3	6.4	15.5	11.3	10.2	7.5	9.3	13.3	14.4
Utilities	0.0	0.0	7.9	11.4	0.0	0.0	2.2	10.2	4.3	0.0	11.4	8.8

The same was true at the end of 1984, but by 1988 all three models were heavily invested in financial stocks. By 1996, all had dropped that weighting substantially.

Utilities' share of the overall universe has stayed reasonably constant, but its share of the various model quintiles has varied quite a bit. Only in 1984 did any utilities make the cut for ESR, but that year the group was 8.8% of the top PSR quintile and 31% of the low P/E category . At the end of 1992, utilities were underweighted (or zero weighted) on all three models. Consumer services (largely the retailers) have been overweighted compared with the overall universe in each of the five year-ends on PSR and ESR, but underweighted as part of the lowest P/Es. Technology has remained consistently underweighted in the top PSR quintile, but jumped around based on ESR and P/E. These sector weightings have a big effect on the performance of the models and on how effectively an investor can use them. (Some of the suggested weightings could be extreme for many portfolio managers, unless they have a very strong conviction about using them).

The ESR Model Worked Fairly Well in Most Sectors

Another way to look at this issue is to determine how well a model works at distinguishing stocks within a sector (as opposed to across sectors). To avoid presenting an excessive number of charts, we chose to focus our sector work on the ESR model (Figure 4.4). The top quintile of ESR out paced the sector average for every group except health care. Only bottom-quintile stocks in technology and financial services failed to lag the sector. The average spread between top- and bottom-quintile returns was positive for every sector, although just barely so for financial services (as was the case for this sector in the price/sales model's test). Some sectors had long strings of poor model performance as well.

Sector returns were more or less monotonically decreasing, and the performance charts looked best for capital spending, consumer cyclical, energy, and utilities. The best top-to-bottom spreads appeared in consumer cyclical and energy.

Figure 4.4

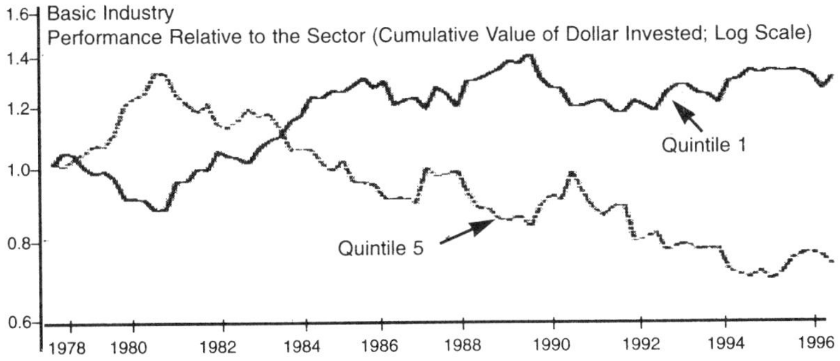
Basic Industry
Performance Relative to the Sector (Cumulative Value of Dollar Invested; Log Scale)
1.6
1.4
1.2
1.0
0.8
0.6
Quintile 1
Quintile 5
1978
1980
1982
1984
1986
1988
1990
1992
1994
1996

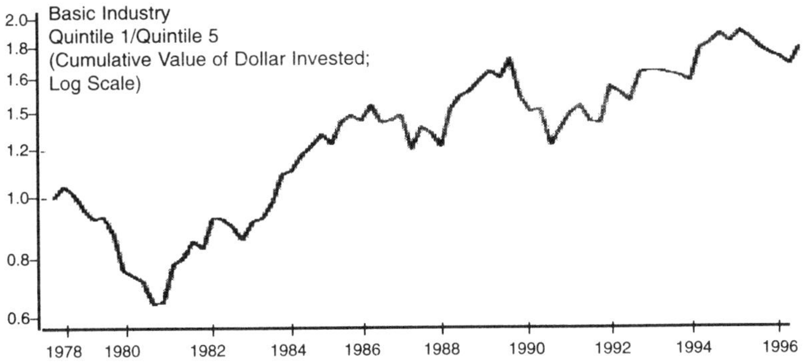
Basic Industry
Quintile 1/Quintile 5
(Cumulative Value of Dollar Invested;
Log Scale)
2.0
1.8
1.6
1.5
1.2
1.0
0.8
0.6
1978
1980
1982
1984
1986
1988
1990
1992
1994
1996

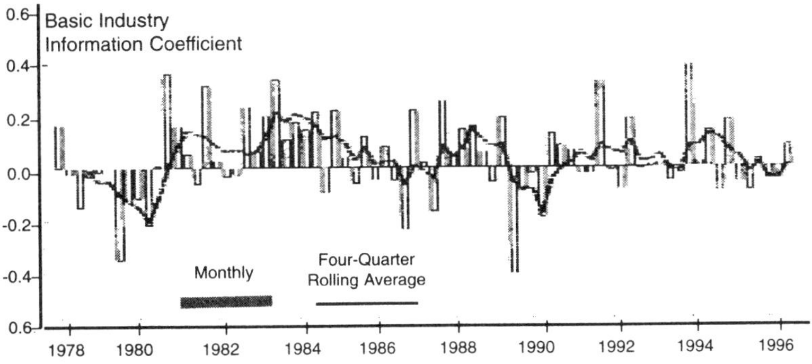
Basic Industry
Information Coefficient
0.6
0.4
0.2
0.0
-0.2
-0.4
0.6
Monthly
Four-Quarter
Rolling Average
1978
1980
1982
1984
1986
1988
1990
1992
1994
1996

Figure 4.4, *Cont'd*

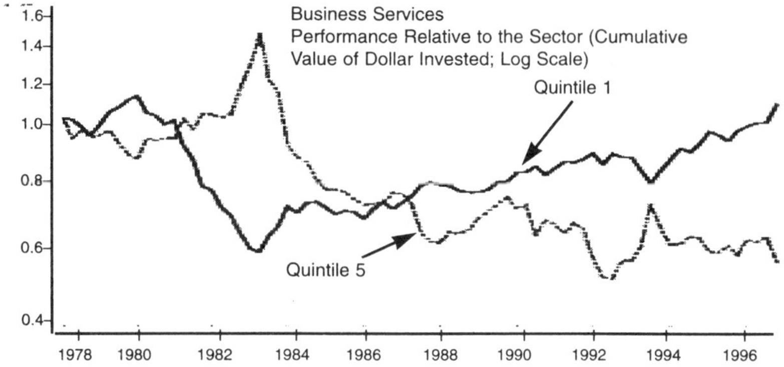

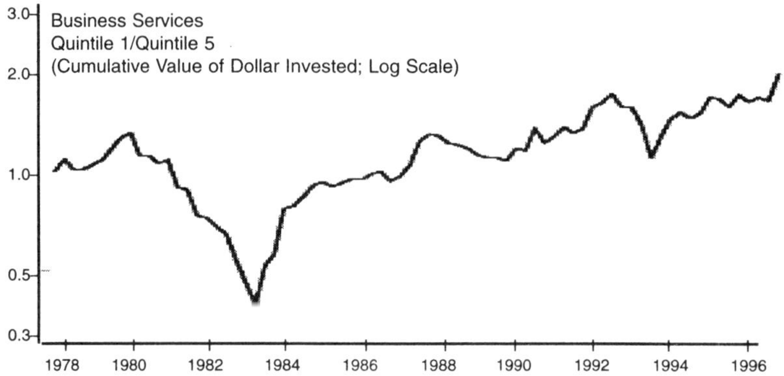

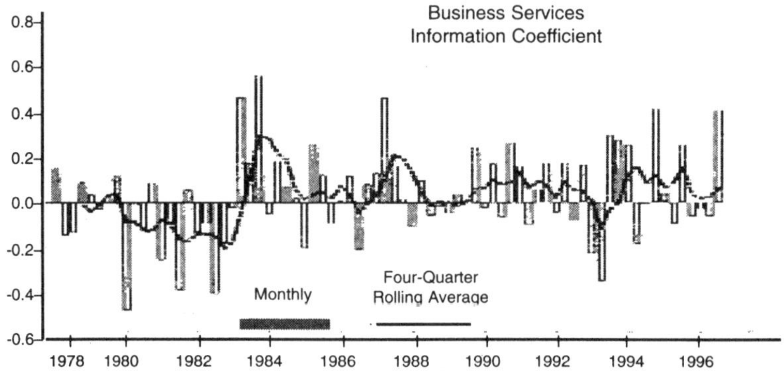

Figure 4.4, *Cont'd*

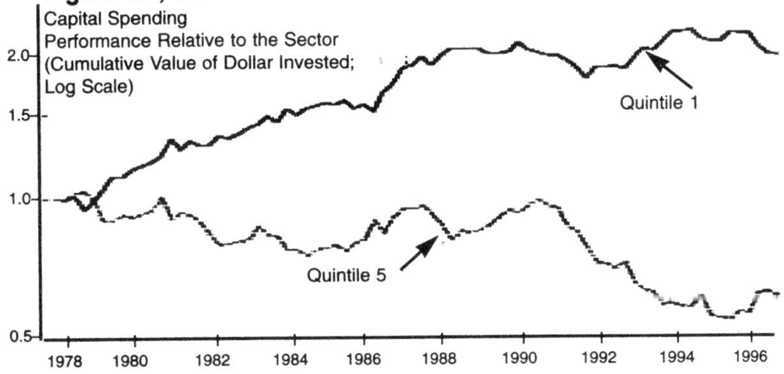

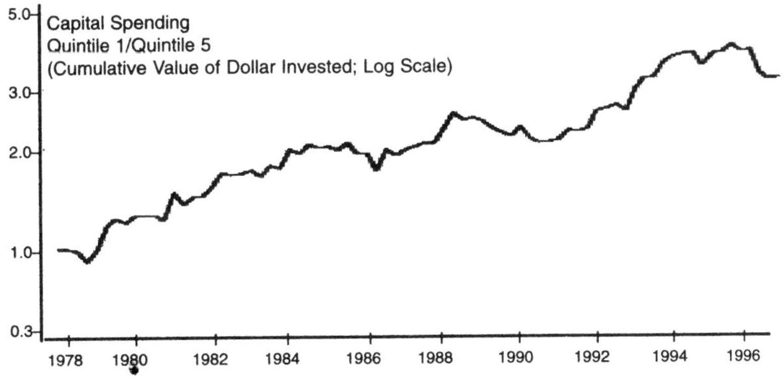

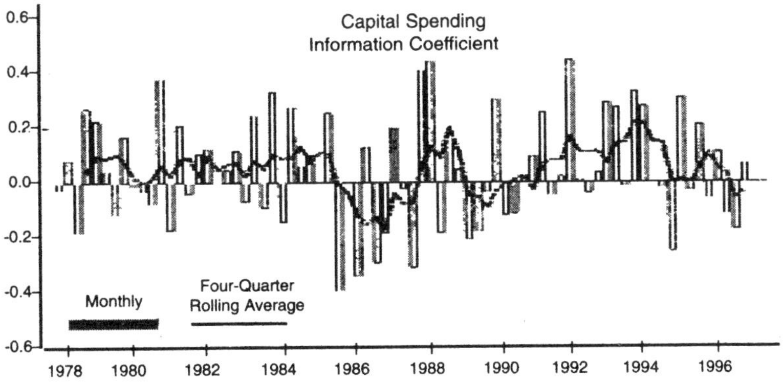

Figure 4.4, *Cont'd*

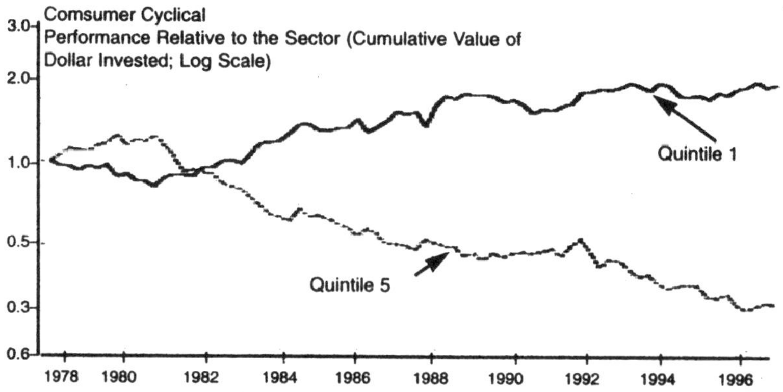

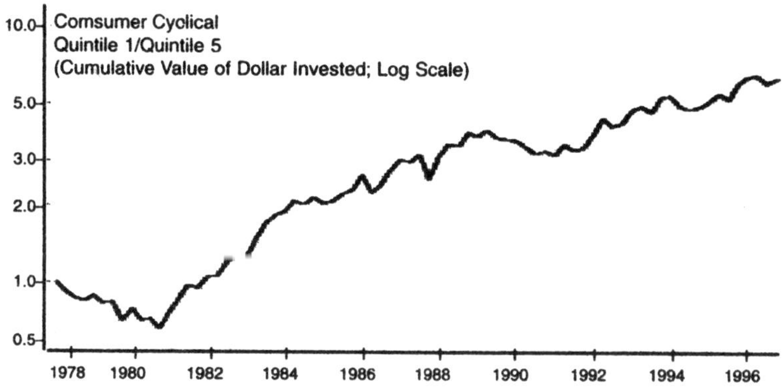

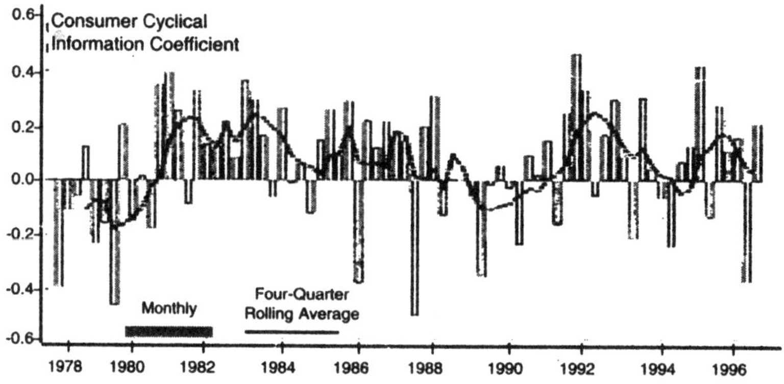

Figure 4.4, *Cont'd*

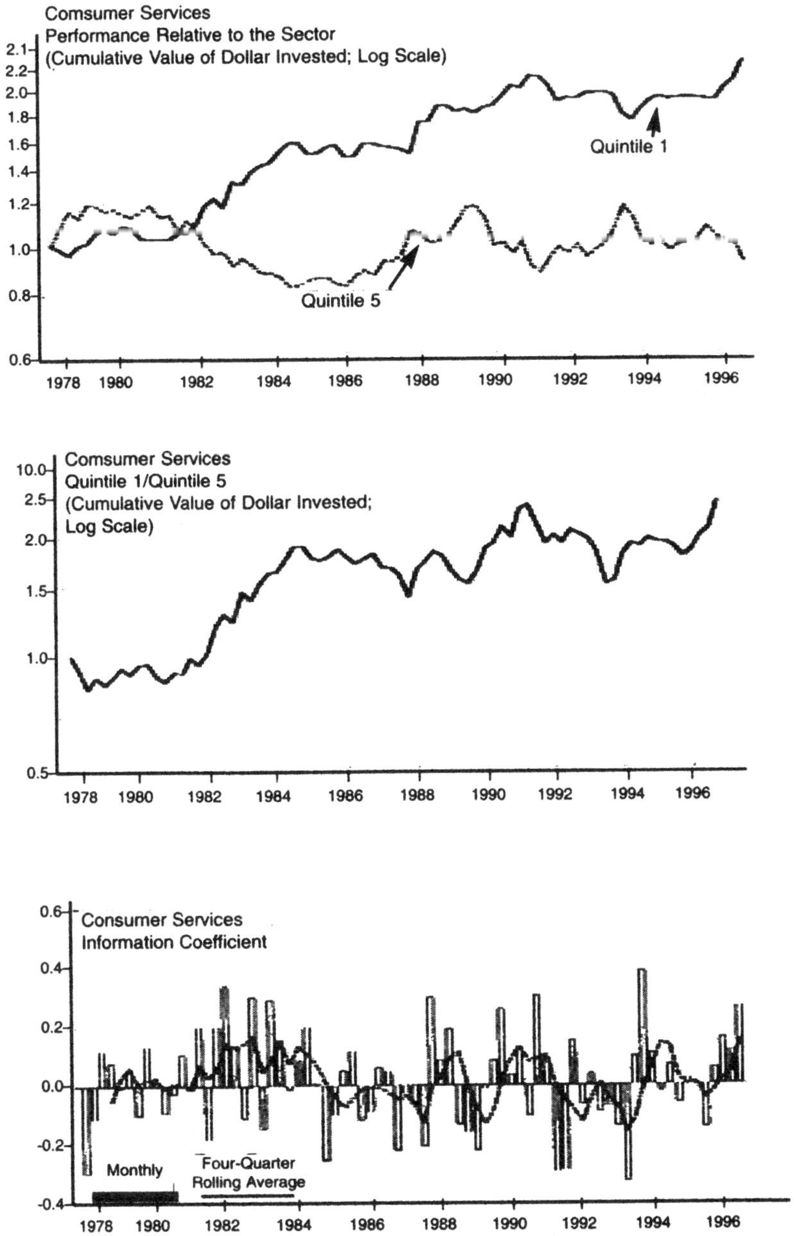

Figure 4.4, *Cont'd*

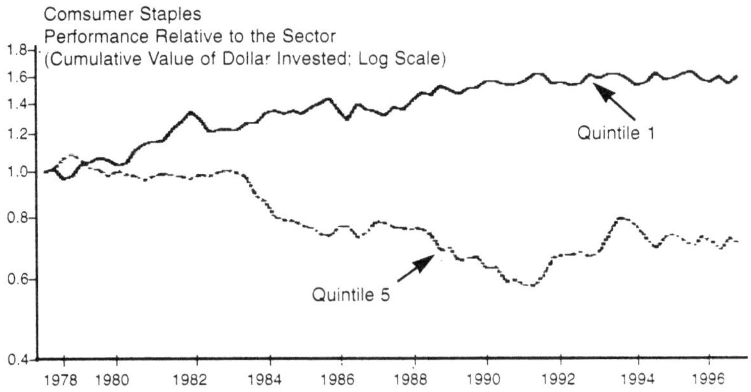

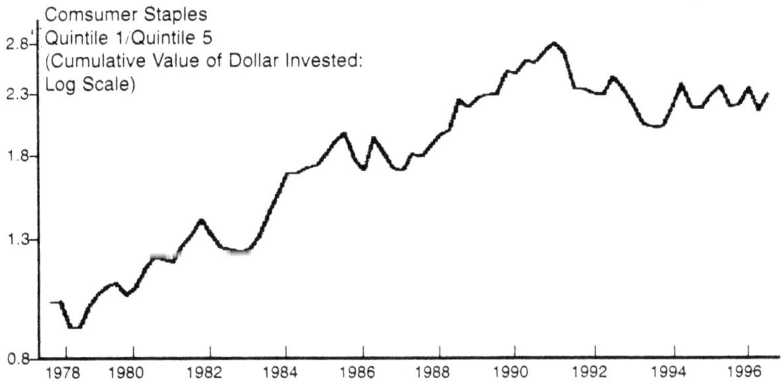

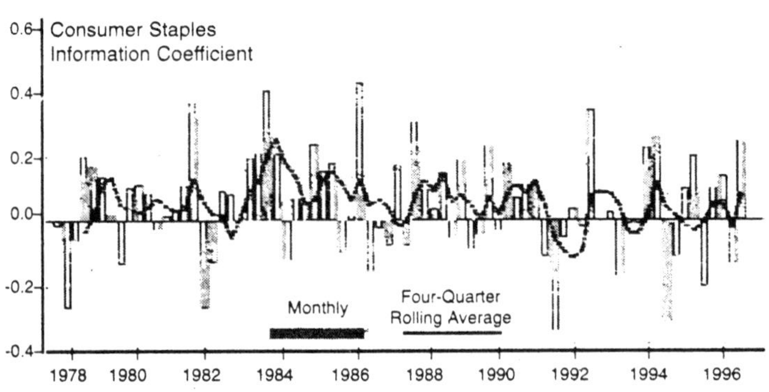

Figure 4.4, *Cont'd*

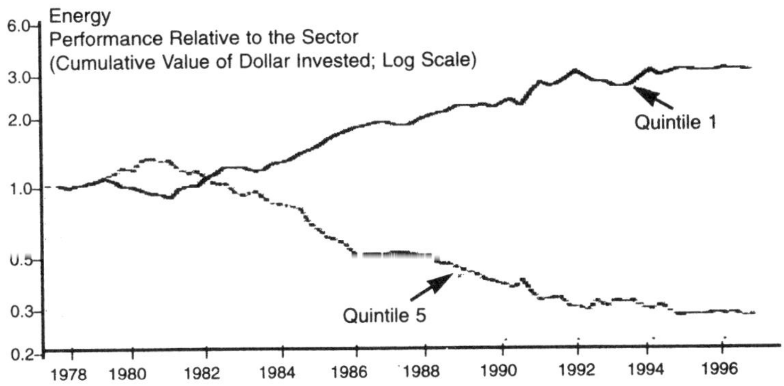

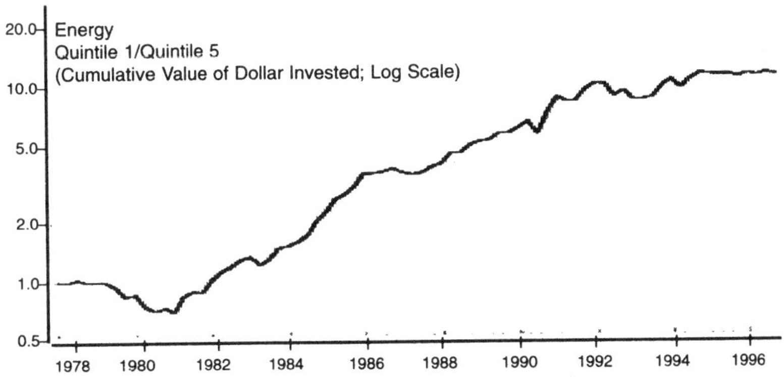

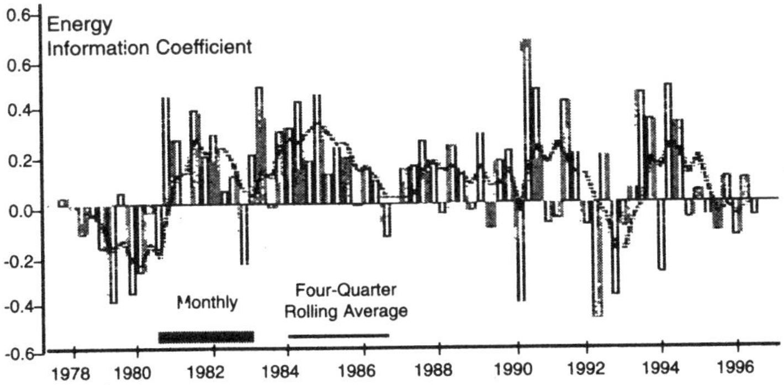

Figure 4.4, *Cont'd*

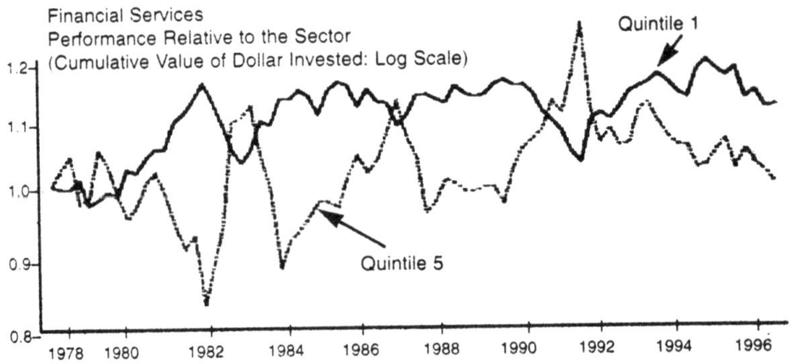

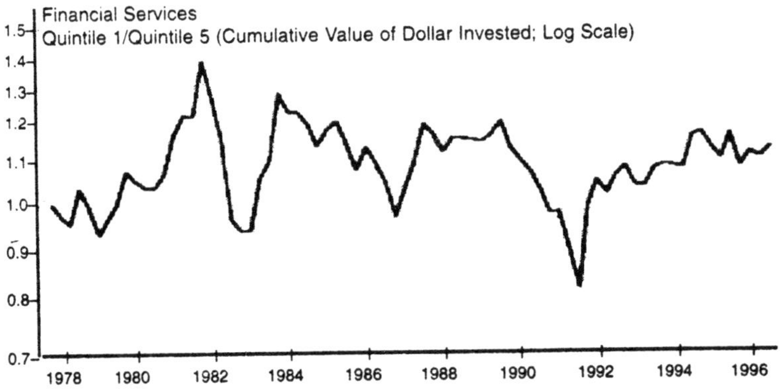

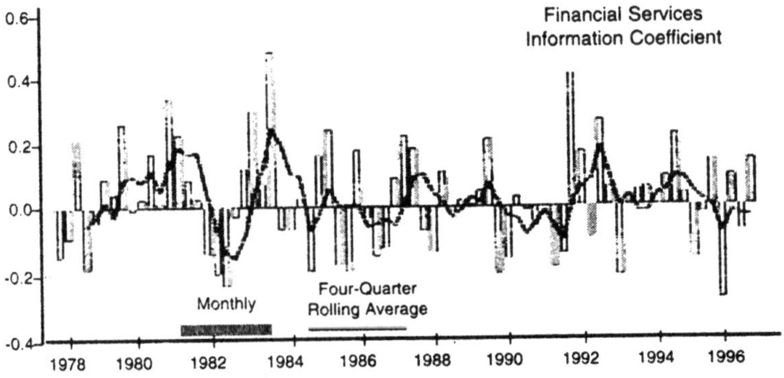

Figure 4.4, *Cont'd*

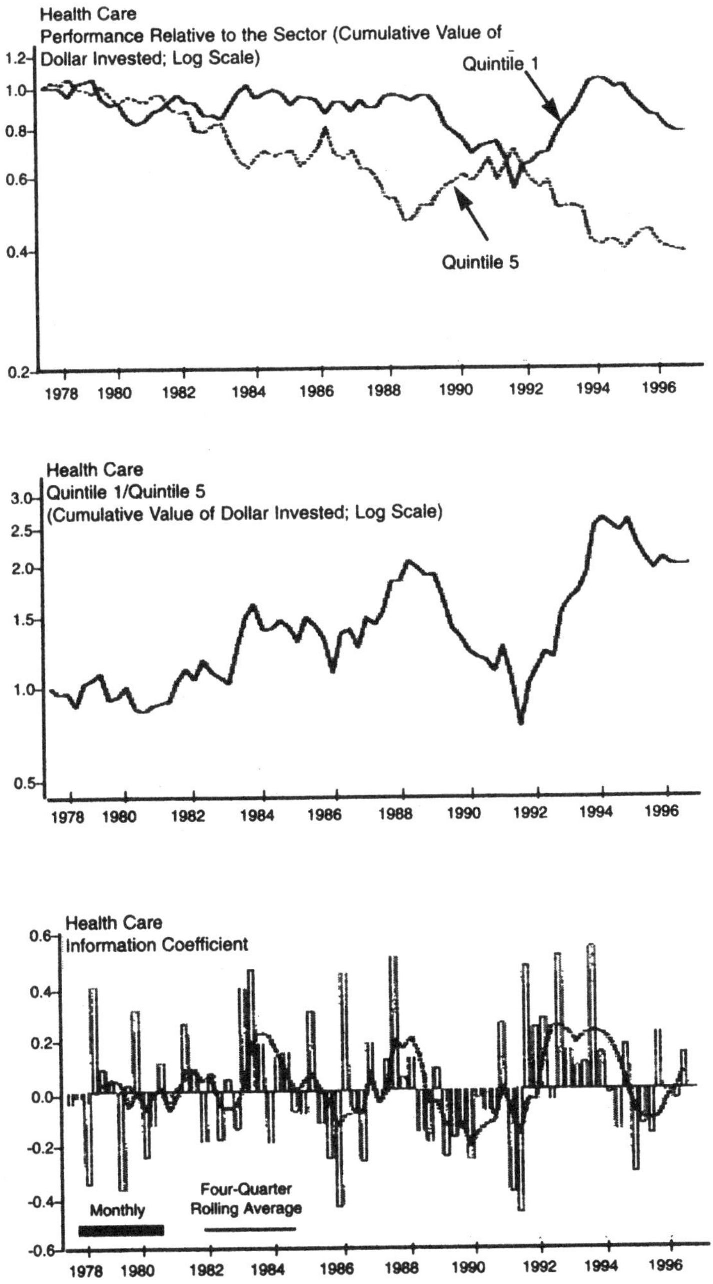

Figure 4.4, *Cont'd*

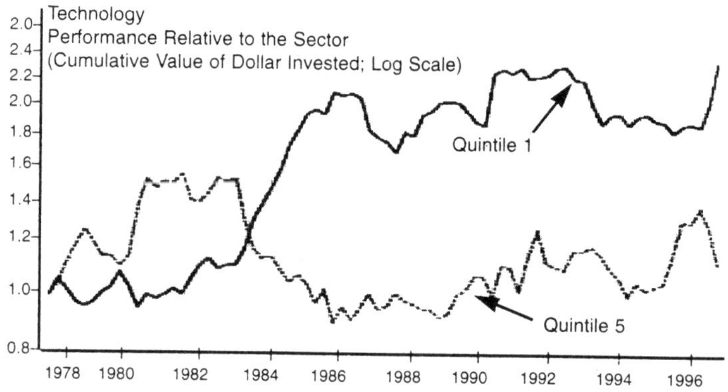

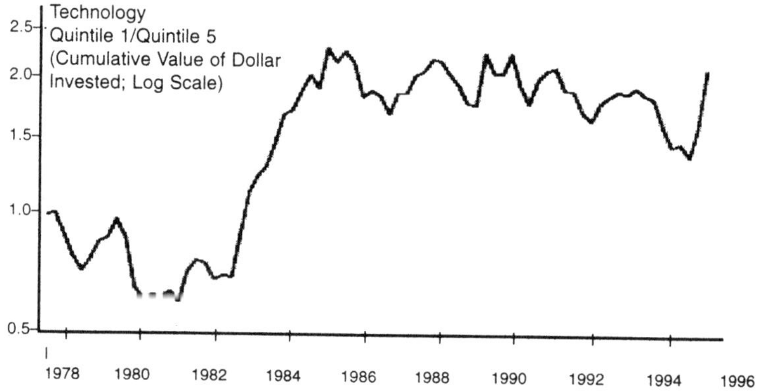

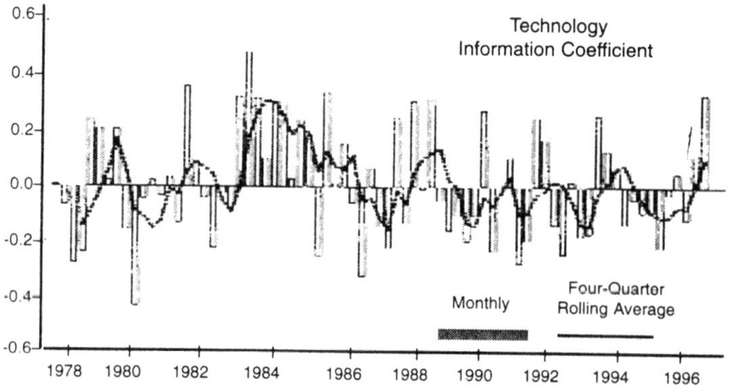

Figure 4.4, *Cont'd*

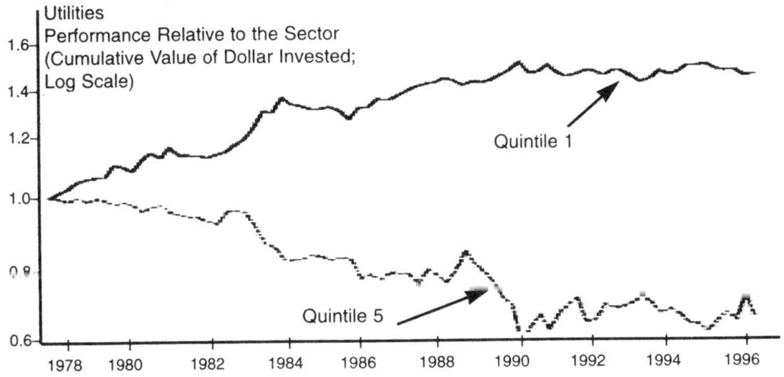

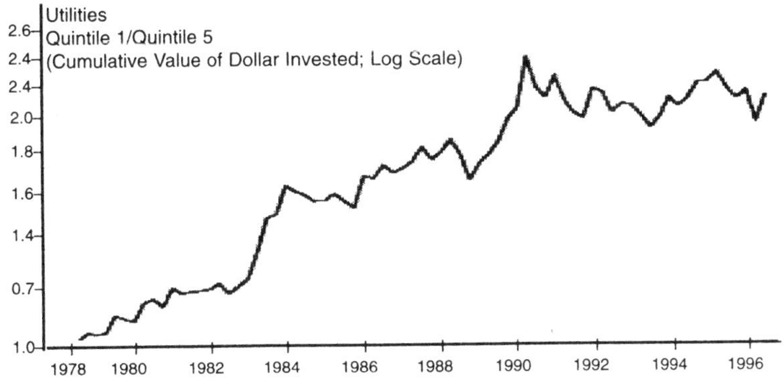

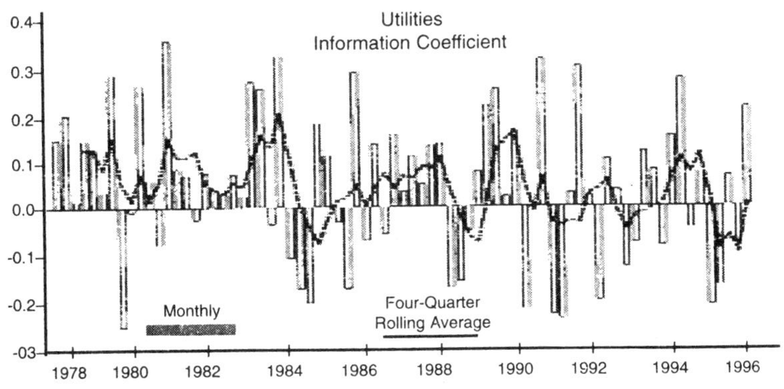

Q1 beat the sector most frequently in energy, capital spending, and utilities. Energy's lowest quintile also lagged the universe most often, followed by consumer cyclical and health care. Energy also comes out on top in terms of the frequency with which Q1 beat Q5; consumer staples and utilities follow closely.

The performance charts seem to indicate a rather random pattern of return for financial services, health care, and technology. Business services had a long period of Quintile 5's beating Quintile 1 from 1979 to 1983, but performance has been pretty good since then.

Q1 stocks were more likely to outpace the S&P Composite than the overall sector in all sectors except financial services and health care. Similarly, Q5 stocks had a higher probability of lagging the market than did the sector in all sectors except consumer services, financial services, and technology. And in every sector except financial services and technology, a Q1 stock had a higher chance of beating the market than did a Q5 stock.

Conclusion

All three of these models could be used as effective tools for stock selection. The user must be aware that none of them work all the time or for every stock and that different models do well in different market environments. Based on a number of criteria, however, not the least of which is intuitive appeal, enterprise value/sales appears to be the best of the lot.

CHAPTER 5

Normalized Value

Ross Paul Bruner
Managing Director
Istituto Mobiliare Italiano (IMI) Group

Overview

Normalized Value Is Quality

Normalized value is based on the notion that quality is as important as cost in selecting individual shares. In essence, it represents an effort to bring the principles of value investing to the process of selecting a highly profitable business to invest in. Given the excess total return of 300 percentage points over 26 years, we think such a framework is essential to consistently outperform benchmarks such as the S&P 500. In this chapter, we focus on ROE divided by P/B (return on equity/price-to-book ratio) as one measure of identifying undervalued shares in profitable companies. As with value strategies in general, extreme valuation can often be a proxy for risk.

Table 5.1 Growth, Quality, and Valuation by Sector

	11-Aug-97 % of Total	5-Year EPS Growth	5-Year Avg ROE	F'cast EPS Growth	F'cast ROE FY 1	5-Year Avg P/B
BASIC MATERIAL						
WTD AVERAGE		0.2	13.4	35.4	22.1	4.1
TOTAL	5.8					
CONSUMER DURABLE						
WTD AVERAGE		10.8	5.5	17.1	22.3	3.0
TOTAL	3.6					
CONSUMER MERCHANDISE						
WTD AVERAGE		17.2	15.0	16.5	18.2	4.1
TOTAL	4.8					
CONSUMER NON-DURABLE						
WTD AVERAGE		12.4	29.8	20.8	38.7	7.4
TOTAL	10.3					
CONSUMER SERVICE						
WTD AVERAGE		11.7	8.8	19.1	17.2	3.7
TOTAL	5.4					
ENERGY						
WTD AVERAGE		0.5	12.7	15.6	17.5	3.7
TOTAL	7.0					
FINANCIAL						
WTD AVERAGE		13.2	14.2	13.9	10.0	3.0
TOTAL	16.3					
HEALTH CARE						
WTD AVERAGE		16.1	22.3	20.5	32.3	8.4
TOTAL	9.9					
INDUSTRIAL						
WTD AVERAGE		6.9	13.9	17.8	20.3	4.1
TOTAL	6.5					
TECHNOLOGY						
WTD AVERAGE		26.2	12.9	26.0	28.3	5.5
TOTAL	21.0					
UTILITY						
WTD AVERAGE		-0.2	15.2	10.5	18.7	2.8
TOTAL	9.4					
OVERALL WTD AVERAGE		13.1	15.7	19.5	24.8	4.7
OVERALL TOTAL	100.0					

Source: Compustat, First Call & IMI estimates.

Quality Is Neither Growth nor Value

Quality shares rank high on profitability but not necessarily on EPS (earnings per share) growth (see Table 5.1). Notice that technology that has the highest historical EPS growth rate (26%) has a below-market return on equity (13%). Also, consumer non-durable has a below average EPS growth rate (12%) and a substantially above-average return on equity (30%). In short, although highly profitable companies tend to produce higher EPS growth as well, it is not a purely linear function. In terms of the relationship between quality and value, relatively unprofitable shares can also be associated with above-average valuations. Technology, for example, is below average on a historical basis in terms of profitability (13%) and well above average in terms of historical valuations (5-year historical price-to-book ratio = 5.5x versus 4.7x for the market). It is interesting to note that the equal-weighted normalized value strategy outperformed the pure value strategy by 156 percentage points, but the cap-weighted normalized value strategy underperformed the pure value index by 13 percentage points. Our pure value strategy (ranked by P/B ratio) outperformed the S&P 500 by 144 percentage points from 1970 through 1996 (see Figure 5.3).

Normalized ROE Adds Value

Over the 26 years in our study, normalized ROE added value in the top two quintiles on an equal- and capitalization-weighted basis. (See Figures 5.1 and 5.2.) We ranked a contemporaneous universe of the largest 500 stocks by trailing ROE divided by P/B ratio in order to normalize profitability relative to value. We believe the equal-weighted and cap-weighted excess relative total returns across quintiles 1 and 2 demonstrate the effectiveness of normalized value, and suggest, as with value strategies in general, extremely low valuation is often a proxy for risk. In other words, stocks that trade at extremely low valuations relative to profitability are inherently riskier investments. It is for this reason that we use quantitative tools to support an active management process.

Figure 5.1

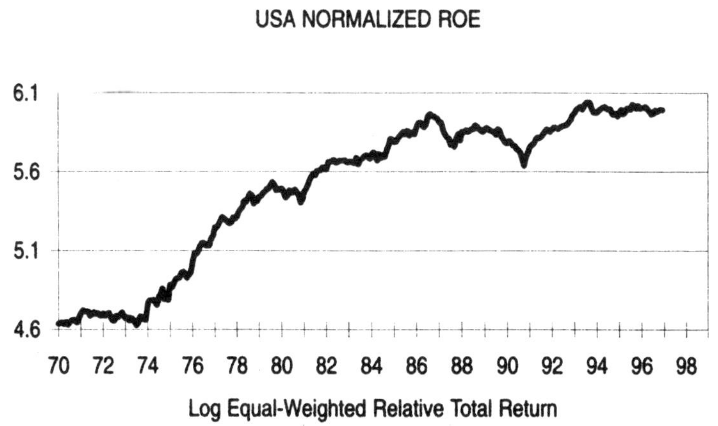

Figure 5.2

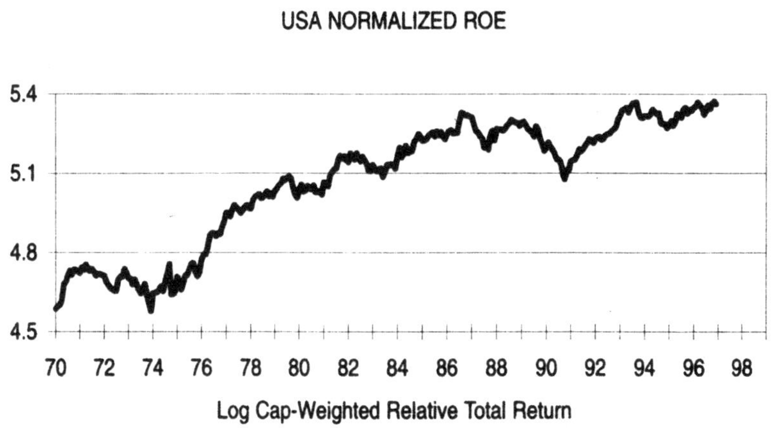

Figure 5.3

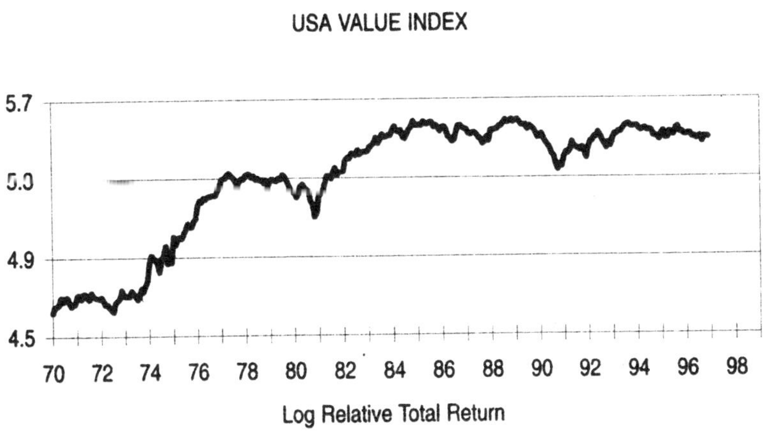

Figure 5.4

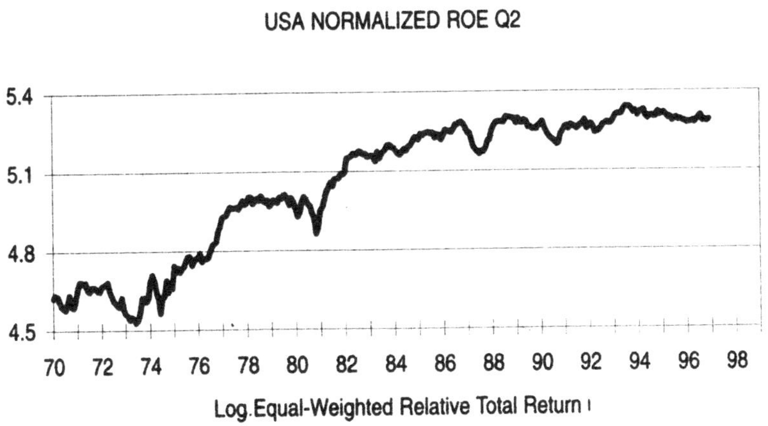

Figure 5.5

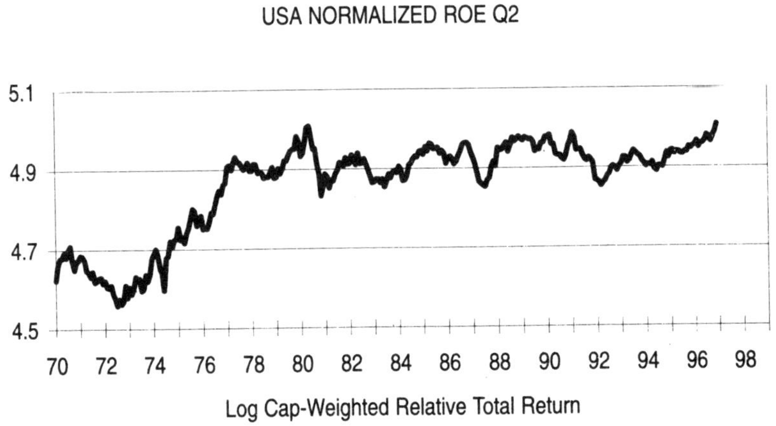

Figure 5.6

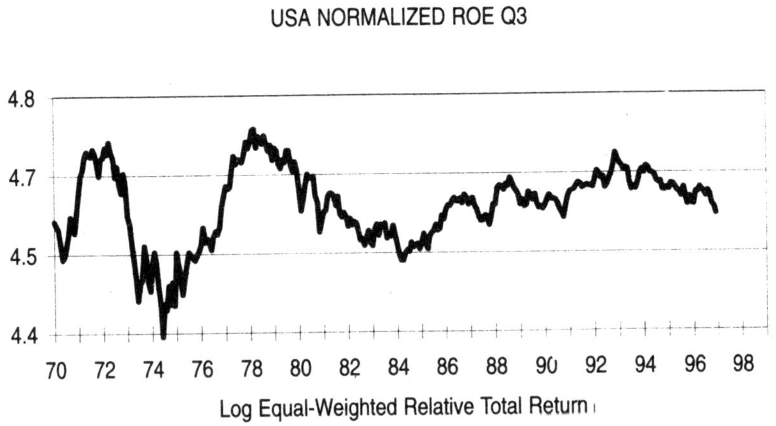

Figure 5.7

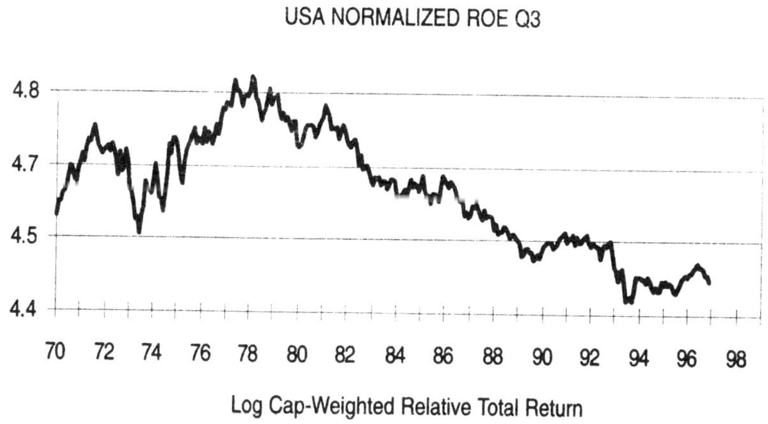

Figure 5.8

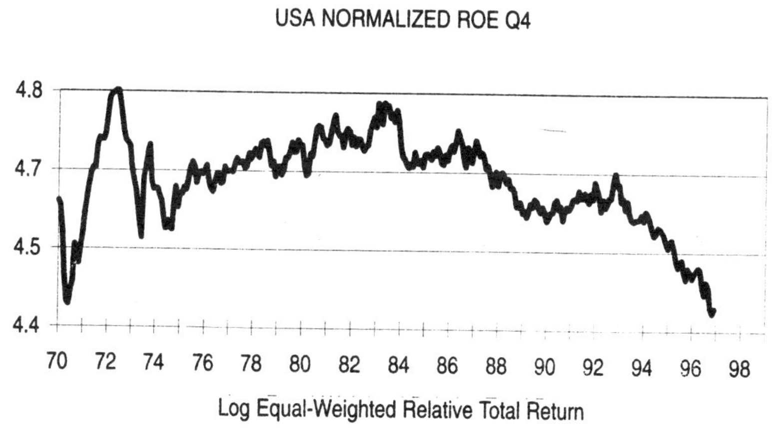

Methodology

ROE Divided By Price-To-Book

We ranked our large-cap universe of 500 stocks by ROE divided by price-to-book. We assigned companies with negative EPS or BPS (book value per share) to the low normalized value quintile. Companies that trade at an 80% or greater discount-to-book value are also assigned to the low normalized value quintile. Here too, we find that extremely low valuation is often a proxy for risk. We think it makes sense to treat such "sick" companies as not meaningful in terms of understanding the relationship between profitability and valuation.

Controlling Turnover

We control turnover by using an annual selection process that results in turnover ranging from 40% to 70%. Because we define quality in terms of financial characteristics, the natural rate of turnover is slower than for pure value strategies, which we define in terms of price. Quality is, at best, a quarterly strategy, while value strategies can be run as frequently as the price changes. Our value benchmarks are created from an annual price-to-book ranking from a large-cap contemporaneous universe of shares. Normalized ROE extends the frequency of quality investing to a monthly or even continuous basis.

Dividends Matter Over Time

The underperformance in total return for the bottom two quintiles compared with outperformance for the top two quintiles illustrates the fact that dividends matter over time (see "Analytical Approaches To Stock Selection.") (See Figures 5.8 through 5.11.) The high and second normalized value quintiles command 40% and 30% premiums to the market dividend yield, respectively, compared with 50% and 30% discounts for the low normalized value and fourth quintiles, respectively. (See Figures 5.12 through 5.15.) A dividend stream is far less volatile than a capital appreciation stream, and thus benefits from the effect of consistency on the compounding process. This is not to say that investors should entirely avoid low normalized value shares, but rather that buying quality stocks successfully over time requires some of the same skills as value investing. Often stocks that score well on normalized ROE pay dividends but are not necessarily the highest-growth companies in the market. By putting the quality in context of cost (expressed by the P/B multiple), normalized value strategies can take advantage of larger and more mature

Figure 5.9

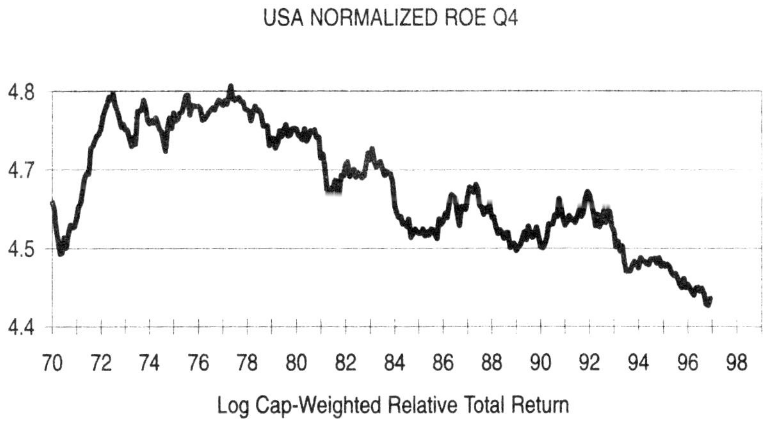

Figure 5.10

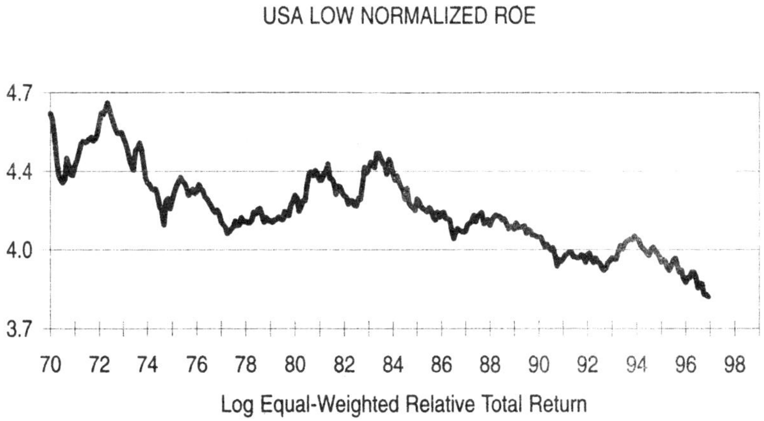

Figure 5.11

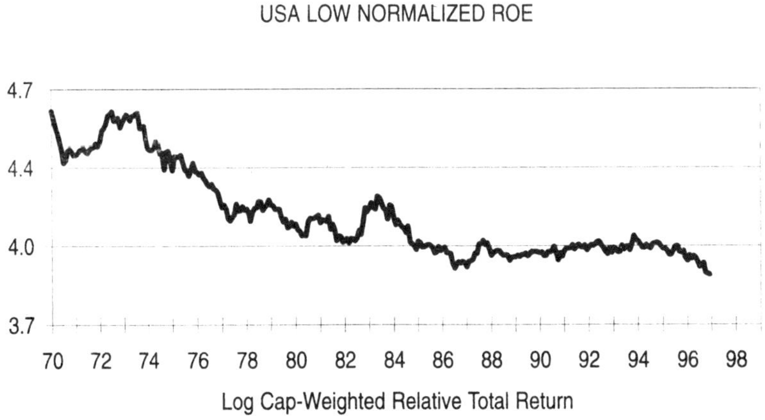

shares that often pay significant dividends. We believe this is the reason why normalized value investing adds performance consistently over time.

Small-Capitalization Effects

The process of equal-weighting positions introduces a small-capitalization bias into portfolio returns. In our view, the small-capitalization effect exists because there are structural limits to growth. Truly superior growth does not continue forever, largely because at some point a stock becomes the whole sector, market, or economy. Smaller shares can grow profits faster than larger companies and, as a result, can support faster-growing share prices as well.

Construction

Equal-Weighting Versus Capitalization-Weighting

Equal-weighting company exposure reduces company-specific risk and introduces a small-capitalization effect into portfolio returns. The results of the normalized value study confirm the previous experience that equal-weighted strategies outperform capitalization-weighted strategies. Equal-weighting company exposure, however, implies that a portfolio overweight with respect to sectors can only be constructed if there are a large number of companies available to choose from. We integrate risk management into the construction process by controlling company-specific risk through an equal-weighting discipline. Equal-weighting company exposure ensures that one position does not determine the performance of the entire portfolio. It also reduces the upside benefit from a single decision. We are long-term investors, and are comfortable with the implications of such an approach.

Contemporaneous Composition

Our 26-year normalized-value strategy is developed from a contemporaneous selection universe, which means that we focus on what a fund manager could have owned rather than on companies that survived over time. We believe this to be an effective way of dealing with the issue of "survivor bias," although it has been our experience that current composition strategies can yield largely the same results and have a compelling rationale as well. For example, a fund manager implementing a strategy today is more concerned with today's selection possibilities rather than in the past. In essence, the fact that some companies survive over time is just as significant as the fact that others do not. When we find strategies that work under a variety of different scenarios or methods, we feel more comfortable with the effectiveness of the process.

Annual Selection

We recalculate the composition of our value and normalized value strategies on an annual basis with the information that was available at the time of selection. Annual rebalancing using lagged data ensures that performance results are achievable (i.e., relatively low turnover) and fair given the information available at the time. In practice, we use the preceding year's financial data so that the portfolio simulation is inherently a process that can be replicated going forward. It is our experience that increasing the rebalancing frequency to a monthly basis produces approximately the same rate of turnover per month and does not work particularly well outside the American equity market.

Results

Performance, Valuation, and Composition

Stocks at the top of our normalized value ranking are trading at outstanding valuations relative to quality. High normalized value shares outperformed significantly on an equal-weighted and capitalization-weighted basis: +300 p.p. and +113 p.p., respectively. (See Figure 5.1 and 5.2.) The second quintile results were also very strong, outperforming the market on an equal- and capitalization-weighted basis: +98 p.p. and +49 p.p., respectively. (See Figure 5.4 and 5.5.) Third quintile, however, underperformed on an equal- and capitalization-weighted basis: -1 p.p. and -13 p.p., respectively. (See Figure 5.6 and 5.7.) Fourth quintile performance was a bit worse than the third on an equal- and capitalization-weighted basis: -15 p.p. and -15 p.p., respectively. (See Figure 5.8 and 5.9.) As we expected, the fifth quintile results were significantly better than the other groups on an equal- and capitalization-weighted basis: -54 p.p. and -50 p.p., respectively. (See Figure 5.10 and 5.11.) The results for all five quintiles are consistent with dozens of value studies we have developed across markets where relative performance travels down the ranking consistently. In other words, we view this linear return distribution as a kind of cross-check on the effectiveness of the process.

The foregoing performance results illustrate the effect of dividends on total return over time. Over the 26 years in the study, the high normalized value quintile averaged a 5.2% dividend yield, compared with 4.9%

Figure 5.12

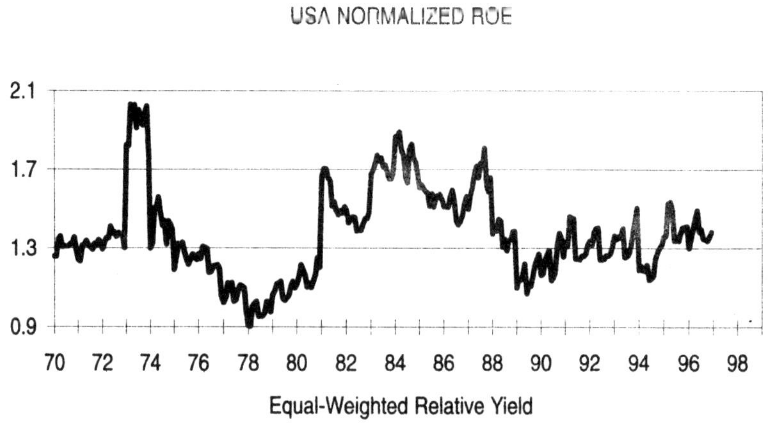

Figure 5.13

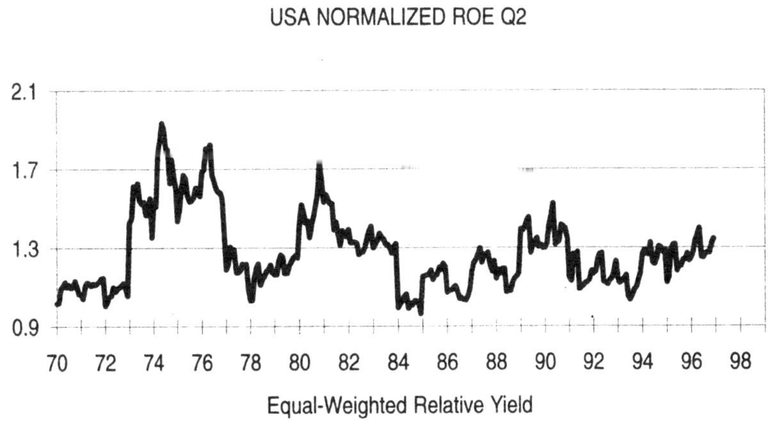

Figure 5.14

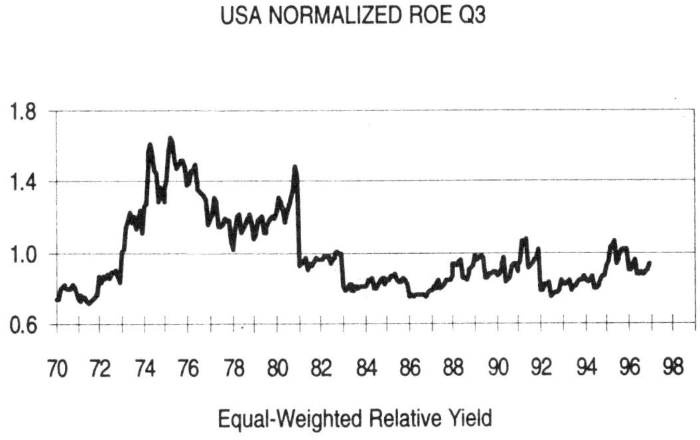

Figure 5.15

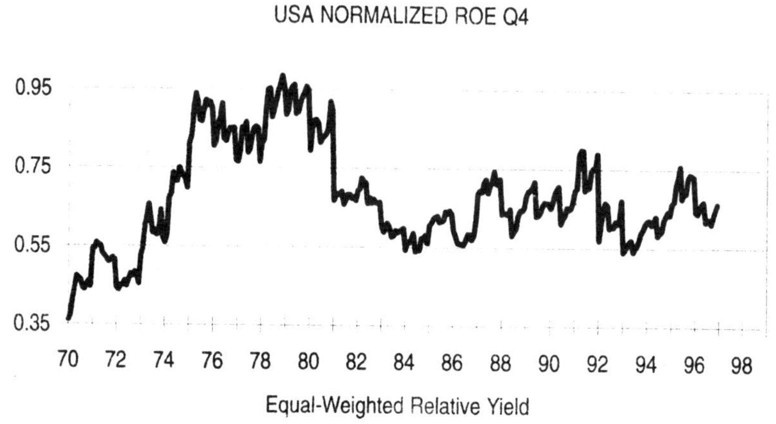

Figure 5.16

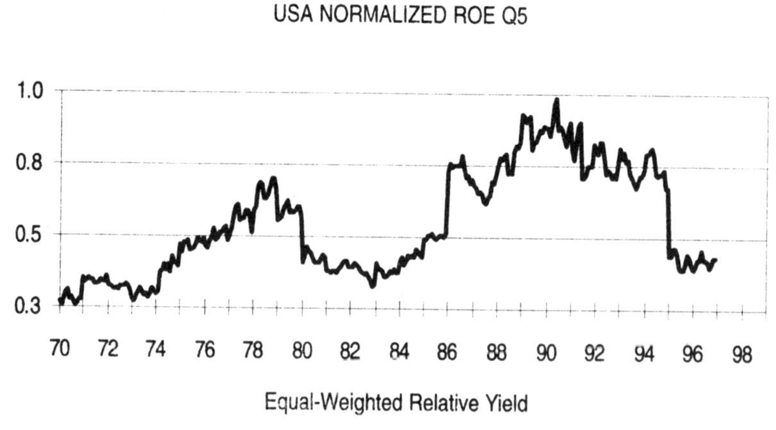

for the second quintile, 3.9% for the third quintile, 2.7% for the fourth quintile, 2.1% for the low normalized value quintile and 3.8% for the S&P 500. (See Figures 5.12 through 5.16.) We believe this is why the high normalized value strategy outperformed the market and the low normalized value strategy did not. Currently, the high normalized value quintile has a dividend yield of 2.8%, compared with 2.8% for the second quintile, 1.9% for the third, 1.4% for the fourth, 0.9% for the low normalized value quintile and 2.0% for the S&P 500. In short, reduce the yield differential versus the market, and then enhance the relative quality of the portfolio.

The composition of our high normalized value strategy illustrates the fact that we placed a size restriction on the selection process. (See Tables 5.2 through 5.5.) The impact of size, therefore, did have some effect on the effectiveness of the strategy, which is evidenced by the difference between the equal-weighted and cap-weighted results (+300 p.p. and +113 p.p., respectively) for the high normalized value strategy. However, because the cap-weighted total returns confirm the equal-weighted results and value can be added across quintiles one and two, the strategy can still be employed on a very large portfolio. For example, in 1970, Exxon Corp. ($13,280 million), Texaco Inc. ($8,344 million), Mobil Corp. ($4,669 million), Ford Motor Co. ($4,496 million) and Chevron Corp. ($4,337 million) were the five largest companies in our normalized value portfolio. (See Table 5.2.) In 1980, Exxon Corp. ($24,190 million), General Motors Corp. ($14,468 million), Chevron Corp. ($9.638 million), Texaco Inc. ($7,838 million), and Ford Motor Co. ($3,846 million) were the largest names in our normalized value strategy. (See Table 5.3.) In 1990, General Motors Corp. ($25,590 million), Ford Motor Co. ($20,626 million), Dow Chemical ($19,221 million), Atlantic Richfield Co. ($18,286 million) and Texaco Inc. ($15,600 million) were the largest companies in our high normalized value strategy. (See Table 5.4.) In 1995, Philip Morris Cos. Inc. ($49,039 million), General Motors Corp. ($31,777 million), Ford Motor Co. ($28,516 million), Federal Natl Mortgage Assn. ($19,880 million) and Chrysler Corp. ($17,398 million) were the largest companies in the high normalized value portfolio. (See Table 5.5.)

Table 5.2 USA Normalized Value 1970

		Market Cap $	1-Year % Chg	1-Year Return	P/E LTM	P/B 12/-1	DY LTM	ROE 12/-1	ROE / P/B
	HIGH NORMALIZED VALUE								
MD	MCDONNELL DOUGLAS CORP	724	-20.0	-18.2	6.5	1.3	1.9	19.5	15.5
WHX	WHX CORP	68	-38.7	-38.7	23.5	0.3	0.0	4.1	15.4
COE	CONE MILLS CORP	47	53.6	63.5	7.0	0.4	4.7	4.9	14.1
NSC1	NORFOLK SOUTHERN RAILWAY VA	316	35.6	44.3	8.3	0.4	5.1	6.1	13.6
IK	INTERLAKE CORP	112	4.4	3.0	10.1	0.5	7.4	7.3	13.5
AOS	SMITH (A O) CORP	109	8.0	12.3	16.1	0.8	2.9	10.5	13.3
BS	BETHLEHEM STEEL CORP	1,194	-15.7	-9.1	11.2	0.6	7.9	8.0	13.1
HRL	HORMEL FOODS CORP	72	31.1	37.4	9.5	0.9	3.5	12.1	12.9
CMA	COMERICA INC	146	7.6	12.8	8.3	1.1	4.4	13.4	12.7
HSC	HARSCO CORP	151	-5.2	0.3	8.9	1.2	5.5	14.6	12.6
OXY	OCCIDENTAL PETROLEUM CORP	1,255	-23.3	-19.0	6.6	4.6	5.4	56.2	12.3
F	FORD MOTOR CO	4,496	36.8	44.5	11.8	0.9	4.3	10.4	12.2
RHR	ROHR INC	86	-33.7	-30.8	6.0	1.4	5.2	17.3	12.1
RIGS	RIGGS NATL CORP WASH D C	79	-4.7	0.5	7.3	1.1	5.2	13.2	11.9
90290510	USX CORP	1,828	-3.3	3.9	12.0	0.5	7.4	6.3	11.9
FBN	FURNITURE BRANDS INTL INC	193	51.5	57.1	12.2	1.2	3.0	14.0	11.8
FCN	FIRST CHICAGO NBD CORP	289	4.3	9.0	8.3	1.1	4.4	12.5	11.6
GY	GENCORP INC	326	20.0	27.0	10.5	0.8	4.6	9.7	11.6
STT	STATE STREET CORP	86	8.[illegible]	14.4	9.7	1.1	5.2	12.5	11.6
TKR	TIMKEN CO	301	16.4	23.8	12.2	0.9	5.5	10.8	11.5
AAV	AVATEX CORP	676	3.9	10.8	12.6	0.8	5.8	9.2	11.5
DI	DRESSER INDUSTRIES INC	241	34.7	41.5	11.3	2.2	4.1	25.5	11.5
EY	ETHYL CORP	244	-3.1	1.1	7.7	1.4	3.6	16.2	11.4
VMC	VULCAN MATERIALS CO	93	23.5	30.3	11.7	0.9	4.8	10.6	11.4
LUC	LUKENS INC	63	-12.1	-7.4	14.3	0.7	5.0	8.4	11.3

continued on next page

Table 5.2 USA Normalized Value 1970

		Market Cap $	1-Year % Chg	1-Year Return	P/E LTM	P/B 12/-1	DY LTM	ROE 12/-1	ROE / P/B
IAD	INLAND STEEL INDUSTRIES INC	493	2.8	10.9	10.4	0.7	7.2	7.7	11.3
FSR	FIRSTAR CORP	129	8.7	13.8	8.7	1.1	4.4	12.2	11.3
CAG	CONAGRA INC	51	-37.5	-35.2	9.1	1.8	4.0	20.4	11.1
FES	FIRST EMPIRE STATE CORP	62	-6.3	na	8.0	1.0	6.7	11.6	11.1
DCN	DANA CORP	316	23.8	30.9	13.3	1.2	4.3	13.9	11.1
IR	INGERSOLL-RAND CO	528	28.5	35.3	11.7	1.5	4.4	16.8	11.1
NSC	NORFOLK SOUTHERN CORP	721	-13.9	-6.4	8.5	0.6	7.5	7.1	11.1
NOC	NORTHROP GRUMMAN CORP	169	-33.8	-30.9	6.0	1.3	4.3	14.7	11.0
WMB	WILLIAMS COS INC	180	20.1	20.1	10.3	2.0	0.0	21.9	10.9
UVV	UNIVERSAL CORP/VA	66	25.5	32.4	10.6	0.9	4.4	10.0	10.9
UTX	UNITED TECHNOLOGIES CORP	475	-14.0	-9.3	9.0	0.9	5.3	9.5	10.7
B	BARNES GROUP INC	58	8.2	12.7	11.5	1.2	3.6	12.9	10.7
STB	STAR BANC CORP	87	10.1	16.0	10.9	1.2	4.5	13.0	10.7
LUK	LEUCADIA NATIONAL CORP	58	1.9	9.0	15.1	1.1	5.5	11.3	10.7
UCL	UNOCAL CORP	1,082	-5.9	-0.8	11.3	1.3	4.4	13.4	10.7
BOR	BORG-WARNER SECURITY CP	461	18.6	23.7	13.1	0.9	4.2	9.6	10.7
ASO	AMSOUTH BANCORPORATION	74	-4.0	1.7	8.3	1.3	5.5	14.1	10.6
AR	ASARCO INC	937	-15.1	-9.2	8.7	1.5	6.9	15.4	10.6
AS	ARMCO INC	827	-26.2	-20.7	12.9	0.8	7.6	8.9	10.5
CHV	CHEVRON CORP	4,337	6.6	13.1	10.2	1.0	5.1	10.2	10.5
RLM	REYNOLDS METALS CO	493	-9.7	-6.0	10.3	0.9	4.1	8.9	10.4
GWF1	ARISTAR INC	75	na	na	na	1.3	na	13.9	10.3
FO	FORTUNE BRANDS INC	959	26.2	33.5	11.2	1.3	4.7	13.2	10.2
MDA	MAPCO INC	53	48.9	55.0	12.9	1.1	3.2	11.3	10.2
FMO	FEDERAL-MOGUL CORP	130	8.6	17.6	12.8	1.1	6.7	11.7	10.2
NWSW	NORTHWESTERN STL&WIRE	186	-10.4	-7.6	9.8	1.9	3.3	19.6	10.1

continued on next page

Table 5.2 USA Normalized Value 1970

		Market Cap $	1-Year % Chg	1-Year Return	P/E LTM	P/B 12/-1	DY LTM	ROE 12/-1	ROE / P/B
WAC	WARNACO GROUP INC -CL A	63	19.0	-14.0	16.2	1.1	3.6	10.8	10.1
KR	KROGER CO	374	31.9	37.8	12.4	1.2	3.5	12.2	10.1
ADP	ALLIED PRODUCTS	56	-47.5	-45.3	22.2	1.2	4.3	12.4	10.0
TEN	TENNECO INC	1,282	3.2	10.2	11.4	1.9	5.5	18.8	10.0
TEN5	TENNESSEE GAS PIPELINE CO	1,282	3.2	10.2	11.4	1.9	5.5	18.8	10.0
DRV	DRAVO CORP	64	20.7	26.9	20.2	0.9	3.8	8.8	10.0
GCO	GENESCO INC	280	5.5	13.1	15.0	1.5	5.9	14.9	10.0
ALD	ALLIED SIGNAL INC	681	-1.0	4.8	15.5	0.9	5.0	9.0	10.0
ARV	ARVIN INDUSTRIES INC	57	20.8	26.6	25.9	1.0	3.9	10.0	10.0
MOB	MOBIL CORP	4,669	25.0	31.9	12.1	1.1	4.2	10.6	9.8
4108A	SHELL OIL CO	2,982	7.1	13.2	13.5	1.1	5.1	10.9	9.8
CRS	CARPENTER TECHNOLOGY	115	-17.3	-11.4	12.6	1.2	7.2	11.4	9.7
SOC	SUNBEAM CORPORATION	168	-23.2	-17.0	22.0	1.3	8.8	12.7	9.7
SON	SONOCO PRODUCTS CO	70	19.2	22.5	13.2	1.2	2.4	11.7	9.7
CBT	CABOT CORP	151	49.6	52.5	13.3	0.9	1.6	8.7	9.6
ROK	ROCKWELL INTL CORP	514	-7.0	-0.3	8.8	1.1	6.0	10.6	9.6
FWC	FOSTER WHEELER CORP	47	7.1	12.1	10.9	0.9	4.3	9.1	9.6
CLF	CLEVELAND-CLIFFS INC	157	43.3	49.3	12.3	0.9	3.1	8.6	9.5
ASH	ASHLAND INC	552	-9.0	-4.4	11.2	1.9	5.0	17.7	9.5
SNG	SOUTHERN NEW ENG TELECOMM	345	9.3	17.4	10.8	0.9	6.6	9.0	9.5
PNC	PNC BANK CORP	193	9.[illegible]	12.5	10.0	1.3	4.1	12.5	9.5
AN	AMOCO CORP	3,320	9.6	15.6	11.6	1.0	4.4	9.8	9.5
CMZ	CINCINNATI MILACRON INC	156	-3.4	0.3	20.9	1.2	3.3	11.1	9.4
CNF	CNF TRANSPORTATION INC	153	11.8	16.4	22.0	1.9	3.3	18.3	9.4
CSN	CINCINNATI BELL INC	125	22.8	30.6	11.9	0.9	5.3	8.5	9.4
XON	EXXON CORP	13,280	18.8	26.2	12.4	1.3	5.1	12.3	9.4

continued on next page

Table 5.2 USA Normalized Value 1970

		Market Cap $	1-Year % Chg	1-Year Return	P/E LTM	P/B 12/-1	DY LTM	ROE 12/-1	ROE / P/B
WOA	WORLDCORP INC	100	-40.0	-40.0	19.4	1.6	0.0	15.3	9.3
NAV	NAVISTAR INTERNATIONL	686	11.1	19.2	14.3	0.6	6.5	5.5	9.3
CR	CRANE CO	101	-13.4	-9.4	10.7	0.7	4.7	6.4	9.3
SPW	SPX CORP	47	-12.0	-7.6	10.4	1.3	4.2	12.0	9.3
TX	TEXACO INC	8,344	13.9	20.6	11.5	1.4	4.6	13.1	9.2
SXI	STANDEX INTERNATIONAL CORP	53	1.7	3.8	10.7	1.6	1.9	14.6	9.2
CZM	CALMAT CO	90	62.4	67.7	15.6	1.2	2.9	11.3	9.2
EPIHQ	EAGLE-PICHER INDS	115	-2.9	0.7	11.5	1.6	3.6	14.7	9.1
CFL	CORESTATES FINANCIAL CORP	195	11.8	17.2	10.3	1.3	4.5	12.3	9.1
NWAC	NORTHWEST AIRLINES CORP	586	-24.1	-22.4	10.1	1.4	2.1	12.5	9.1
CTS	CTS CORP	52	21.3	24.5	14.0	1.3	2.2	11.9	9.0
CSX	CSX CORP	301	17.9	26.3	11.9	0.5	5.6	4.1	9.0
FLT	FLEET FINANCIAL GROUP INC	103	-14.5	-10.3	10.2	1.4	4.9	12.6	9.0
ENSO	ENVIROSOURCE INC	188	-40.7	-39.5	na	0.9	0.0	7.9	9.0
MRIS	MARSHALL & ILSLEY CORP	53	2.7	na	8.4	1.2	4.7	10.7	9.0
CDP	CONSOLIDATED PAPERS INC	59	-20.7	-16.4	13.8	0.6	5.5	4.9	9.0
UST	UST INC	71	46.4	54.1	13.5	1.7	4.3	15.1	9.0
SUN	SUN CO INC	1,240	15.3	17.9	14.9	1.9	2.0	17.0	8.9
FTX	FREEPORT MCMORAN INC	320	-15.2	-10.0	17.2	1.4	4.6	12.2	8.9
APZ	APPLIED INDUSTRIAL TECH INC	47	-11.4	-9.1	10.7	1.9	2.4	17.3	8.9
KSU	KANSAS CITY SOUTHERN INDS	70	-0.4	5.9	12.0	0.6	5.7	5.0	8.9
UAL	UAL CORP	497	-18.1	-15.1	na	0.9	0.0	7.6	8.9
BNL	BENEFICIAL CORP	542	11.1	15.1	12.1	1.9	3.1	16.4	8.8
	AVERAGE		4.3	9.7	12.1	1.2	4.4	12.4	10.5
	WTD AVERAGE		10.4	16.8	11.7	1.2	4.8	12.6	10.2

Source: Compustat & IMI estimates.

Table 5.3 USA Normalized Value 1980

		Market Cap $	1-Year % Chg	1-Year Return	P/E LTM	P/B 12/-1	DY LTM	ROE 12/-1	ROE / P/B
	HIGH NORMALIZED VALUE								
LTV	LTV CORP	208	153.1	153.1	4.8	0.5	0.0	31.1	62.7
SP	SPELLING ENTERTNMT GRP INC	703	-44.1	-41.5	10.2	1.3	5.1	57.3	42.8
ASH	ASHLAND INC	1,218	1.2	7.2	8.5	1.3	5.9	53.9	42.8
KMB	KIMBERLY-CLARK CORP	954	30.7	39.6	6.8	0.8	6.0	25.6	33.0
CNP.B	CROWN CENTRAL PETROL -CL B	222	-25.8	-21.7	10.3	1.3	2.6	40.8	32.3
TSO	TESORO PETROLEUM CORP	237	12.4	14.1	3.5	2.1	1.4	64.1	30.9
CSX	CSX CORP	431	23.8	137.5	6.7	0.3	3.4	10.0	30.8
NAV	NAVISTAR INTERNATIONL	1,204	-34.5	-29.4	na	0.6	4.7	17.2	30.7
F	FORD MOTOR CO	3,846	-37.5	-31.5	na	0.4	6.0	11.3	30.5
MXP	MESA INC	964	114.8	115.4	22.8	2.4	0.2	72.1	29.9
BS	BETHLEHEM STEEL CORP	922	24.9	33.4	9.5	0.4	6.1	10.7	29.9
CNA	CNA FINANCIAL CORP	552	0.0	0.0	5.9	0.8	0.0	22.7	29.4
LTR	LOEWS CORP	725	35.9	38.1	5.0	0.7	1.4	20.2	28.9
RLM	REYNOLDS METALS CO	616	8.5	15.5	3.8	0.5	6.8	15.1	28.5
MMG	METROMEDIA INTERNATIONAL GRP	236	-21.6	-19.0	23.4	0.9	3.4	25.2	27.3
OXY	OCCIDENTAL PETROLEUM CORP	1,962	27.6	36.6	3.9	1.6	6.4	42.9	26.9
PCAR	PACCAR INC	458	27.5	33.2	7.2	0.9	4.2	24.9	26.3
AA	ALUMINUM CO OF AMERICA	1,930	3.7	14.3	4.6	0.8	5.4	20.4	26.0
AMR	AMR CORP/DE	291	-11.1	-10.3	na	0.4	0.0	9.8	26.0
AHC	AMERADA HESS CORP	1,798	77.9	83.9	6.7	1.1	2.5	26.7	24.9
GR	GOODRICH (B F) CO	323	26.8	36.3	7.0	0.4	6.3	8.9	24.9
AAV	AVATEX CORP	504	-5.2	3.4	5.7	0.4	8.0	8.8	24.8
AHM	AHMANSON (H F) & CO	485	-7.7	-2.1	9.4	0.6	6.2	14.1	24.2
USG	USG CORP	505	4.8	12.7	5.7	0.8	7.3	20.3	24.1
BKB	BANKBOSTON CORP	354	23.3	33.3	4.3	0.5	7.0	13.0	23.8

continued on next page

Table 5.3 USA Normalized Value 1980

		Market Cap $	1-Year % Chg	1-Year Return	P/E LTM	P/B 12/-1	DY LTM	ROE 12/-1	ROE / P/B
PPG	PPG INDUSTRIES INC	942	41.1	50.7	6.4	0.7	5.3	16.5	23.5
BNI	BRLNGTN NTHRN SANTA FE	710	129.4	136.2	8.5	0.4	1.9	8.5	23.4
NSC	NORFOLK SOUTHERN CORP	850	49.5	59.6	5.5	0.6	5.4	14.4	23.3
CMB	CHASE MANHATTAN CORP	546	16.4	27.1	3.8	0.5	8.2	11.7	23.3
BT	BANKERS TRUST NEW YORK CORP	433	54.4	65.2	3.6	0.6	6.0	12.9	23.2
ETN	EATON CORP	669	11.2	18.5	6.6	0.7	6.0	16.8	23.0
AR	ASARCO INC	1,105	15.7	20.8	5.9	1.0	3.6	22.4	22.9
OI	OWENS-ILLINOIS INC	576	25.9	33.0	5.0	0.5	5.5	11.4	22.5
TX	TEXACO INC	7,838	66.2	77.8	5.8	0.7	5.4	16.5	22.4
CUM	CUMMINS ENGINE	259	-2.4	3.4	na	0.5	6.0	12.0	22.1
MEA	MEAD CORP	643	5.1	12.7	5.4	0.8	7.3	18.2	21.9
TA	TRANSAMERICA CORP	1,111	10.3	18.1	5.5	0.8	6.8	18.0	21.5
FG	USF&G CORP	1,070	10.1	17.7	5.2	1.0	6.6	22.0	21.5
WH	WHITMAN CORP	393	24.7	34.6	5.1	0.4	6.5	8.4	21.5
FCN	FIRST CHICAGO NBD CORP	360	-16.9	-10.3	4.0	0.6	8.2	12.5	21.1
Z	WOOLWORTH CORP	740	-1.5	5.6	4.9	0.7	7.3	14.7	21.1
AET	AETNA INC	2,681	6.4	12.9	5.6	0.9	6.0	19.5	20.8
CB	CHUBB CORP	472	3.9	10.7	4.6	0.8	6.8	17.4	20.7
ALT	ALLEGHENY TELEDYNE INC	1,804	101.5	101.5	9.5	1.4	0.0	29.1	20.6
FI	FINA INC -CL A	409	53.9	64.3	6.0	1.0	5.5	19.4	20.4
CNF	CNF TRANSPORTATION INC	323	-1.0	4.9	6.1	0.9	5.7	19.2	20.4
WFC	WELLS FARGO & CO	613	6.0	14.3	5.3	0.7	6.7	14.9	20.3
BOR	BORG-WARNER SECURITY CP	747	19.2	26.9	7.3	0.7	5.8	14.2	20.2
UK	UNION CARBIDE CORP	2,781	19.6	28.6	5.0	0.7	6.4	13.9	20.2
GM	GENERAL MOTORS CORP	14,468	-10.0	-4.4	na	0.8	5.3	15.4	20.1
BK	BANK OF NEW YORK CO INC	227	-2.1	6.2	4.6	0.6	8.6	12.5	19.9

continued on next page

Table 5.3 USA Normalized Value 1980

		Market Cap $	1-Year % Chg	1-Year Return	P/E LTM	P/B 12/-1	DY LTM	ROE 12/-1	ROE / P/B
IAD	INLAND STEEL INDUSTRIES INC	656	-11.9	-4.7	20.2	0.5	7.2	10.0	19.8
ANV	AEROQUIP-VICKERS INC	269	-5.7	1.4	10.5	0.7	5.2	13.1	19.8
CHA	CHAMPION INTERNATIONAL CORP	1,300	2.6	9.0	7.5	0.9	6.0	16.9	19.7
IP	INTL PAPER CO	1,786	13.5	20.5	7.0	0.7	5.7	13.5	19.6
VVI	VIAD CORP	632	-3.5	4.5	5.2	0.8	8.6	15.9	19.5
DCN	DANA CORP	899	-17.0	-10.9	10.2	1.0	7.5	18.7	19.3
BCC	BOISE CASCADE CORP	901	0.7	6.0	6.7	0.8	5.1	14.8	19.2
NSC1	NORFOLK SOUTHERN RAILWAY VA	828	49.1	57.3	7.0	0.8	4.6	15.0	19.2
OG	OGDEN CORP	286	35.2	43.0	6.9	0.8	4.8	15.1	19.2
COT	COLTEC INDUSTRIES	561	3.1	10.2	6.1	1.0	6.4	18.7	19.1
WX	WESTINGHOUSE ELECTRIC CORP	1,711	47.2	55.6	6.3	0.8	4.7	14.5	19.1
CI	CIGNA CORP	1,426	34.8	40.0	6.1	0.7	3.3	14.2	19.0
CDP	CONSOLIDATED PAPERS INC	291	18.3	26.3	6.6	1.2	6.2	21.9	18.9
GWF	GREAT WESTERN FINANCIAL	494	-15.3	-11.2	10.7	0.8	4.7	14.6	18.9
HPC	HERCULES INC	874	-7.9	-1.8	7.3	0.9	6.3	17.4	18.9
SAFC	SAFECO CORP	724	-3.0	2.0	6.5	1.0	5.0	17.9	18.8
PPL	PP&L RESOURCES INC	772	-12.0	0.0	5.9	0.7	13.6	13.0	18.7
CSN	CINCINNATI BELL INC	215	-9.0	-0.2	5.9	0.8	10.0	14.6	18.7
EIX	EDISON INTERNATIONAL	1,590	4.6	17.4	7.3	0.7	11.6	13.2	18.6
ED	CONSOLIDATED EDISON OF NY	1,517	2.6	14.9	5.3	0.6	10.8	10.3	18.6
MST	MERCANTILE STORES CO INC	224	-10.5	-6.8	5.5	0.9	4.4	16.5	18.5
CMA	COMERICA INC	219	-18.4	-11.3	5.0	0.7	9.5	13.0	18.5
CHV	CHEVRON CORP	9,638	76.5	84.8	7.1	1.0	4.0	19.2	18.5
HI	HOUSEHOLD INTERNATIONAL INC	839	-10.3	-1.6	5.6	0.7	9.8	13.1	18.4
ZLC	ZALE CORP	221	36.4	43.7	8.6	0.8	4.2	15.0	18.3
CCI	CITICORP	2,942	2.1	9.2	6.0	0.8	5.9	14.9	18.3

continued on nex page

Table 5.3 USA Normalized Value 1980

		Market Cap $	1-Year % Chg	1-Year Return	P/E LTM	P/B 12/-1	D[illegible] LTM	ROE 12/-1	ROE / P/B
IBP	IBP INC	227	104.3	108.4	9.3	1.0	1.3	17.3	18.2
GPU	GPU INC	528	-42.0	-42.0	14.7	0.4	0.0	6.9	18.1
BN	BORDEN INC	744	7.9	16.4	5.4	0.6	7.4	11.3	18.0
AS	ARMCO INC	1,326	52.0	59.8	8.0	0.7	4.3	11.9	18.0
AGC	AMERICAN GENERAL CORP	933	1.7	4.6	5.7	0.9	2.7	16.8	18.0
ACLM	ALLIS-CHALMERS CORP	429	5.1	12.6	10.2	0.7	5.5	12.0	18.0
LCE	LONE STAR INDUSTRIES	298	12.2	18.5	6.1	0.8	5.1	15.2	18.0
FBN	FURNITURE BRANDS INTL INC	554	22.4	29.9	6.4	0.9	5.5	16.2	18.0
NGE	NEW YORK STATE ELEC & GAS	412	-5.6	6.0	5.5	0.7	12.6	13.0	18.0
TKR	TIMKEN CO	571	18.6	25.6	7.3	0.8	5.4	14.5	17.9
SPC	ST PAUL COS	854	-4.9	0.6	5.4	0.9	6.0	16.4	17.9
BC	BRUNSWICK CORP	269	15.9	23.9	na	0.6	5.8	10.8	17.9
NEM	NEWMONT MINING CORP	996	17.4	22.4	6.1	1.4	3.8	24.2	17.8
MAY	MAY DEPARTMENT STORES CO	695	10.4	17.7	7.0	0.9	5.8	15.2	17.8
NB	NATIONSBANK CORP	247	-0.9	4.8	5.3	0.8	5.9	14.6	17.8
MEL	MELLON BANK CORP	544	14.4	22.5	5.5	0.7	6.4	11.7	17.7
FO	FORTUNE BRANDS INC	1,805	14.2	23.7	5.5	1.3	8.0	22.1	17.7
XON	EXXON CORP	24,190	46.3	57.7	6.2	1.1	7.4	19.0	17.7
Y	ALLEGHENY CORP	251	22.2	27.2	6.9	0.9	3.3	15.5	17.6
FMC	FMC CORP	836	17.3	24.1	7.3	0.7	5.2	12.8	17.5
PNC	PNC BANK CORP	259	6.6	14.1	5.7	0.8	6.7	14.1	17.5
FNM	FEDERAL NATL MORTGAGE ASSN	946	-26.4	-20.4	49.7	0.6	5.4	11.0	17.4
NSI	NATIONAL SERVICE INDS INC	242	8.6	15.8	5.7	1.1	6.4	19.7	17.4
	AVERAGE		16.7	23.6	7.4	0.8	5.6	18.2	22.3
	WTD AVERAGE		25.5	33.4	7.0	0.9	5.8	18.3	21.0

Source: Compustat & IMI estimates.

Table 5.4 USA Normalized Value 1990

		Market Cap $	1-Year % Chg	1-Year Return	P/E LTM	P/B 12/-1	DY LTM	ROE 12/-1	ROE / P/B
	HIGH NORMALIZED VALUE								
BHC	BHC COMMUNICATIONS -CL A	1,545	-12.6	-12.6	2.7	1.3	0.0	70.5	52.5
LYO	LYONDELL PETROCHEMICAL	1,720	-32.0	-14.7	3.3	191.1	10.9	4151.1	21.7
CYM	CYPRUS AMAX MINERALS CO	1,014	-30.2	-27.5	7.8	0.9	4.3	19.8	21.4
STO	STONE CONTAINER CORP	1,431	-51.3	-49.5	7.2	1.1	6.3	21.2	19.9
F	FORD MOTOR CO	20,626	-39.0	-34.0	14.3	0.9	11.3	17.1	18.8
AR	ASARCO INC	1,243	-9.2	-3.6	7.5	0.9	5.9	15.9	18.4
UK	UNION CARBIDE CORP	3,292	-29.6	-25.7	7.5	1.4	6.1	24.2	17.5
MWD	MORG STAN DEAN WTTR DSCVR&CO	2,392	-15.9	-13.6	8.1	1.4	2.8	23.4	17.3
RLM	REYNOLDS METALS CO	3,182	6.3	9.7	11.4	1.2	3.2	20.3	17.2
GGC	GEORGIA GULF CORP	1,094	-76.3	64.6	3.5	3.3	0.0	56.1	16.9
PCAR	PACCAR INC	1,492	-24.6	-22.4	17.6	1.5	3.1	23.9	16.1
BS	BETHLEHEM STEEL CORP	1,392	-20.3	-18.0	na	0.8	2.7	13.1	15.8
GD	GENERAL DYNAMICS CORP	1,866	-43.7	-41.8	na	0.9	4.0	13.7	15.6
GR	GOODRICH (B F) CO	1,051	-9.0	-4.0	8.9	0.9	5.6	14.0	15.5
TX	TEXACO INC	15,600	2.8	8.1	11.7	1.8	5.3	28.4	15.5
GP	GEORGIA-PACIFIC CORP	4,203	-23.2	-20.1	8.7	1.5	4.3	23.7	15.3
GM	GENERAL MOTORS CORP	25,590	-18.6	-12.7	na	0.7	8.7	11.0	15.0
HON	HONEYWELL INC	3,470	2.6	9.3	9.1	1.8	3.4	26.9	14.9
WFC	WELLS FARGO & CO	3,786	-21.9	-16.7	4.3	1.5	6.9	22.9	14.9
CHA	CHAMPION INTERNATIONAL CORP	2,975	-19.9	-16.6	12.1	0.8	4.3	11.8	14.3
AA	ALUMINUM CO OF AMERICA	6,566	-23.2	-19.3	16.9	1.3	5.2	18.0	14.2
BAC	BANKAMERICA CORP	5,626	-0.9	3.0	6.9	1.1	3.8	16.2	14.2
BOW	BOWATER INC	988	-23.1	-18.8	9.2	1.1	5.6	15.2	14.0
BCC	BOISE CASCADE CORP	1,684	-41.4	-38.4	16.0	1.1	5.8	15.0	13.9
SB	SALOMON INC	2,781	4.3	7.1	11.7	1.0	2.6	13.5	13.9

continued on next page

Table 5.4 USA Normalized Value 1990

		Market Cap $	1-Year % Chg	1-Year Return	P/E LTM	P/B 12/-1	DY LTM	ROE 12/-1	ROE / P/B
CIN1	CINCINNATI GAS & ELECTRIC	1,608	-5.2	2.7	7.3	1.3	8.0	17.3	13.8
CIN	CINERGY CORP	1,608	-5.2	2.7	7.3	1.3	8.0	17.3	13.8
SPC	ST PAUL COS	2,915	6.1	10.7	7.3	1.2	3.8	17.1	13.8
DAL	DELTA AIR LINES INC	3,483	-18.3	-16.8	na	1.2	2.2	16.5	13.7
WLL	WILLAMETTE INDUSTRIES	1,398	-21.8	-18.9	8.4	1.6	3.7	21.2	13.7
IP	INTL PAPER CO	6,142	-5.3	-2.1	10.3	1.2	3.1	16.3	13.7
PCH	POTLATCH CORP	1,061	-21.1	-18.3	8.5	1.3	4.6	16.7	13.0
DOW	DOW CHEMICAL	19,221	-33.5	-30.0	9.3	2.4	5.5	31.1	12.9
PD	PHELPS DODGE CORP	2,047	-4.2	0.9	4.3	1.5	5.3	19.5	12.8
FLT	FLEET FINANCIAL GROUP INC	2,845	-57.9	-54.4	na	1.3	7.3	16.8	12.8
TXU	TEXAS UTILITIES CO	6,435	4.3	13.3	8.3	1.0	8.1	12.8	12.6
PVT	PROVIDENT COS INC	1,196	-31.7	-28.7	4.5	1.0	5.3	12.2	12.4
AMR	AMR CORP/DE	3,608	-16.6	-16.6	na	1.0	0.0	11.8	12.3
SAFC	SAFECO CORP	2,442	-14.9	-12.1	7.5	1.3	4.1	16.2	12.3
TXT	TEXTRON INC	2,190	11.2	16.0	8.6	0.9	3.7	10.6	12.3
AHC	AMERADA HESS CORP	3,939	-4.9	-3.7	7.8	1.5	1.3	18.5	12.0
ROK	ROCKWELL INTL CORP	5,862	16.8	20.8	10.8	1.5	3.1	17.5	12.0
UCC	UNION CAMP CORP	2,540	-3.1	1.4	10.7	1.4	4.4	17.1	11.8
ALEX	ALEXANDER & BALDWIN INC	1,729	-40.7	-38.7	8.9	2.9	4.0	33.4	11.7
LPX	LOUISIANA-PACIFIC CORP	1,644	-36.7	-34.7	11.1	1.4	3.9	16.3	11.7
RCM	ARCO CHEMICAL CO	3,476	-2.8	4.3	11.0	2.2	7.1	25.4	11.6
MEL	MELLON BANK CORP	1,044	-17.0	-11.9	8.4	0.9	5.9	10.0	11.6
FTU	FIRST UNION CORP (N C)	2,210	-25.5	-20.6	6.1	1.1	7.0	12.4	11.6
RTN	RAYTHEON CO	4,561	0.9	4.6	8.2	1.9	3.4	21.7	11.5
STI	SUNTRUST BANKS INC	2,928	-0.5	3.5	8.3	1.4	4.0	16.0	11.4
W	WESTVACO CORP	1,966	-12.0	-8.4	9.2	1.3	3.9	15.1	11.4

continued on next page

Table 5.4 USA Normalized Value 1990

		Market Cap $	1-Year % Chg	1-Year Return	P/E LTM	P/B 12/-1	DY LTM	ROE 12/-1	ROE / P/B
CSX	CSX CORP	3,505	-1.5	-7.6	8.7	1.1	4.4	12.3	11.4
HI	HOUSEHOLD INTERNATIONAL INC	1,832	-36.6	-32.9	5.4	1.5	6.7	17.4	11.3
BBI	BARNETT BANKS INC	2,279	-47.8	-44.8	17.8	1.3	7.0	15.2	11.3
PVN	PROVIDIAN FINANCIAL CORP	2,399	-24.8	-22.8	11.5	1.8	2.8	19.8	11.2
FCN	FIRST CHICAGO NBD CORP	2,303	3.1	7.9	8.8	1.4	4.2	15.4	11.2
IIN	ITT INDUSTRIES INC	7,227	-18.5	-15.8	6.0	0.9	3.6	10.4	11.1
NCC	NATIONAL CITY CORP	2,373	-20.1	-15.2	8.1	1.6	6.0	17.5	11.1
BSC	BEAR STEARNS COMPANIES INC	1,204	-12.4	-8.1	10.3	1.3	5.5	14.6	11.0
FRE	FED HOME LOAN MTG CO	4,033	-27.4	-25.4	7.1	2.1	3.3	22.8	10.8
S	SEARS ROEBUCK & CO	13,058	-33.4	-29.2	9.8	1.0	7.9	10.4	10.8
TIN	TEMPLE-INLAND INC	1,906	-8.6	-6.3	7.6	1.5	2.5	16.3	10.8
DPL	DPL INC	1,381	-4.9	3.2	8.6	1.4	8.1	14.8	10.8
AGC	AMERICAN GENERAL CORP	3,444	-1.6	6.2	6.6	0.8	10.4	9.0	10.7
GPU	GPU INC	2,616	-3.7	2.0	9.1	1.3	5.7	13.4	10.6
CDO	COMDISCO INC	1,009	-25.8	-24.7	8.9	1.8	1.5	19.3	10.6
XRX	XEROX CORP	5,274	-38.0	-33.6	6.4	1.0	8.5	11.1	10.6
HBAN	HUNTINGTON BANCSHARES	1,024	-38.8	-35.2	7.7	1.4	7.2	15.0	10.5
NL	NL INDUSTRIES	1,610	-59.0	-57.0	7.0	12.2	6.0	128.3	10.5
PPG	PPG INDUSTRIES INC	4,325	13.2	22.7	10.6	1.9	3.6	19.9	10.5
KM	K MART CORP	6,992	-13.9	-14.3	17.0	1.4	6.1	14.4	10.5
DTE	DTE ENERGY CO	3,727	11.3	19.0	8.7	1.6	6.3	16.5	10.4
CB	CHUBB CORP	4,021	13.9	17.2	8.9	1.5	2.4	15.9	10.3
BNL	BENEFICIAL CORP	1,098	-11.5	-6.9	8.7	1.4	5.5	14.1	10.2
PE	PECO ENERGY CO	4,902	-22.2	-15.5	na	1.3	6.7	13.4	10.2
JR	JAMES RIVER CORP OF VIRGINIA	2,302	-7.5	-5.0	39.8	1.1	2.3	11.0	10.2
ALD	ALLIED SIGNAL INC	5,057	-22.6	-18.2	8.1	1.5	6.7	15.1	10.2

continued on next page

Table 5.4 USA Normalized Value 1990

		Market Cap $	1-Year % Chg	1-Year Return	P/E LTM	P/B 12/-1	DY LTM	ROE 12/-1	ROE / P/B
BNI	BRLNGTN NTHRN SANTA FE	2,375	-8.7	-5.3	9.9	2.2	4.2	22.3	10.1
ARC	ATLANTIC RICHFIELD CO	18,286	11.0	15.6	12.1	2.8	4.0	28.2	10.1
NTRS	NORTHERN TRUST CORP	1,073	-4.5	-1.7	9.5	2.0	2.8	20.4	10.1
AET	AETNA INC	6,327	-31.0	-26.3	7.1	0.9	7.1	9.2	10.1
TRV	TRAVELERS GROUP INC	3,153	-19.7	-18.6	7.0	1.2	1.7	12.2	10.1
OLN	OLIN CORP	1,140	-37.1	-33.9	9.4	1.7	5.8	17.2	10.0
OCAS	OHIO CASUALTY CORP	991	-13.2	-8.2	9.4	1.3	5.7	12.8	10.0
CMS	CMS ENERGY CORP	3,107	-26.6	-25.6	na	1.6	1.7	15.9	10.0
NB	NATIONSBANK CORP	4,682	-50.5	-48.3	6.7	1.6	6.5	15.8	10.0
LNC	LINCOLN NATIONAL CORP	2,539	-29.4	-25.2	10.0	1.2	6.0	11.5	10.0
CNA	CNA FINANCIAL CORP	6,061	-30.0	-30.0	11.9	1.5	0.0	15.0	9.9
90290510	USX CORP	9,137	-14.7	-11.0	9.7	1.7	4.6	16.8	9.9
NCE	NEW CENTURY ENERGIES INC	1,386	-11.4	-3.1	9.3	1.5	8.6	15.1	9.9
NKE	NIKE INC -CL B	1,991	51.2	53.0	10.6	3.0	1.4	29.6	9.9
AEP	AMERICAN ELECTRIC POWER	6,387	-15.2	-7.8	10.6	1.5	8.6	14.3	9.8
UTX	UNITED TECHNOLOGIES CORP	6,569	-11.8	-8.6	8.1	1.4	3.8	13.6	9.8
ETN	EATON CORP	2,104	12.5	-8.9	10.5	1.8	4.4	18.0	9.8
CPQ	COMPAQ COMPUTER CORP	3,122	41.8	41.8	11.0	2.7	0.0	26.0	9.8
USBC	U S BANCORP	1,551	-22.2	-18.7	6.8	1.5	4.9	14.4	9.8
LTR	LOEWS CORP	9,326	-21.0	-20.2	8.9	1.9	1.0	18.8	9.7
AMH	AMDAHL CORP	1,565	-1.7	-1.0	8.5	1.3	0.7	12.9	9.7
IPL	IPALCO ENTERPRISES INC	990	1.4	8.9	10.4	1.4	6.7	13.5	9.6
AAPL	APPLE COMPUTER INC	4,413	22.0	23.5	10.5	2.9	1.1	27.8	9.6
	AVERAGE		-15.7	-10.4	9.4	3.5	4.8	60.5	12.8
	WTD AVERAGE		-15.3	-10.8	10.0	2.4	5.3	36.6	12.7

Source: Compustat & IMI estimates.

Table 5.5 USA Normalized Value 1995

		Market Cap $	1-Year % Chg	1-Year Return	P/E LTM	P/B 12/-1	DY LTM	ROE 12/-1	ROE / P/B
	HIGH NORMALIZED VALUE								
C	CHRYSLER CORP	17,398	12.5	17.1	9.9	1.6	4.4	33.6	20.6
F	FORD MOTOR CO	28,516	3.6	8.3	8.1	1.3	4.8	23.5	17.8
CCI	CITICORP	16,346	62.5	66.3	9.3	1.2	1.8	20.8	17.3
SLM	SLM HLDG CORP	2,389	103.1	109.4	12.4	1.9	2.4	29.4	15.5
GM	GENERAL MOTORS CORP	31,777	25.5	28.5	7.4	2.5	2.3	36.5	14.7
BKB	BANKBOSTON CORP	2,757	78.7	84.8	11.1	1.0	3.2	15.3	14.6
LIL	LONG ISLAND LIGHTING	1,821	6.5	19.0	7.8	0.8	10.9	10.6	14.0
KEY	KEYCORP	6,009	45.0	51.7	11.0	1.3	4.0	18.3	13.8
BAC	BANKAMERICA CORP	14,662	63.9	69.5	10.0	0.9	2.8	12.6	13.6
NB	NATIONSBANK CORP	12,475	54.3	59.8	9.8	1.1	3.3	15.4	13.6
BK	BANK OF NEW YORK CO INC	5,442	68.1	74.6	10.7	1.3	3.0	17.6	13.5
CUM	CUMMINS ENGINE	1,882	-18.2	-16.3	6.7	1.8	2.7	23.7	13.5
CMA	COMERICA INC	2,850	64.1	70.9	11.3	1.2	3.5	16.0	13.5
MER	MERRILL LYNCH & CO	6,488	42.7	45.7	9.4	1.3	2.0	16.9	13.3
SEG	SEAGATE TECHNOLOGY	1,712	97.9	97.9	10.1	1.2	0.0	16.4	13.2
BT	BANKERS TRUST NEW YORK CORP	4,323	20.1	28.1	32.8	1.0	6.0	13.0	12.9
CMB	CHASE MANHATTAN CORP	8,772	63.8	68.7	9.4	0.9	3.4	12.2	12.9
RNB	REPUBLIC NEW YORK CORP	2,381	37.3	40.9	13.3	1.2	2.3	15.5	12.8
FTU	FIRST UNION CORP (N C)	7,283	34.4	39.8	11.0	1.3	3.7	17.0	12.6
FCN	FIRST CHICAGO NBD CORP	4,264	44.3	51.6	11.4	1.3	3.6	16.3	12.6
BBI	BARNETT BANKS INC	3,724	53.2	58.6	11.1	1.3	3.2	15.9	12.4
FOA	FIRST OF AMERICA BANK CORP	1,885	47.9	54.9	11.9	1.2	4.0	14.7	12.3
PNC	PNC BANK CORP	4,927	52.7	61.4	27.1	1.1	4.3	13.6	12.2
AMD	ADVANCED MICRO DEVICES	2,374	-33.7	-33.6	10.4	1.4	0.0	16.6	12.1
CI	CIGNA CORP	4,595	62.3	68.0	36.1	0.8	2.9	9.5	12.0

continued on next page

Table 5.5 USA Normalized Value 1995

		Market Cap $	1-Year % Chg	1-Year Return	P/E LTM	P/B 12/-1	DY LTM	ROE 12/-1	ROE / P/B
LMT	LOCKHEED MARTIN CORP	8,871	77.3	31.6	24.1	1.7	1.8	20.8	11.9
PCAR	PACCAR INC	1,720	-4.8	4.2	6.5	1.5	9.5	17.4	11.9
BBK	BB&T CORP	1,955	37.3	42.6	15.9	1.3	3.5	15.5	11.8
PNW	PINNACLE WEST CAPITAL	1,716	46.5	52.4	12.6	1.0	3.5	11.3	11.7
FO	FORTUNE BRANDS INC	7,545	18.7	24.7	15.3	1.6	4.5	19.1	11.7
ED	CONSOLIDATED EDISON OF NY	6,049	23.3	32.3	10.8	1.1	6.4	13.2	11.6
LPX	LOUISIANA-PACIFIC CORP	3,052	-11.0	-9.1	na	1.7	2.3	19.1	11.6
SPC	ST PAUL COS	3,768	24.3	28.1	9.3	1.4	2.9	15.8	11.4
GT	GOODYEAR TIRE & RUBBER CO	5,091	34.9	38.1	11.3	1.8	2.2	20.3	11.2
FSR	FIRSTAR CORP	2,015	47.4	53.7	13.2	1.4	3.4	15.0	11.1
MBI	MBIA INC	2,336	33.6	36.2	11.7	1.4	1.8	15.1	11.0
TA	TRANSAMERICA CORP	3,452	46.5	51.2	11.1	1.4	2.7	15.7	11.0
HBAN	HUNTINGTON BANCSHARES	2,246	46.1	51.7	13.5	1.6	3.3	17.2	10.8
LYO	LYONDELL PETROCHEMICAL	2,070	-11.6	-8.4	4.7	32.9	3.9	353.0	10.7
JPM	MORGAN (J P) & CO	10,535	43.0	49.2	12.5	1.2	4.0	12.5	10.7
FNM	FEDERAL NATL MORTGAGE ASSN	19,880	70.0	75.3	15.8	2.1	2.2	22.3	10.7
MD	MCDONNELL DOUGLAS CORP	5,526	94.4	96.5	na	1.4	0.9	15.2	10.7
TMK	TORCHMARK CORP	2,495	29.7	32.6	11.9	2.0	2.6	21.4	10.7
OEC	OHIO EDISON CO	2,823	27.0	35.9	11.5	1.2	6.4	13.0	10.6
NU	NORTHEAST UTILITIES	2,702	12.1	20.8	10.8	1.2	7.3	12.4	10.6
NSM	NATIONAL SEMICONDUCTOR CORP	2,402	13.5	13.5	10.0	2.0	0.0	21.1	10.6
MU	MICRON TECHNOLOGY INC	4,505	79.6	80.3	8.4	3.7	0.5	39.5	10.6
DE	DEERE & CO	5,725	59.6	63.9	13.0	2.2	2.3	23.7	10.6
GWF	GREAT WESTERN FINANCIAL	2,149	58.6	65.4	14.8	1.0	3.6	10.4	10.6
FRE	FED HOME LOAN MTG CO	9,128	65.3	68.2	14.7	1.8	1.4	18.8	10.5
GDW	GOLDEN WEST FINANCIAL CORP	2,065	56.7	57.9	13.8	1.0	0.7	10.9	10.5

continued on next page

Table 5.5 USA Normalized Value 1995

		Market Cap $	1-Year % Chg	1-Year Return	P/E LTM	P/B 12/-1	DY LTM	ROE 12/-1	ROE / P/B
PEG	PUBLIC SERVICE ENTRP	6,484	15.6	24.5	11.9	1.2	7.1	12.8	10.5
DI	DRESSER INDUSTRIES INC	3,470	29.1	33.1	20.8	2.1	2.8	22.3	10.5
NOB	NORWEST CORP	7,226	41.2	45.7	12.0	2.2	2.9	22.7	10.5
NCC	NATIONAL CITY CORP	3,818	28.0	33.9	12.4	1.6	4.0	16.5	10.4
EIX	EDISON INTERNATIONAL	6,549	20.5	26.1	10.6	1.1	5.7	11.1	10.4
TRV	TRAVELERS GROUP INC	10,247	93.4	97.7	12.9	1.3	1.3	13.5	10.3
MTL	MERCANTILE BANCORPORATION	1,627	-7.2	51.8	12.3	1.3	2.9	13.7	10.3
MWD	MORG STAN DEAN WTTR DSCVR&CO	4,481	36.7	38.3	11.6	1.2	1.6	12.3	10.3
PGR	PROGRESSIVE CORP-OHIO	2,492	39.6	40.4	15.0	2.3	0.5	24.0	10.3
DTE	DTE ENERGY CO	3,785	32.1	41.2	12.3	1.1	6.0	11.7	10.2
WFC	WELLS FARGO & CO	7,432	49.0	53.0	10.6	2.2	2.1	22.1	10.2
BSC	BEAR STEARNS COMPANIES INC	1,727	35.7	39.7	7.4	1.0	3.0	10.2	10.2
WR	WESTERN RESOURCES INC	1,764	16.6	24.2	12.3	1.2	6.1	11.8	9.9
DCN	DANA CORP	2,322	24.5	28.5	10.3	2.5	3.1	24.3	9.8
AOC	AON CORP	3,447	55.9	61.5	19.4	1.5	2.7	15.1	9.8
AHM	AHMANSON (H F) & CO	1,888	64.3	70.9	7.8	0.6	3.3	6.2	9.8
PVN	PROVIDIAN FINANCIAL CORP	3,011	32.0	35.2	11.3	1.4	2.2	13.9	9.8
AAPL	APPLE COMPUTER INC	4,676	-13.3	-17.3	23.6	1.8	1.5	17.8	9.8
POM	POTOMAC ELECTRIC POWER	2,173	42.9	54.4	40.4	1.1	6.3	10.8	9.7
TXN	TEXAS INSTRUMENTS INC	6,940	37.6	39.1	9.1	2.3	1.3	22.2	9.7
WB	WACHOVIA CORP	5,513	4[illegible].9	46.9	13.1	1.7	3.1	16.3	9.7
JCP	PENNEY (J C) CO	10,372	[illegible].7	11.3	12.3	2.0	4.0	19.3	9.7
HOU	HOUSTON INDUSTRIES INC	4,677	3[illegible].1	46.1	15.2	1.4	6.2	13.4	9.7
LNC	LINCOLN NATIONAL CORP	3,307	5[illegible].6	60.2	11.6	1.2	3.2	11.7	9.6
SAFC	SAFECO CORP	3,274	3[illegible].7	36.2	10.9	1.2	3.1	11.1	9.6
NES	NEW ENGLAND ELECTRIC SYSTEM	2,087	2[illegible].3	31.8	12.6	1.3	6.0	12.6	9.6

continued on next page

Table 5.5 USA Normalized Value 1995

		Market Cap $	1-Year % Chg	1-Year Return	P/E LTM	P/B 12/-1	DY LTM	ROE 12/-1	ROE / P/B
ILN	ILLINOVA CORP	1,655	37.1	42.8	15.3	1.1	3.3	10.9	9.6
FLT	FLEET FINANCIAL GROUP INC	8,294	25.9	31.7	26.0	1.7	4.2	16.1	9.5
ONE	BANC ONE CORP	10,074	48.3	54.4	11.8	1.4	3.6	13.1	9.5
TXT	TEXTRON INC	4,307	34.0	37.4	14.1	1.5	2.3	14.3	9.5
HI	HOUSEHOLD INTERNATIONAL INC	3,586	60.3	64.3	13.8	1.6	2.3	15.5	9.5
MO	PHILIP MORRIS COS INC	49,039	57.0	64.5	13.9	3.8	4.4	36.4	9.5
MYG	MAYTAG CORP	1,610	35.0	39.1	na	2.2	2.8	20.8	9.5
EQ	EQUITABLE COS INC	3,330	32.4	33.6	13.1	1.3	0.8	12.0	9.4
BNI	BRLNGTN NTHRN SANTA FE	4,294	62.1	65.0	47.0	2.3	1.5	21.0	9.3
FON	SPRINT CORP	9,622	43.4	47.7	14.7	2.1	2.5	19.8	9.3
FD	FEDERATED DEPT STORES	2,437	41.6	41.6	na	1.2	0.0	10.9	9.3
STT	STATE STREET CORP	2,360	57.2	60.0	15.1	1.8	1.6	16.4	9.3
NYT.A	NEW YORK TIMES CO -CL A	2,174	33.9	36.9	21.2	1.4	1.9	13.0	9.3
TDM	TANDEM COMPUTERS INC	1,983	-38.0	-38.0	31.3	2.0	0.0	18.2	9.2
CSR	CENTRAL & SOUTH WEST CORP	4,304	23.2	31.8	14.1	1.4	6.2	13.0	9.2
PET	PACIFIC ENTERPRISES	1,745	32.9	40.5	13.3	1.4	4.8	13.2	9.2
STI	SUNTRUST BANKS INC	5,524	43.5	47.0	13.9	1.6	2.3	14.6	9.2
CMS	CMS ENERGY CORP	1,979	30.6	35.4	13.5	1.8	3.2	16.3	9.1
JP	JEFFERSON-PILOT CORP	2,513	34.5	38.7	13.1	1.5	2.8	13.2	9.1
AXP	AMERICAN EXPRESS	14,628	40.3	42.8	13.3	2.3	2.2	21.3	9.1
PCG	PG&E CORP	10,487	16.4	24.8	9.5	1.2	6.9	11.0	9.1
NTRS	NORTHERN TRUST CORP	1,893	60.0	64.0	14.9	1.7	2.2	15.4	9.1
SBK	SIGNET BANKING CORP	1,678	-17.0	61.9	12.8	1.5	3.4	13.7	9.0
	AVERAGE		38.2	43.9	13.9	1.8	3.3	20.1	11.1
	WTD AVERAGE		40.9	46.1	13.1	1.9	3.3	21.5	11.8

Source: Compustat & IMI estimates.

Conclusion

Normalized Value Reflects Risk

The results of our 26-year study illustrate the relationship between normalized value and risk. The high normalized ROE quintile trades at 14.8x normalized value (i.e. ROE / (P/B) = 14.8x) and outperformed significantly on an equal- and capitalization-weighted basis (+300 p.p. and +113 p.p., respectively). The second quintile trades at 10.6x normalized value and outperformed significantly on an equal- and capitalization-weighted basis (+98 p.p. and +49 p.p., respectively), illustrating our concept of a "sweet spot." The third quintile trades at 8.4x normalized value and underperformed on an equal- and capitalization-weighted basis (-1 p.p. and -13 p.p., respectively). The fourth quintile trades at 6.3x and underperformed on an equal-weighted and capitalization-weighted basis (-15 p.p. and -15 p.p., respectively). The fifth quintile trades at 3.6x normalized value and underperformed on an equal- and capitalization-weighted basis (-50 p.p. and -54 p.p., respectively). In short, avoid only the most highly valued shares relative to quality and search for dividend yield within the "sweet spot."

CHAPTER 6

Sector and Style Rotation: A Valuation Approach

Michael F. Wilcox
President, Founder and CEO
Alford Associates, Inc.

Dan Fox
Research Associate
Alford Associates, Inc.

Overview

This chapter describes a methodology for identifying investment opportunities in segments of the global equity markets. These market segments may be defined in any convenient way, by parsing the names in the universe into economic sectors, for example; or by dividing the list of equities in a more statistical fashion, such as ranking all companies by size, by P/E ratio, or by book-to-market value (as is done in so-called "Style" analysis).

Our technique can be used to add value within a single country, in a bloc of related markets, or across the globe, as long as the groups defined have some investment characteristic that will make the equities within them follow a similar trading pattern.

Applications Illustrated Here

We will delineate two different applications of our approach:

1. Sector Rotation: In six different markets around the globe, we have grouped selected lists of equities into economic sectors. We show how a simple valuation measure can be used to identify periods during which portfolio weightings of these sectors should be above or below normal, and that such a strategy can add a significant increment to the returns of the unmanaged universe.

2. Style Rotation: We have chosen to illustrate managing the "Size" dimension of a portfolio to show that a single variable can be used to identify when to invest in certain "Styles." We could just as easily have used the book-to-market ratio as a ranking variable, as is done in many of the popular "Growth versus Value" style measurements, or any other characteristic that is of investment interest.

Other Applications

We have illuminated only two of a nearly infinite number of factors that might be considered relevant by portfolio managers. (See Chapter 9 on "Multifactor Equity Models," by Herbert Blank, for a discussion of other factors that are in common use.)

Whether groups of equities have been determined statistically (as in, for instance, a factor or cluster analysis) to trade together (i.e., past returns have been highly correlated with each other), or are assembled by force of logic (e.g., they are in similar lines of business), the approach outlined here can be used to predict when a portfolio that emphasizes (i.e., overweights) one factor will outperform the relevant performance benchmark for the equity universe being drawn from. The same logic will also be effective in forecasting the performance of more abstract factors, such as those employed in the multi-factor regression framework so popular among money managers these days.

Also, our methodology lends itself nicely to combining diverse measures of portfolio characteristics. With today's sophisticated portfolio analysis software, it is quite easy to determine a portfolio's exposure to a variety of factors. By determining the desirability of these factors with the methods we outline in this chapter, it is a fairly straightforward step to implementing a strategy to capture their value.

Add Value Directly or Indirectly

The methodology recommended in this chapter can be used in two important ways. One is to provide a direct method of adding value to a portfolio by identifying groups of equities that can be overweighted or underweighted to enhance returns. The second use of the information developed by the means we outline is to gain insight into which factors are undervalued in the marketplace at any given time, and thus should be emphasized in an equity portfolio, even if the names used in the analysis are not necessarily the vehicles used to implement the strategy. If, for example, a ranking of the universe by dividend yield shows that high-yielding stocks are more attractive than usual, a portfolio manager would be well advised to be sure that equity portfolios have a higher dividend yield than the performance benchmark being employed.

The examples that we give in this chapter, for ease of exposition and understanding, are all based on very simple valuation techniques. In our experience, success in this enterprise of rotating among predefined sectors or styles (or both) depends first and foremost on having a sound methodology for valuing individual equities, then on having a very clear idea of how to define investment characteristics that can be measured precisely. Once such a system is in place, improvements in valuation technology will naturally boost returns, but the incremental returns will generally be small in proportion to the added effort needed to introduce additional sophistication. Our assumption here is that our readers will have their own favorite valuation approaches, be they single-factor models (such as the one we use here for illustration) or more elaborate multifactor procedures.

There is another class of valuation model that attempts to blend multiple factors in an analytical framework and produce a single expected return forecast for each stock in the universe. We have, for example, successfully used an elaborate present value approach that involves forecasting earnings and dividends with a combination of mechanical rules and analyst forecasts.[1] We have also found strong predictive ability in the PB/ROE valuation model[2] first introduced by Jarrod Wilcox.[3]

---

[1] Michael F. Wilcox and Elizabeth M. MacElwee, "Dramatic Shifts in Sentiment Under Way; Time to Jump on the Bandwagon: Buy Low P/E Cyclicals," *Morgan Stanley Investment Research Report* (December 12, 1990).

[2] Michael F. Wilcox, "A Global Search for Value: Expected Return as a Function of Price to Book Value and Return on Equity," *Morgan Stanley Investment Research Report* (December 11, 1987).

[3] Jarrod W. Wilcox, "The PB-ROE Valuation Model," *Financial Analysts Journal* (January-February 1984).

No matter which basic approach is used in developing a measure of attractiveness for individual equities, incremental value can be added by using a double-relative perspective for evaluating any of these types of equity valuations. By double-relative we mean that current valuations of individual equities must be placed in context by comparing them not only with a benchmark, but with similar comparisons done in the past. While this type of measurement has come into more widespread use in recent years, we believe its value is not yet fully appreciated. To the best of our knowledge, the first publication to mention this technique was our report that introduced the "VAL" (Valuation Attractiveness Level) yardstick back in 1986.[4]

We later expanded this procedure to include characteristics such as the factors mentioned earlier in this chapter.[5] In that context, the stratagem is to create a time series of correlations between exposure to a factor and the valuation measure being employed. This time series is then "normalized" on an open-ended scale centered on zero. A negative reading indicates that the factor being measured is overvalued and therefore undesirable, whereas a positive reading says that the factor is more attractive than usual and thus should be overweighted in an equity portfolio.

Unfortunately, a detailed discussion of these and other valuation issues is beyond the scope of this chapter. We surmise that our readers already have (or at least have in mind) some proven valuation techniques for ranking equities and now wish to convert that information to successful portfolio strategies that will rotate among sectors or styles (or any other factors).

A Simple Example

To illustrate the ease with which our procedure can be put into practice, we show in Figure 6.1 the cumulative excess performance that our simulation obtained in the U.K. equity market over the six-year period ending June 30, 1997 by following the steps we outline on the following pages.

---

[4] Michael F. Wilcox, "A New Valuation Yardstick," *Morgan Stanley Investment Research Report,* (April 10, 1986).

[5] Michael F. Wilcox and Elizabeth M. MacElwee, "Buy Stock with High Yields and Low P/Es," *Morgan Stanley Investment Research Report* (September 14, 1990).

Figure 6.1 Global Equity Market Sector Rotation
UK Equal-Weighted Quintiles

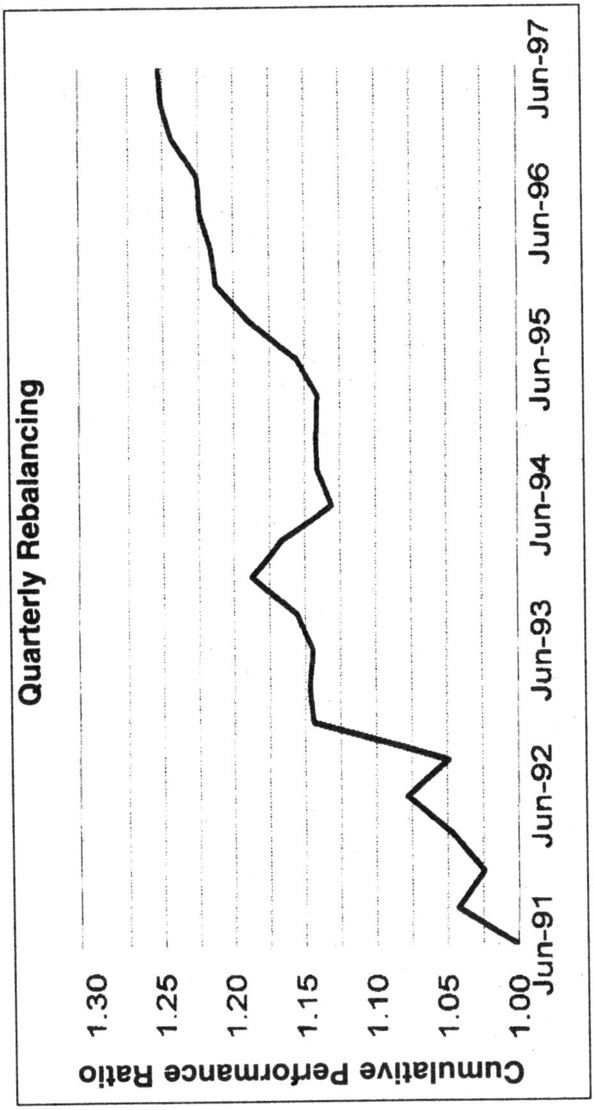

Source: Alford Associates, Inc.

1. We identified all U.K. equities in the Morgan Stanley Capital International (MSCI) universe that were also covered by I/B/E/S (essentially, this provides a list of all companies that are of institutional interest in that marketplace) and computed a forward-looking earnings/price (E/P) ratio based on the consensus of Wall Street analyst forecasts as collected by I/B/E/S. The size of this universe varied over time from a low of 140 to a high of 205. Although studies such as this are always subject to many criticisms of bias (especially survivorship bias), we believe that the names we used throughout this time period were, for all practical purposes, a complete list of the equities that were in fact available for investment by institutional investors.

In any case, our motivation here is not to present an air-tight, academically pure, statistical study, but to demonstrate to our readers that the approach we advocate has exciting possibilities for enhancing portfolio returns. We presume that investors who are convinced by our presentation will want to verify the potential of our approach by testing our ideas on their universe of equities, using their favorite valuation technique(s).

As an aside: the reason for using an E/P ratio rather than the more commonly expressed inverse (P/E ratio) is to provide analytical continuity when the "E" number is very small or negative.

2. We parsed the universe into industry groups. For this, we followed the categorization used by MSCI. The most recent month in the study contained 34 industries, as listed in Table 6.1

3. We calculated the average E/P within each industry. We did this two different ways: first by weighting the stocks within each group by their capitalization, and second by taking an equal-weighted average.

4. We ranked the industry groups by their average E/P and divided the list into quintiles. In any time period in which the number of industries was not evenly divisible by five, we kept an equal number in the first and fifth quintiles. We performed this ranking on both the equal-weighted and the cap-weighted sets of industries.

Table 6.1 Industry Groups in the United Kingdom as of June 30, 1997

Aerospace & Military Technology
Appliances & Household Durables
Banking
Beverages & Tobacco
Broadcasting & Publishing
Building Materials & Components
Business & Public Services
Chemicals
Construction & Housing
Electrical & Electronics
Electronic Components & Instruments
Energy Sources
Financial Services
Food & Household Products
Forest Products & Paper
Health & Personal Care
Industrial Components
Insurance
Leisure & Tourism
Machinery & Engineering
Merchandising
Metals-Non Ferrous
Metals-Steel
Miscellaneous Materials & Commodities
Multi-Industry
Real Estate
Recreation & Other Consumer Goods
Telecommunications
Textiles & Apparel
Transportation-Airlines
Transportation-Road and Rail
Transportation-Shipping
Utilities-Electrical & Gas
Wholesale & International Trade

5. We computed the subsequent performance of each quintile (total return, either weighted by market value or equally weighted, as appropriate) over several intervals; we report here on the results after 3, 6, 9, 12, 15, and 18 months, recording the difference in performance between the first- and fifth-quintile groups.

6. We linked the results of these hypothetical long/short portfolios to estimate the cumulative return differential between the best and worst quintiles over the entire six-year time period studied.

Our Findings

Figure 6.1, referred to earlier, shows the cumulative excess performance that could have been obtained by eliminating the lowest E/P quintile of industry groups from an equal-weighted (with respect to both industry groups and individual equities) portfolio and doubling up in the highest-ranking quintile of industries.

As can be seen, over the six years of the test period, this strategy would have netted an excess return of 25.3%, which on an annualized basis is 3.8%. Although no transaction charges were netted against this result, it is clear that, with quarterly rebalancing, in the extreme and unlikely event that both the top and bottom quintiles are totally replaced each quarter, the maximum annual turnover is 80% of the portfolio. Turnover would in actuality be much lower because groups do not rapidly move from one quintile to another. In any case, no reasonable transaction penalty would come close to negating the highly positive returns to this strategy.

Also, as pointed out earlier, this is a very straightforward valuation methodology. In our experience, more sophisticated schemes generate stronger signals and thus higher returns, although they also tend to produce slightly higher turnover.

Figure 6.2 introduces the capitalization-weighted version of this strategy, which proves to be even more profitable (though it is not as easy to estimate what the maximum turnover of the portfolio would be), compounding at 4.5% over the six-year period. Notice, however, that the returns to the cap-weighted version are not as dependable; nearly all of the excess returns were generated in the last three years of the period under study.

Figure 6.2 Global Equity Market Sector Rotation
Cap- versus Equal-Weighting

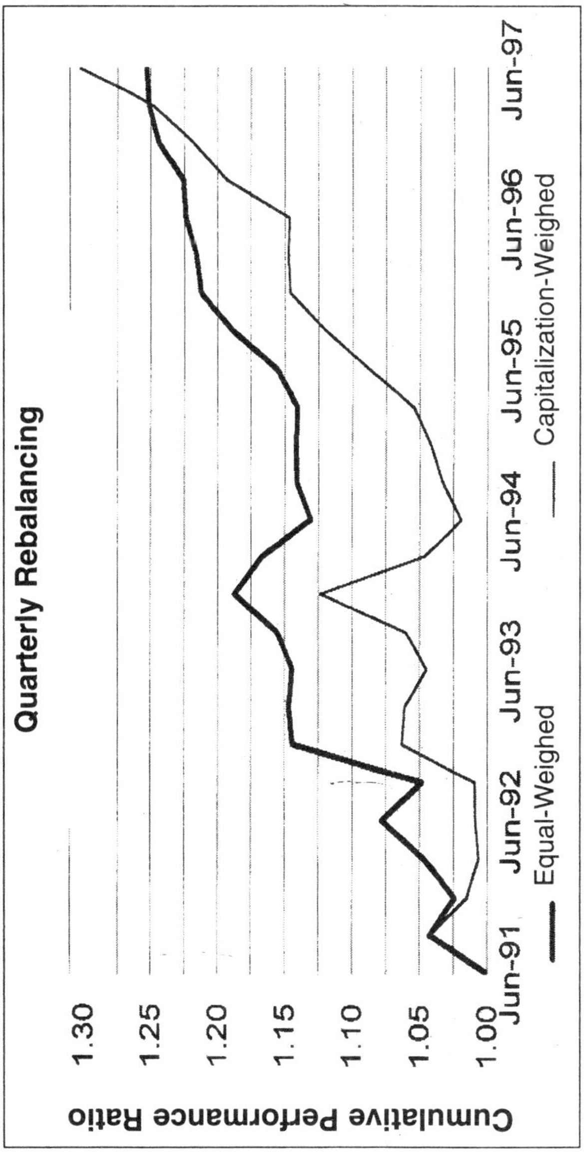

Source: Alford Associates, Inc.

Keep in mind, too, that these two strategies are time-dependent. That is, altering the starting or ending time by even one month can produce somewhat different results. To get a slightly more objective measure of the excess return potential of these two different strategies, we compiled the statistics given in Table 6.2.

In this table, we summarize the excess returns of the highest-ranked quintile of industry groups over the lowest quintile, for all possible holding periods of the lengths shown starting between June 30, 1991, and December 31, 1995.

Table 6.2 Top Quintile versus Bottom Quintile-E/Ps in the UK

Holding Periods (months):	**3**	**6**	**9**	**12**	**15**	**18**
Equal Weighted						
(a) Avg Outperformance (%)	0.95	1.95	2.89	3.80	4.78	5.93
(b) Standard Deviation	2.88	3.72	3.97	4.72	5.50	5.61
Ratio of (a) to (b)	0.33	0.52	0.73	0.81	0.87	1.06
Avg Outperformance	0.32	0.32	0.32	0.32	0.32	0.33
Capitalization Weighted						
(a) Avg Outperformance (%)	0.63	1.04	1.68	2.61	3.82	5.35
(b) Standard Deviation	2.97	3.80	3.98	4.48	5.11	5.46
Ratio of (a) to (b)	0.21	0.27	0.42	0.58	0.75	0.98
Avg Outperformance	0.21	0.17	0.19	0.22	0.25	0.30

These numbers are not annualized. Notice that the equal-weighted approach is superior by every measure, except that its standard deviation exceeds that of the cap-weighted version for the three longer holding periods. Despite its statistical disadvantage, the cap-weighted version of this strategy outperformed its equal-weighted counterpart for all 6 of the holding periods shown when we simulated the same long/short portfolios as illustrated in Figures 6.1 and 6.2. The annualized results of these simulations are given in Table 6.3.

Table 6.3 Top Quintile versus Bottom Quintile E/Ps in the United Kingdom

Holding Periods (months):	**3**	**6**	**9**	**12**	**15**	**18**
Equal Weighted (%)	3.83	3.44	3.48	4.03	2.58	3.59
Capitalization Weighted (%)	4.50	4.17	3.75	4.09	3.04	4.77

Notice that in both the equal-weighted and cap-weighted versions, there is no clear relationship between the holding period and the excess returns. This can also be seen from the data in Table 6.2, where the line labeled "Average Outperformance per Month" makes it obvious that the length of the holding period (at least up to the 18-month interval we tested) has little or no effect on the magnitude of the excess monthly performance. In other words, returns from this strategy tend to continue to accrue for long periods of time, which is a delightful prospect for those worried about trading costs. On the other hand, significantly positive results also begin immediately, which is good news for investors seeking short-term gratification.

It may seem at first blush that these tables contain contradictory information. At 15 months, for example, Table 6.2 shows the average outperformance to be equal to or better than any of the shorter holding periods, but in Table 6.3 the results are decidedly worse. The reason for this apparent contradiction is simply that the Table 6.3 numbers are path-dependent. To use a simplistic example, subsequent returns of +50% and -50% average zero, but result in a 25% loss, while +5% and -5% also average zero, yet result in only a 0.25% loss. Part of the seeming inconsistency in our numbers could be resolved by using the natural logarithms of wealth ratios in computing the Table 6.2 statistics, instead of the more familiar arithmetic averages we have chosen to present. But part of the problem is that the numbers given in Table 6.3 (as well as the results in the graphs shown in this chapter) are specific to the starting and ending points chosen. If we had started the 15-month strategy a few months later, a totally different compound return would have resulted. Delaying the start of the simulation by ten months, for example, would have added 115 basis point to the annualized result! One way to obtain less time-dependent results would be to treat the distribution of excess returns obtained from this study as a sample from a large distribution and run a series of simulations based on random draws from this presumed distribution. By repeating this experiment a thousand times or more, one could obtain reliable statistics as to the likely range of outcomes. For purposes of this chapter, we thought this to be overkill, since we are simply trying to present a methodology and give enough evidence that it works to inspire readers to develop similar strategies based on their own valuation work, which could then be tested by some of the more robust methods we suggest.

Lest the reader be suspicious that this is a strategy that works only in the United Kingdom, we present below a look at some other equity markets around the world, large as well as small. In every case, we found that this approach has promise. For the six markets we studied over this same time period, the average annualized value added ranged from 4% to 7%, depending on the measurement used (simulated results were generally a little lower than the statistics suggested they should be) and whether the equal-weighted or cap-weighted approach was used (the cap-weighted version nearly always did better). Table 6.4 summarizes our results. The first two panels show portfolio simulations of the same fashion as the results displayed in Figures 6.1 and 6.2; the last two panels give the averages of all possible holding periods in the interval studied.

Table 6.4 (Annualized Excess Returns) Top E/P Quintile versus Bottom E/P Quintile

Holding Periods (months):	**3**	**6**	**9**	**12**	**15**	**18**
Long/Short Portfolio Value Added						
Equal Weighted						
United Kingdom (%)	3.83	3.44	3.48	4.03	2.58	3.59
France	2.90	3.21	3.35	3.49	2.81	2.97
Germany	0.37	-0.20	-0.08	0.05	1.17	1.62
Malaysia	10.08	8.91	8.94	7.12	10.91	8.20
Hong Kong	12.61	14.68	12.52	12.53	5.40	12.19
Japan	-1.67	-1.89	-1.96	-0.60	1.65	-1.10
6-Country Average	4.69	4.69	4.37	4.44	4.09	4.58
Capitalization Weighted						
United Kingdom (%)	4.50	4.17	3.75	4.09	3.04	4.77
France	3.28	4.11	4.20	3.78	3.47	3.43
Germany	5.71	5.25	6.35	5.05	5.64	9.27
Malaysia	10.29	8.49	6.95	4.71	4.66	6.20
Hong Kong	16.35	18.80	19.37	18.44	12.63	18.90
Japan	-1.36	-0.93	-1.53	0.09	4.85	-0.84
6-Country Average	6.46	6.65	6.52	6.03	5.72	6.96

continued on next page

Arithmetic Average Value Added

Equal Weighted						
United Kingdom (%)	3.85	3.96	3.93	3.87	3.89	4.02
France	2.31	2.61	2.38	2.58	3.04	3.30
Germany	-1.30	-1.38	-1.06	-0.64	0.05	0.82
Malaysia	12.88	13.51	14.11	15.24	16.44	17.10
Hong Kong	15.99	15.46	14.79	15.37	14.07	13.27
Japan	-1.63	-1.48	-1.35	-1.05	-0.74	-0.48
6-Country Average	5.35	5.15	5.17	5.90	6.12	6.34
Capitalization Weighted						
United Kingdom (%)	2.55	2.09	2.26	2.64	3.10	3.63
France	0.38	0.67	0.98	1.17	1.57	2.11
Germany	1.51	2.70	3.88	4.58	5.63	6.57
Malaysia	12.02	12.11	11.31	11.18	10.99	10.45
Hong Kong	20.90	21.13	21.05	21.69	20.85	20.81
Japan	-0.92	0.36	0.28	1.06	1.32	1.31
6-Country Average	6.07	6.51	6.63	7.05	7.24	7.48

Conclusions on Sector Rotation

Although the results in Japan over the time period we studied were not nearly as good as in the other markets, we do not conclude from this that our approach should not be used there. The period in question has been a particularly difficult one for the Japanese economy and stock market, and the fact that our scheme added only about 100 basis points per year in the cap-weighted version and lost a little ground in the equal-weighted statistics is not surprising in the market environment we have witnessed. Also, almost all of the negative results occurred in the first year of this study period. If we had just left out the first year in Japan, the results would have been quite a bit better.

On the flip side of this coin, our statistics in Hong Kong showing the potential to add 20% per year or more with a cap-weighted ranking scheme are equally unconvincing to us in revealing the long-term value of our strategy. In truth, future results in Japan will likely be better than those shown here, and those in Hong Kong will likely not be as good. But after all, this is what global diversification is all about: a strategy that is not working in one market at any given time may very well be adding value in another.

We believe the average statistics showing the potential to add 5% or 6% per year (before transaction costs) to a global portfolio with this approach represent a reasonable expectation of what can be achieved using the methodology that we have outlined.

Style Rotation

Style investing, in its most basic form, involves measuring the universe of equities along a single continuum (rather than dividing it into discrete groups, as we did in the previous discussion of sector rotation).

One commonly used variable, or factor, is the Book Value to Market Value ratio, often expressed as Book Value per Share (B) divided by Share Price (P), or B/P. If a list of equities is ranked by B/P, the higher-ranked companies are called "Value" stocks (because the investor is getting more "Value," at least as measured by accounting book value per unit of currency paid), and the lower-ranked companies are called "Growth" stocks (on the presumption that investors are willing to pay more for a given unit of book value only if that company is growing its book value at an above-average rate). Obviously, this is a very simplistic way to look at the world, but it can be very useful for many purposes.

Another commonly used factor in style rotation is that of size. The jury is still out on whether (among the universe of institutionally acceptable stocks, anyway) small stocks have a higher expected rate of return (i.e., whether the "small-cap" effect is a real economic phenomenon), but there is no question that there are extended periods when small-cap stocks outperform their large-cap counterparts, and the other way around.

Figure 1.3 shows the results of applying our analysis to the same universe of U.K. stocks that we described in the section on Sector Rotation. The left y-axis scale shows the ratio of the valuation measure we described (in this illustration, the cap-weighted average for the entire universe was divided by its equal-weighted equivalent). The right scale shows the ratio of the subsequent three-month performance of the universe; again, the cap-weighted performance was divided by the equal-weighted performance.

Figure 6.3 Global Equity Market Sector Rotation Style Prediction

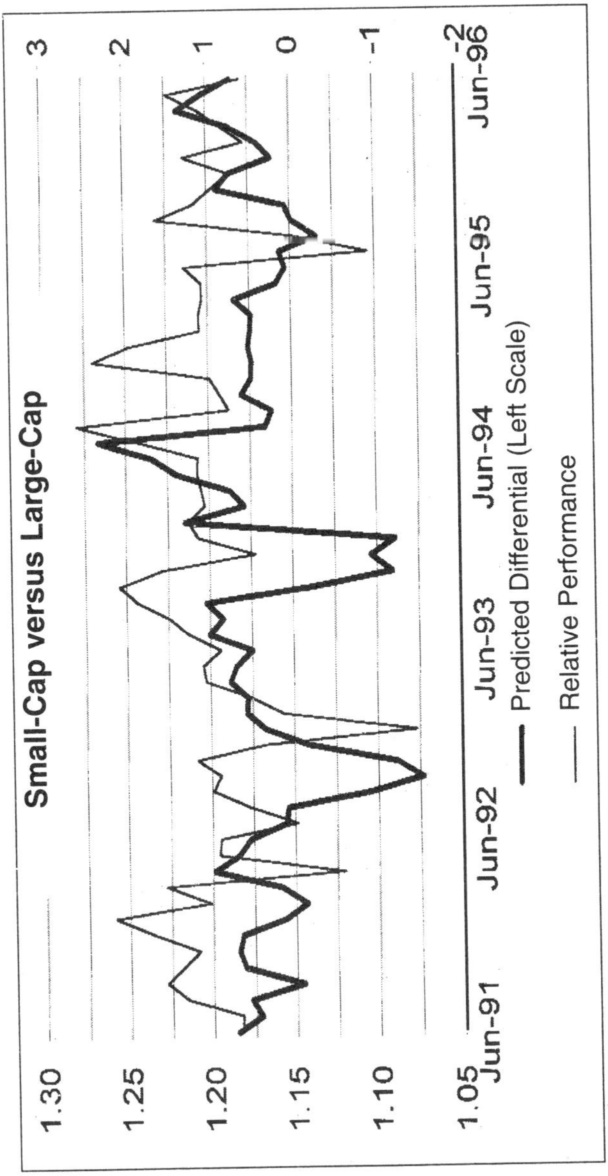

Source: Alford Associates, Inc.

In the case of the predicted performance (the darker line), a high reading indicates a prediction that large-cap stocks will outperform small-cap ones. Note that in many cases, an increase in this line is indeed followed by a rise in the lighter line, indicating that large-cap stocks did, in fact, outpace small-cap stocks. The phenomenon works in reverse, of course; when the lines decline they are favoring small-cap equities.

Although the visual evidence in this case may not be terribly compelling, we did compute a correlation between these two lines and found that statistic to be approximately 0.10. In our experience, this is high enough to indicate that there is sufficient information in this forecasting series to add value to a portfolio by tilting it one way or the other, as the forecast dictates. (In practice, many quantitative practitioners are happy with models of this sort that can give them a correlation of 0.05 or better.)

We leave it to the reader to envision applying this same logic to any number of other factors. These factors can be of limitless variety: sensitivity (as measured in a multiple regression) to economic factors such as interest rates or GDP growth, statistical factors such as are developed in an Arbitrage Pricing Theory (APT) risk model, financial or market characteristics such as those mentioned already (P/B and size), and many others (e.g., sales growth, dividend yield, return on equity, past earnings growth).

As long as the valuation measure being employed has some predictive ability (such as the value we have demonstrated in using forward-looking E/P ratios), it is useful to correlate it with any of the factors mentioned above. By observing when the correlation between any given factor and the valuation measure being used is above its norm, the portfolio manager can emphasize that factor when it is undervalued and underweight it when it is expensive. (See our discussion of the VAL measure at the beginning of this chapter.)

Summary

We have demonstrated that by using a straightforward approach relying on only a single factor (forward-looking E/P ratios), it is reasonable to expect to be able to add several hundred basis points per year to the performance of a global equity portfolio. The reader is invited to test our ideas in the context of other valuation techniques.

Our methodology involves grouping or ranking equities according to a pre-identified characteristic, such as industry affiliation or capitalization, and measuring the relative value that each group or characteristic offers. An equity portfolio can then be overweighted with equities that have desirable exposure to the group or factor found to be undervalued, while at the same time underweighting the least desirable groups or characteristics.

In this fashion, a portfolio will rotate into and out of sectors of the markets in which it is invested in such a way as to consistently outperform a passive approach that holds all stocks regardless of their exposures.

Enhanced Index Portfolio Construction Using Full Covariance Optimization for a Small-Capitalization Portfolio

Bernard V. Tew
Chairman
Q.E.D. Investments, LLC

The investment in a portfolio of small-capitalization stocks is a commitment to the future of relatively new, unproven companies and to the uncertainties commonly associated with these companies. The small-cap stock manager must by necessity "forecast" the future of many variables for each of the companies being considered and, more importantly, must accurately assess the variability of each forecast. All the typical classes of management styles such as fundamental analysis, technical analysis, traditional value and growth biases, and the more unusual mathematical/statistical methodology can be operative in the small-stock universe, and each can generate significant amounts of alpha. While each approach encompasses unique strengths and weaknesses, all require the forecasting and assessment of variables for an acceptable set of stocks. This discussion focuses on the use of mathematical analysis exclusively as a management methodology for a small-stock portfolio and the implementation of a full-covariance approach for an enhanced index assignment.

The portfolio construction process has five basic components for the mathematical manager, including first developing a set of decision criteria. These criteria include an investment philosophy that defines allowable portfolio risk, finding an acceptable portfolio holding period, selecting an appropriate investment time horizon, and assessing expectations of portfolio return. Second, the target universe of acceptable stocks must be clearly defined and the dynamic nature of the selection universe must be described. Procedures for accommodating the dynamic aspect of the selection universe must be defined. Third, modeling and estimation procedures for model inputs must be developed with clearly defined expectations, confidence limits, and general limitations described per asset class. The strengths and weaknesses of each model developed relative to general types of market environments must be defined. Fourth, a portfolio compilation algorithm or optimization method must be selected, and finally, the timing and choice of portfolio rebalancing and revision policies must be determined.

Although each component of the construction process is important to achieving acceptable results, the focus of this discussion is the third element, the input estimation procedure. This component is often considered the most important part of the process. In fact, reasonable precision in statistical input modeling will result in alpha-producing portfolios even if much less precision is achieved in the other elements of the construction process. Alternatively, poor input estimation can result in negative alpha production even though significant precision in all other areas of the process is achieved. The existence of statistical input estimation risk was recognized by Markowitz (see references at the end of this chapter) in the conclusion of his article, when he suggested using historical information as a basis for estimation of expected returns and variability for each security. This suggestion to use point estimates originating from historical data for the variance-covariance construction has been widely disregarded due to the rigorous data requirements. For example, a portfolio containing 1,000 stocks would conventionally need at least 1,000 data points for each security to obtain a nonsingular estimate of the full variance-covariance matrix. The difficulties and lack of robustness of using sample estimates have been widely noted in the finance literature.

One method commonly used to reduce the effects of estimation risk is tightly constraining each security holding, thereby limiting the benefits of "good" parameter estimates and the damage of "bad" estimates. Another method is the reduction of the dimensionality of the portfolio selection problem by using a simple structural model such as the single-index model first introduced by Sharpe, or by using more complex structural models such as the multifactor models often developed and used by various quantitative equity managers today. Although Sharpe did not explicitly describe the computation of multiple beta model coefficients, it has become common to estimate the parameters of the model using ordinary least squares by defining the model as a multivariate regression model. These estimates, when computed using historical data or hypothetical data, are minimum variance linear unbiased estimators of true parameter values. Thus, conventional thought is that statistical input parameter estimation risk is greatly reduced, as opposed to estimating each element of a variance-covariance independently.

Typical alternative approaches use a fundamental approach to statistically forecast future price movements by incorporating economic, social, accounting, and/or behavioral factors chosen by the modeler in the estimation procedure, while a more technical approach would attempt to assess and incorporate past price trends and patterns in the estimation method on a single-stock basis or a market-relative basis. A mathematical approach would seek to estimate future price directions only by evaluations of the stochastic price process.

There are significant differences among these three methods of input estimation, although each method does use past data to some extent and in some form. For example, the fundamental approach may experience frequent omissions of data in small companies that only recently originated. In this case, much effort must be devoted to modifying and calibrating the modeling procedures to accommodate missing data. The correlation between the fundamental factors and future price directions may frequently be highly subjective rather than quantitative, or highly sensitive to structural changes either in the individual companies or in the market environment. The technical approach typically uses only the past price data, with comovements being difficult to assess among more than a few securities. Portfolios managed in this style are typically held in equal-portion format or much less often in capitalization-weighted format. Finally, the last approach, mathematical/statistical input estimation, uses only the past price history and usually incorporates an optimization process. In its purest implementation this method has the potential to optimize "input estimation error" rather than portfolio alpha.

The pricing and copricing process of stocks is a complex, dynamic, nonstationary time-series phenomenon. Modeling these processes inherently must incorporate autocorrelationships as well as cross-sectional correlationships among a very large number of securities. Mathematical/statistical implementation of these processes can incorporate financial theory in the form of the APT multifactor model or the CAPM. These approaches in classical form, however, are static one-period models with the usual and obvious limitations. More recent implementations use multivariate time series methods, nonlinear estimation formulations, ARCH and GARCH models and all the recent variations, Kalman filter models, stochastic coefficient techniques, multivariate regression methods in OLS and/or robust forms, and individually designed vector autoregressive approaches. Each of these methods has definable strengths and weaknesses and is an acceptable choice. However, even after a modeling method is selected, the length of the data sample period relative to the investment holding period remains an extremely important factor in the portfolio construction process and must be determined properly to preserve the predictive power of the chosen estimation method. This can imply that the data sample period selected for modeling stock time-series processes can be relatively short or surprisingly long.

Following a brief assessment of the value of historical information as a model input and a review of one particular implementation of Markowitz optimization methods, an example of the development of the three most important mathematical/statistical inputs is described. The discussion concludes with the presentation of actual composite quarterly performance results for a small-capitalization portfolio developed and managed in this style for an enhanced index assignment.

Historical Probability Beliefs as Inputs

The problem of creating optimal investment portfolio statistical inputs via a mathematical process has three primary components. These are (1) producing estimates of the centrality, variability, and covariability of future returns for each security in the optimization universe; (2) estimating these statististical parameters for a large array of possible portfolios; and (3) selecting that particular portfolio that meets the optimality criterion. The Markowitz approach to portfolio theory and construction takes the statistical inputs as given:

> "Various types of information concerning securities can be used as the raw material of a portfolio analysis. One source of information is the past performance of individual securities."

Markowitz further explained that portfolios constructed with inputs formulated from historical data were portfolios that performed particularly well in the past, and portfolios made with more subjective inputs reflect the implications of the subjective beliefs. In practice, probability beliefs that are the basis of the statistical inputs for the optimization process can take any form and can originate from any number of sources. These beliefs are simply a forecast of various possible future states of nature for each security in the selection set. If one assumes that a random process generates the historical data for each stock and that the same random process is expected to remain for some defined portfolio holding period in the future, then the assumption is that the historical performance of securities is at least a workable representation of the future performance. As a result, historical price data can be used as the foundation for the statistical inputs to the analysis (Samuelson). This assessment of validity must be made for each security in the selection universe independently and must be repeated at regular predetermined intervals.

Constructing Markowitz Efficient Portfolios

Briefly for review, the expected return of a portfolio of n securities in the optimization universe is:

(1) $$E = \sum_{i}^{n} x_i R_i$$

where **E** is the expected return of the selected portfolio, x_i is the percentage of the portfolio invested in security i, and R_i is the periodic expected return of security i computed as:

(2) $$R_i = E[(P_{i,t+1} + D_{i,t+1} - P_{i,t})/P_{i,t}] + 1.0$$

where $P_{i,t+1}$ is the periodic closing price for security i in time period t+1, $D_{i,t+1}$ is the dividend received by the close of time period t+1, and $P_{i,t}$ is the periodic closing price for security i in period t. The variance of the portfolio about the expected return of the portfolio is:

(3) $$V = \sum_{i}^{n} \sum_{j}^{n} x_i x_j \sigma_{ij}$$

where σ_{ij} is the covariabilty of securities i and j.

The original formulation of the mean-variance approach to portfolio selection defined by Markowitz may be described in the context of computing an efficient set of portfolios. The problem becomes maximizing a quadratic function subject to a linear equality constraint. In matrix notation this is accomplished by maximizing:

(4) $\mathbf{L} = \sigma \mathbf{E} - \mathbf{V}$

where σ is always greater than or equal to zero. The problem then is to:

(5) solve $\mathbf{x} = A^{-1}$ b

where A^{-1} is the inverse of an n by n matrix of covariance estimates, b is a column vector of n-1 length with elements as functions of $\frac{1}{2}\sigma r_i$, and x is a vector of efficient portfolios. Iterating σ from a large positive value to zero determines the complete set of efficient portfolios, with more risk-averse investors preferring portfolios at or near the minimum variance portfolio $(\sigma = 0)$. Individually optimal portfolios are determined by input probability beliefs and selected by assessing individual investor risk aversion.

If the expected returns of all the securities in the optimization universe are equal, the variances of the securities are also all equivalent, and at least two of the stocks are not perfectly positively correlated, there exists a minimum variance portfolio that has the same expected return as any security in the selection universe but has a variance less than any security. The minimum variance portfolio is the only efficient portfolio in this case, and the expected return of the portfolio cannot be changed by changing the proportions invested in each stock. Furthermore, if all the covariances are equal, then the portfolio exhibits symmetric interdependence and the optimal weight for each security is 1/n. It seems reasonable that while managers employing different styles may agree with the assumptions typically used by the mathematical manager, all equivalent covariances seems highly unlikely. If one security has an expected return that is higher than the others and at least some of the covariances are not equal, then changing the proportions invested in each stock will change the expected returns of the portfolio. Thus, for portfolios with few stocks relative to the index, the expected return input is critical (Fama). However, recall that as the number of securities increases to infinity, the expected return of the portfolio approaches the "market return" and the variance of the individual stocks becomes insignificant. The result is that covariances among the securities in the selection universe remain the only significant input to the construction process and full covariance implementations may be the most robust.

Other nonstatistical inputs required in the construction process after the mathematical inputs are computed include but are not limited to:

- appropriate upper and lower potential holding limits for each stock in the selection universe,
- maximum acceptable portfolio turnover and/or maximum turnover per several selected issues in the existing portfolio,
- short selling as a percent of the total portfolio value and for which stocks in the selection universe,
- allowable tracking error,
- industry and sector constraints,
- factor-loading constraints such as yield, P/E, etc., and
- constraints reflecting legal and/or social management.

Geometric Mean Input Estimation and Optimization

The portfolio selection problem previously described is static, with no guidance about the optimal portfolio holding period or revision intervals. Theoreticians such as Tobin asserted that market imperfections in the form of transaction costs make the optimal revision schedule relevant. Markowitz, Lantane, and many others illustrated that the portfolio with the highest geometric mean during any particular subperiod maximizes multiperiod return. However, the process described in the previous section is applicable only insofar as the statistical inputs are robust for a predetermined subholding period. As the holding period is exceeded, revisions must occur to preserve the effectiveness of the input estimation methods.

Much research effort has been devoted to analyzing various implementations of the geometric rate of return as an appropriate input to an optimization construction process. These begin with Markowitz and include among many others: Young and Trent, and Lantane and Tuttle. For this discussion consider r_i through r_n as all positive numbers and periodic rates of return for a stock. Equation (6) illustrates the geometric rate of return for this stock, noting that the logarithm of the geometric mean equals the arithmetic mean of the periodic logarithms.

$$(6)\quad \log R_g = 1/n * (\log r_1 + \ldots. + \log r_n)$$

Estimating (6) for all of the stocks in the selection universe provides reasonable inputs to the optimization process.

More robust input estimates can be created using equation (6) estimates as a foundation because it has been shown that uniform improvement can be made, as measured by total mean squared error risk, when estimating several parameters from independent normal observations (Stein). Originating from the fact that if the means being estimated, R_g, are a sample from a prior distribution, say the expected rates of return for all tradable stocks in the selection universe that are distributed in approximately a normal distribution, then the Baysian estimate of R_g is the best apiori estimate of the mean for the data in hand. Furthermore, a simple estimator was developed that makes very substantial improvements out-of-sample if more than two parameters under consideration are estimated (James and Stein). Still other improvements were made by Bartlett; Atchison and Martz; West and Harrison; Elderton and Johnson; and Efron and Morris in an empirical Baysian context.

The method presented in this discussion is based on an application of the first fundamental James-Stein estimator (Efron and Morris). The basis of this estimator is that although sample means all regress toward some measure of central tendency, some regress more rapidly than others. The essential part of the James-Stein estimator, then, is the "shrinkage" factor that describes this regression to the "master mean" of the sample means and proper estimation of the central grand mean. The actual value of the shrinkage factor is determined by all the observed averages. It always must be greater than zero but less than one in positive part formulation.

The first step is to determine the grand mean of the sample geometric means for each stock denoted by Φ as follows:

$$(7) \quad \Phi = E[R_g]$$

where R_g are estimated as previously described for each stock in the selection universe. The shrinkage factor "c" is calculated as follows:

$$(8) \quad c = 1.0 - (k - 3)\,\sigma^2 / \sum (R_g - \Phi)_2$$

where k is the number of means in the sample, σ^2 is the square of the standard deviation, and $\sum(R_g - \Phi)^2$ is the sum of the squared deviations of each sample average from the master mean. As the shrinkage factor becomes smaller, shrinking is more drastic because the denominator gets smaller. Alternatively, as "c" increases, the shrinking is less drastic. The James-Stein ex-anti estimates for each stock's geometric average rate of return become:

(9) $$\sigma_1 = \Phi + c * (R_g - \Phi)$$

Formulation of the corresponding James-Stein estimators for the variance of each security and the covariance between stocks are:

(10) $$\sigma_{ii} = E[(r_i - \sigma_i)(r_i - \sigma_i)]$$

(11) $$\sigma_{ij} = E[(r_i - \sigma_i)(r_j - \sigma_j)]$$

Equations (9), (10), and (11) can now be used to estimate all the statistical inputs to the optimization model.

The Results of "Mathematical" Equity Management

A portfolio of small-capitalization stocks has been managed using a purely mathematical methodology similar to this discussion for the past several years. The beginning selection universe of stocks consists of all of the stocks in the RUSSELL2000 index existing in December of each year. Statistical inputs estimated in December include 2,000 estimates of expected return, 2,000 estimates of variability and 3,998,000 individual estimates of covariance. The portfolio is optimized and held passively, with no rebalancing until the next optimization 12 months later. More than 425 stocks are typically held in the portfolio annually, with no single stock position exceeding 0.25% of the portfolio value. Daily oversight of the portfolio is computer driven, with no other input such as analyst reports, investment committee consensus, etc., ever being used. No stocks are removed or added to the optimized portfolio during the intraoptimization period with the exception of stocks that experience some form of corporate action that stops trading, such as delisting or a complete buyout of the company. In the event of an announcement of a corporate purchase, the position was most often liquidated at the time of the announcement.

Additional money received during the intraoptimization period is invested in the same optimized portfolio that originated at the beginning of the year. The portfolio remains approximately fully invested at all times, with the cash holding never exceeding 0.5% of the total portfolio value. Dividends received during the year are invested in those issues that most differ from the respective optimized proportions as trading costs allow. Annual turnover averages approximately 40 to 65%, with a substantial portion caused by turnover in the index.

Table 7.1 presents the live composite results for this portfolio. Index returns do not include transaction costs. Quarterly and annual optimized returns do include transaction costs as actually experienced in all the accounts. Table 7.2 contains a comparative presentation of Q.E.D.'s current portfolio with the RUSSELL2000 index as of the December 1996 optimization. During the first year of management for the method, the portfolio performance was reduced largely due to limitations of this manager as systems were developed for handling a portfolio with so many different positions. Still, the portfolio outperformed the index substantially. The performance during the second year was very typical, with the index experiencing a poor year and the optimized portfolio displaying its characteristic "downside" protection. Performance during the third and fourth years of management has been well within the defined parameters of the method. Finally, a brief examination of Table 7.2 illustrates the characteristic "structured contrarianism" of the method.

Table 7.1 Optimized Small-Cap Composite*

	RUSSELL2000	Small Cap		
	Quarterly		Annual	
Mar-93	1.78%	6.62%		
Jun-93	2.18%	-0.95%		
Sep-93	8.74%	6.81%		
Dec-93	2.63%	0.69%	16.07%	13.59%
Mar-94	-2.66%	-2.27%		
Jun-94	-3.90%	0.27%		
Sep-94	6.94%	3.96%		
Dec-94	-1.86%	-1.63%	-1.83%	0.22%
Mar-95	4.61%	5.11%		
Jun-95	9.37%	6.71%		
Sep-95	9.88%	8.77%		
Dec-95	2.18%	4.44%	28.46%	27.42%
Mar-96	5.10%	3.30%		
Jun-96	5.00%	3.79%		
Sep-96	0.35%	2.96%		
Dec-96	5.20%	9.15%	16.50%	20.50%
Mar-97	-5.52%	0.27%		
Jun-97	15.70%	12.49%	9.31%	12.80%
Sharpe Ratio	0.97	1.46		
Annualized Return		14.84%	16.28%	
Annual St. Dev.	10.45%	7.90%		
Tracking Error		5.80%		
Beta		0.62		
Alpha		4.84%		

* All performance for periods prior to June 1997 was achieved while Dr. Tew was employed by Weiss, Peck and Greer. Dr. Tew was responsible for the specific stock selection and weights for equity portfolios of managed accounts.

Table 7.2 Q.E.D. Small-Cap 1997 Comparative Characteristics

	RUSSELL 2000	Small Cap
Stocks	2000	450
Average Market Cap	693mm	577mm
Beta	1.00	0.62
Price/Book Value Ratio	2.60	2.00
Price/Earnings Ratio	26.20	17.60
Yield %	1.20	2.80

References

Atchison, T. A. and H. F. Martz Jr., *Empirical Bayes Estimation and Computing in Statistics*, Texas Tech University Press, Lubbock, Texas, 1969.

Bartlett, M.S., *Empirical Bayes Methods*. Spottiswoode, Ballantyne & Co. Ltd., London, 1970.

Efron, B. and C. Morris, "Stein's Paradox in Statistics," *Scientific American* 236, 5, May 1977: 119-127

Elderton, W. P. and N. L. Johnson, *Systems of Frequency Curves*, Cambridge University Press, London, 1969.

Fama, E. F., *Foundations of Finance*, New York: Basic Books, 1976.

James, W. and C. Stein, "Estimation with Quadratic Loss," *Proceedings of the Fourth Berkeley Symposium Mathematical Statistics and Probability,* University of California Press, Berkeley, 1961.

Lantane, H. A., "Criteria for Choice Among Risky Ventures," *Journal of Political Economy*, 62, 1959: 144-155.

Lantane, H. A. and D. L. Tuttle, "Criteria for Portfolio Building," *Journal of Finance* 24, 1967: 359-373.

Markowitz, H. M., "Portfolio Selection," *Journal of Finance,* 7, 1952: 71-91.

Markowitz, H. M., *Portfolio Selection: Efficient Diversification of Investment,* Cowles Foundation Monograph #16, New Haven: Yale University Press, 1959.

Markowitz, H. M., *Mean-Variance Analysis in Portfolio Choice and Capital Markets,* New York: Basil Blackwell, 1987.

Samuelson, P. A., "Proof that Properly Anticipated Prices Fluctuate Randomly," *Industrial Management Review*, 6, Spring 1965: 41- 49.

Sharpe, W. F., "A Simplified Model for Portfolio Analysis," *Management Science,* January, 1963.

Stein, C., " Estimation of the Mean of a Multivariate Normal Distribution," *Annals of Statistics* 9, 81: 1135-1151.

Tobin, J., "Liquidity Preferences as Behavior Towards Risk," *Review of Economic Studies* 26, 1958: 65-86.

West, Mike and Jeff Harrison. *Bayesian Forecasting and Dynamic Models,* Springer-Verlag Publishing, New York, New York, 1989.

Young, W. E. and R. H. Trent, "Geometric Mean Approximations of Individual Security and Portfolio Performance," *Journal of Financial and Quantitative Analysis* 4, 1969: 179-199.

CHAPTER 8

Multifactor Equity Models

Herbert Blank
Quantitative Consultant
Worldscope\Disclosure

Any discussion of multifactor equity models must commence with a definition of terms. In the broadest and most literal sense, a multifactor equity model is any system that combines more than one variable to analyze equities. By this definition, even the simplest and most common of screening mechanisms, utilizing two or more fundamental ratios (usually as pass/fail tests) to narrow an overall universe of stocks, qualifies as a multifactor equity model. Indeed, this elementary type of multifactor model is one of the most commonly used quantitative tools in asset management today.

The Value Line Timeliness Ranking System

This chapter will focus on the evolution and implementation of analytic and formulaic quantitative multifactor models currently in use by the world's equity community. In many ways, the "grandfather" of all such models is the Value Line Timeliness Ranking System, founded in 1965 — at the same time that the efficient market theory and the Capital Asset Pricing Model (CAPM) were taking root in academia. Value Line's Sam Eisenstadt pored over years of historical data with a slide rule and a "Bowmar Brain" calculator in order to rank each stock covered by the *Value Line Investment Survey* from 1 (highest) to 5 (lowest) in relative attractiveness. The variables assigned to each stock were calculated purely on the basis of that stock's historical price and earnings time series relative to the Value Line universe. The coefficients for each variable were determined annually on the basis of a regression equation fitting historical price change as the dependent variables to the independent variables, which consisted of some measurements of price rank, price momentum, earnings rank, and earnings momentum.

At a time long before the founding of the Association for Investment Management and Research, when most investors were unable to obtain rates of return from their investment managers, the Ranking System constituted a major quantitative innovation in the investment world. With minor adjustments, including the addition of an earnings surprise variable in 1971, the Ranking System is still in use today. For more than three decades, it has confounded academics who have sought to reconcile its long-term track record for above-average price performance with the tenets of market efficiency. Yet, there have been years, especially 1988 and 1992, where the system has fared very poorly. Moreover, Value Line Asset Management, which has applied the Ranking System to money management since 1979, has experienced a mediocre performance record relative to other asset management firms. The major historical significance of the Ranking System is that its success opened the door to legitimize the concepts of multifactor equity models and quantitative stock selection.

Regression Models

The Ranking System is an example of a regression model. More narrowly, it is a form of price-performance-only-oriented regression model. It does not attempt to account for risk, and it does not attempt to account for total returns, including dividends—only price performance. These two drawbacks have contributed to the fact that the Ranking System has, for the most part, been left out of the evolution of mainstream institutional investment thinking throughout the past three decades. But regression models of all descriptions have been, and continue to be, applied toward the goal of using a multifactor model to map the sources of projected equity returns. Indeed, regression models are the most common types of multivariate equity model used in the equity industry today. For example, many of William O'Neill's momentum scores shown graphically in *Investors Business Daily* are derived from regression equations.

Form and Assumptions of Multiple Regression Models

The basic equation of the multiple regression analytic model takes the following form:

$$y_i = \alpha + \Sigma \beta_{ij} * x_{ij} \text{ for } i=1,\ldots,n; j=1,\ldots,m ;$$

where n = the number of observations variables; m = the number of independent variables; α = the x-intercept (a constant), and β_{ij} = the coefficient for the ith observation of the jth independent variable. The regression model, then, always takes the form of a straight line.

Typically, in equity modeling, the dependent variable (y) is some time series of total returns. Accordingly, the independent x's are "m" number of time series, calibrated at identical time intervals with the dependent variable, that the modeler believes somehow contribute to the determination of the independent series of total returns. This is a powerful statement, with definitive implications that these independent variables, taken together, explain—according to a precise mathematical formula—the causes of total return.

The x-intercept (α) and the independent variables' coefficients (the β's), are outputs of the model. Other important outputs include the coefficient of determination (r-squared) and the error term for each β, (μ). Deriving its name from the simple correlation coefficient (also known as Pearson's r), r-squared (quite literally a correlation coefficient squared for a single-factor model) is the most commonly cited statistic pertaining to regression models. The r-squared conveys how tight a fit the actual data really are to the straight-line equation from which they were derived. Each μ relates the distance between the observed β and the value of β needed to make the straight-line equation true. In actual capital markets research, a "Holy Grail" equation has yet to be found that works in all cases; therefore, multiple regression models should be viewed as approximations that, hopefully, provide reasonably useful projections in most cases.

Limitations of Regression Models

It is important to note that regression models are rather rigid in their construction. The multiple regression model makes many important assumptions. A list of these assumptions and their implications in dealing with time series of investment data follow.

- The distributions of dependent variables and independent variables are continuous.
- The relationships between the independent variables and the dependent variables can be characterized linearly.
- The independent variables are linearly independent from each other.
- The independent variables are devoid of serial autocorrelation (the error terms, m's, are not correlated; correlation between the error terms frequently occurs in time series data where cycles exist.).
- The distribution is not abnormally skewed in one direction or another.
- The distribution is marked by heteroscedasticity (the expected error term is not constant throughout the distribution).

The extent to which these assumptions accurately apply affects the validity of the model's application to the distributions. Most computer-resident statistical programs utilized today supply statistics automatically with this information. In practice, it is rare to find time series distributions where these assumptions hold entirely. Multicolinearity between independent variables is tough to completely avoid. Indeed, referring back to the Timeliness Ranking System, even at face value, all four of the dependent variables (price rank, price momentum, earnings rank, and earnings momentum) are heavily multicolinear. Likewise, autocorrelation and skewness are problems frequently encountered in time series that are correlated significantly with total returns. Still, imperfection does not equal uselessness. Many such models have been demonstrated to add value in helping to explain the sources of asset returns.

Data Quality Issues: Garbage In – Garbage Out

A model is only as good as the data used to create it. Many dimensions of this issue apply to multifactor equity modeling, the first being the quality and the sources of the data. Financial reporting is not an exact science. The recording of revenues, net income, shares outstanding, earnings per share, cash flows, total returns, and many other important equity variables is highly source dependent. That is, one electronic data source (such as Compustat) may list different shares-outstanding figures than another source (such as Value Line or Disclosure). And many times, the differences are more a matter of interpretation than accuracy. This problem is even more pronounced with international data, because foreign accounting practices and regulatory requirements are less exacting than in the

United States. Sample bias is another problem that needs to be avoided when attempting to build a robust regression model. All empirically derived, multifactor equity models work on the assumption that the data upon which the model was constructed is representative of the entire population to which it will be applied.

Factor Selection—the Perils of Data Mining

How does one select the independent factors that explain total returns? In the best of all possible worlds, the answer is pure and simple intuition. The modeler knows in his or her heart and mind which independent factors are explanatory of the dependent variable and simply applies these time series to a regression model. When, as per usual, this is not the case, then an alternative method must be found. In the 1970s, one popular approach was what is now derisively referred to as the "kitchen sink" method. That is, throw every conceivable independent variable into the mix. Since a model's r-squared can only go up with each added variable, the more a modeler indulged in this practice, the tighter the fit he or she could proclaim. The problem is that such models are not robust; that is, they do not tend to endure well in time periods other than the one in which the model is fitted. One of the explanations for the lack of persistence is that such models are generally rife with co-linearity, rendering one of the basic assumptions of the regression model invalid. This process is known as "data mining." One of the quirks of statistical analysis is that one may be able to find a factor that seems very highly correlated with the dependent variable during a specific time period, but such a relationship turns out to be spurious when tested in other time periods. Such spurious correlations produce the iron pyrite ("fool's gold") of data mining. However, even when adjustments are made for excessive co-linearity by removing less explanatory, co-linear variables from the model, many such models have trouble withstanding the test of time.

Sometimes, Timing Is Everything

No discussion of the potential perils and pitfalls inherent in multifactor modeling would be complete without discussing time-period dependency. It is important to note that data mining still may be a problem in the total absence of "mad regression" techniques. Frequently, a modeler's own market experience will prompt the inclusion of a potential factor. Since recent history makes the largest impact in most of our minds, this may result in a type of mental data mining. It is always advisable to test the robustness of such relationships in multiple, distinct periods if at all possible.

One example of the perils of data mining is demonstrated by the ill-fated experience suffered by the Columbine Ranking System of Columbine Investment Research in Missouri. This multifactor model performed quite well in the inflationary period of 1977-1981, but performed very poorly in the disinflationary period from 1983-1989. The relationships emphasized by the Columbine model turned out to be too time-period specific. This inability to withstand the test of time means that the Columbine variables were merely variables, not explanatory factors. Although modelers such as this author tend to use the words "variable" and "factor" interchangeably, Ferguson and Moffatt ("Myth and Reality in the World of Factors," *Journal of Investing*, Summer 1995) make the distinction that factors are variables that have proven to be explanatory in actual practice for more than a decade.

Nevertheless, empirical study can serve as fruitful ground for the exploration of relationships and potential factors. One of the issues that modelers must address critically is whether such indicated factors have legitimate theoretical underpinnings. In other words, are the factors fundamentally sound? When regression analysis discovers a strong empirical relationship between two seemingly unrelated variables, the relationship warrants further investigation. One methodologically sound technique is to review the relationship in several, distinct time periods. While many such attempts will prove fruitless, it is still a worthwhile endeavor. In many noteworthy cases, such analysis actually has led to the identification of previously unrecognized, important relationships.

The Modern Portfolio Theory Revolution

Thus far, this chapter has focused almost exclusively on the return side of the equation. That is only half of the story. The largest tax-free accounts in the United States focus most of their analytic attention on the relationships between the risk exposures of equity portfolios and total returns. In his book, *Capital Ideas,* Peter L. Bernstein detailed the chronology of the modern portfolio theory revolution and its impact on the U.S. investment community. Mr. Bernstein covered the period from the early 1950s through the early 1990s, detailing the exploits of the true modern luminaries of the field, including: Harry Markowitz, William Sharpe, Merton

Miller, Barr Rosenberg, Fischer Black, Stephen Ross, and many others. We will certainly not attempt to cover these gentlemen's contributions in the tiny space allotted within this chapter. However, it is necessary to spotlight the contribution of each briefly in the context of its effect on the evolution of multifactor equity models.

The cornerstone of Modern Portfolio Theory, developed by Harry Markowitz, is the efficient frontier consisting of portfolios with a maximum level of expected return, given some investor-selected level of risk. In his landmark *Journal of Finance* paper, "Portfolio Selection," published in 1952, Markowitz legitimized the concept of risk diversification. He demonstrated that the riskiness of a portfolio depends on the covariance of its holdings, not on the average riskiness of the separate investments. Aggregate portfolio risk for all potential portfolios is determined by the sum of the covariances of its holdings. For a given level of risk, only the portfolio with the maximum level of expected return belongs on the efficient frontier. Importantly, such a portfolio could be determined through a new construct he developed, called portfolio optimization.

Yet this landmark concept, by itself, had little effect on investment management practices of its day. The state of 1950s computer technology, and the lack of availability of such technology, made the calculation of mean-covariance efficient portfolios difficult and, thus, the implementation of Markowitz' efficient frontier impractical.

The Capital Asset Pricing Model

William Sharpe made Markowitz's concepts implementable by developing a single-factor model that quantified the relationship between market risk and return. In 1963, he published a paper in *Management Science* called "A Simplified Model of Risk and Return." In 1964, he refined this model by specifically defining each stock's sensitivity to movements of the entire market as this solitary factor. He dubbed his new offspring the Capital Asset Pricing Model (CAPM).

$$R_i - r = [\alpha_i + \beta_i * (R_m - \rho)]$$

For an individual stock, the CAPM's equation is:
where:

R_i = the holding period return for asset i
R_m = the holding period return for the market
ρ = the risk-free rate of return

α_i = the nonmarket excess return on asset i
β_i = the sensitivity of the excess return of asset i to the return for the market
$R_i - \rho$ = the excess holding period return for asset i
$R_m - \rho$ = the excess holding period return for the market

Alpha, the nonmarket excess return, can be positive or negative. In industry terminology, it is also frequently referred to as idiosyncratic, nonsystematic, or stock-specific risk. Beta, the common risk that affects all assets, is also referred to as systematic or market risk. It is basically a measure of sensitivity or relative volatility. For a significantly diversified equity portfolio, the aggregate are α s expected to cancel each other out, and the equation should simplify to:

$$E(R_p) - \rho = \beta_p * (R_m - \rho)$$

where:

$E(R_p)$ = the expected holding period return for diversified portfolio p
R_m = the holding period return for the market
β_p = the systematic (market) risk of the portfolio
ρ = the risk-free rate of return

Since, during a given holding period, R_m and ρ are constant for all portfolios, the CAPM indicates that a portfolio's return is directly determined by a single risk factor, beta. The CAPM, therefore, is a single-factor model. But it is vital to the understanding of this chapter because the most widely used multifactor equity risk models are variations on the basic CAPM construct.

Sharpe applied his model to Markowitz's efficient frontier construct to develop what has become known as the Efficient Market Hypothesis. By extrapolation of the CAPM equation, the ultimate efficient portfolio must be the entire market itself. Simply put, in the words of Robert Hagin (*The Dow Jones-Irwin Guide to Modern Portfolio Theory*, 1979) this hypothesis states, ". . . it would be impossible to consistently outperform the market . . . in an environment characterized by many competing investors, each with similar objectives and access to the same information." In other words, in an efficient market, the only way that an investor could expect to make an above-average return is to be willing to assume above-average market risk.

Implementation of the Capital Asset Pricing Model

The Modern Portfolio Theory revolution may never have transpired if attempts to implement the theory had not proven successful almost immediately. The pioneers behind this implementation were John McQuown, James Vertin, and William Fouse. James Vertin, the Director of Research, was a convert who was swayed by the empirical evidence produced by McQuown's quantitative group. Together, they established Wells Fargo Investment Advisors. They also managed the first index fund for a pension account, Samsonite. The results were remarkable, to say the least. Almost from the outset, the index funds outperformed an average of 64% of active managers—and with less risk. There is nothing like solid, quantitative proof to make people sit up and take notice. Once started, the indexing business grew substantially, from Samsonite's $6 million in 1971 to about $10 billion in 1980 to more than $200 billion in 1990 and an estimated $400 billion at the end of 1996. The undeniable success of index funds gradually eroded the resistance of the investment community to other quantitative constructs focusing on the relationships between risk and return. The mammoth explosion of retail dollars committed to index funds in John Bogle's Vanguard Group has demonstrated conclusively that it is not necessary to understand the principles of Modern Portfolio Theory to enjoy and appreciate its fruits.

Multifactor Risk Models: The Next Logical Step

Multifactor risk models have strong intuitive appeal relative to the classic, single-factor Capital Asset Pricing Model. Although academia preached the CAPM as if it were gospel, and star-system die-hards considered all quantitative constructs to be heresy, a third camp of investment professionals emerged who saw value in the new theories but refused to accept them completely as the ultimate solution. These professionals bristled at the idea of a single factor, beta, being sufficient to explain systematic market risk. The crux of their argument was that asset price movements are far too complex to be explained completely by a single-factor model. But at the time, more emphasis was placed on how beta should be specified and calculated than on potential alternatives to the single-factor CAPM. Between 1975 and 1989, however, the floodgates opened and multifactor risk models gradually gained acceptance in the institutional equity community. The first, most intuitively pleasing, and most widely used of the multifactor risk models is the BARRA E-model series. Three other significant multifactor equity risk models discussed in this chapter are the Roll-Ross APT model, the APTI, and the Salomon Brothers Risk Attribution Measurement (RAM) model.

Important Applications

Although somewhat dissimilar methodologically, these four models tend to be employed in similar ways. The models facilitate the following important applications:

- Analyzing a portfolio to determine its risk (or tracking error) relative to some benchmark.
- Creating or revising stock portfolios that track any user-specified index, portfolio, or benchmark.
- Creating or revising stock portfolios to exploit some desired tilt (e.g., low price-book) while simultaneously controlling risk relative to some user-specified benchmark.
- Finding the closest risk-equivalent substitute for an existing portfolio security that meets certain user-specified criteria.
- Cross-temporal analysis—that is, analyzing the changes in factor exposures of an individual stock, a portfolio, or an entire stock market over time.

These applications are facilitated because multifactor equity risk construct models lend themselves easily to the usage of linear and quadratic optimizers. These optimizers are much simpler mathematically and tend to converge toward a solution much more easily than the mean-covariance optimizer originally developed by Markowitz. By explicitly identifying the relationships that exist between factor sensitivities and returns, an optimizer has a straightforward objective function to maximize and well-defined constraints to obey. Furthermore, in general, the more factors with which an optimizer has to work, the more statistical degrees of freedom it has available to derive an optimal solution.

The BARRA E-Model

With ERISA adopting the Modern Portfolio Theory tenets emphasizing the importance of risk control for pension fund accounts, pension plans found themselves in need of experts to advise them if these new standards were being satisfied. This requirement brought about the evolution of the U.S. pension-fund industry. Dr. Barr Rosenberg, founder of BARRA (originally, Barr Rosenberg Associates), was the most innovative early practitioner of this new craft. Dr. Rosenberg gleaned quickly that the CAPM allowed the performance analyst to measure how closely a manager's returns tracked the predictions of the model, but provided no insights as to why.

Rosenberg scrutinized the determinants of a manager's residual returns—defined as the difference between actual returns and CAPM-indicated returns. In order to explain the residual returns, Dr. Rosenberg developed a concept he dubbed extra-market covariance. This notion, in turn, added a new dimension to Sharpe's single-factor CAPM model. Dr. Rosenberg postulated that the CAPM was right as far as it went, but it left too much unexplained. To address this problem, he designed the E-model, first available for client use in 1977, as a tool for explaining the systematic risk of a security in terms of its sensitivities to certain important, fundamental factors. To select the original fundamental factors utilized in the E-model, he formed a list of variables that he intuitively thought should influence stock prices (industry, size, financial condition, earning growth history, etc.) and tested their significance in multiple-regression models. The variables with the most aggregate explanatory power became E-model factors. To derive the factor sensitivities for a portfolio or a security, the appropriate time series of returns is regressed against the BARRA factors. To use this new analytical tool most effectively, Dr. Rosenberg also developed a new, more user-friendly optimizer that he made available for direct client usage.

Mathematically, the BARRA fundamental factor model begins with observations on firm characteristics at the beginning of every period. These firm characteristics constitute ct measured at the beginning of period t. The factor returns, ft, and the nonmarket (idiosyncratic) returns, et, are estimated by regressing the excess returns, rt , on the sensitivities:

$$\phi_t = [\chi_t^{\,k} * W_k^{-1} * \chi_t]^{-1} * \chi_t^{\,k} * W_k^{-1} * \chi_t$$

and

$$\varepsilon_{t,} = r_t - (\chi_t * \phi_t)$$

where:

W_k = weighting matrix for Generalized Least Squares (GLS) regression

The resultant time series of estimated factor and specific returns are then used to estimate the factor covariance matrix. This last estimation may include weighting the observations and scaling the variance estimates to better match the volatility of a market index. The mathematical construct requires the weighting matrix to be diagonalized so that it may be inverted.

The Many Uses of BARRA

The combination of versatility, flexibility, and power inherent in the E-model made it virtually indispensable in the large-plan sponsor and asset management community almost immediately. In combination with the BARRA optimizer, the E-model was truly a landmark empowerment tool. The most prevalent application was, and still is, to analyze the sources of portfolio risk. The E-model allows plans to measure what implicit factor "bets" their managers are taking currently. Or, viewed as a time series, sponsors can identify tendencies that an individual manager or some group of managers have displayed over a specific period of time. It also gives managers the ability to gauge the potential impact that trades under consideration would have on the factor exposures (or loading) of the portfolio. In combination with the optimizer, users who have forecasts for one or more of the factors may create portfolios to replicate a user-specified benchmark precisely; or alternatively, make a conscious decision to emphasize a particular factor loading. Similarly, the E-model makes it possible to create model portfolios that optimize any user-defined variable while specifying that factor risks be benchmark-equivalent within some user-selected tolerance. And, working in the opposite direction, every market security can be defined and quantified in terms of its factor-risk profile—also referred to as its "factor signature." Of course, the usefulness of all these applications is directly contingent upon the user accepting the BARRA factors as accurately representing market risk.

In the early 1980s, Dr. Rosenberg responded to another sponsor need by creating an offshoot program, MULMAN, which allowed sponsors to analyze and optimize the factor signatures of any combination of asset managers. The subsequent analyses led Dr. Rosenberg and others to counsel sponsors to monitor how closely their asset managers, individually or collectively, created a risk/return profile that was the equivalent of, or inferior to, their benchmark of choice. Dr. Rosenberg characterized such a profile as "closet indexing." The implication to sponsors was clear. Why pay active managers substantial fees to deliver results that in the aggregate were less than or equal to their benchmarks when index funds could deliver the same with less variance in a much more cost-effective manner? By this reasoning, the only justification for paying active management fees was to improve the overall risk/return profile by combining an array of specialty managers, each of whom contributed expected return potential by taking large bets in their areas of expertise. This analysis led directly to the common practice among many plans of indexing a "core" portion of their portfolios and employing a handful of active managers to take aggressive positions in their specialty fields.

A Year of Change

Essayist Jonathan Swift wrote in 1792, ". . . the only thing in this whole world constant is change." That statement was certainly true of BARRA in 1985. That year, three major events occurred at BARRA. First, Dr. Rosenberg left the firm to form Rosenberg Capital Management. Second, years of statistical analysis in a changing investment environment led to a respecification of the factors in the E-Model. The new model was called E2, or more precisely U.S. E2, since the third major event was the introduction of country models for the United Kingdom and Japan. U.S. E2 and its factors are still in use as of this printing, although a newly specified U.S. E3 was due to be released sometime in 1997. The 13 factors of U.S. E2 are:

Variability in markets	***Earnings variability***
Success	***Financial leverage***
Size	***Foreign income***
Trading activity	***Labor intensity***
Growth	***Yield***
Earnings/price	***Locap***
Book/price	

Global Applications

BARRA certainly did not rest on its laurels after developing the U.K. and Japan models. It soon developed models for 12 other developed foreign markets. The fact that BARRA models can analyze markets as portfolios has given rise to a spate of BARRA-model-based global research, much of it from BARRA itself. The research has provided insights into the factors influencing global stock price movements and global asset allocation. For example, in 1989, Grinold, Rudd, and Stefek (*Journal of Portfolio Management*, Fall 1989) demonstrated that, on average, country factors are more important than industry factors. This held especially true in major markets. Yet, they also found that the most important industries were stronger determinants of return than the least important countries. Six years later, Beckers, Connor, Curds et. al. (*BARRA Newsletter*, Autumn 1995) took these findings even further, concluding, "Country factors are much more powerful than industry factors in explaining worldwide security returns. In terms of international portfolio management, country factors affect risk analysis, asset allocation, and security valuation. In fact, even after allowing for the effect of country factors, local industries are better determinants of return than global industries."

Co-linearity and Other Criticisms

The BARRA E-models have not been without their critics, however. The most frequent and serious criticism concerns the significant co-linearity present among the 13 factors, which undermines, to some extent, the robustness and consistency of the model. It also implies that the BARRA factors are not completely independent. BARRA has asserted that this shortcoming has been addressed in the E-3 model. They have also provided studies showing that, in most common applications of the system, distortions due to co-linearity are minimal. Minor statistically oriented complaints include the strictness of the assumptions implied by using the basic CAPM structure and the process by which outlier values are assigned factor sensitivities.

Customer Applications

More than three times as many asset managers and plan sponsors use BARRA than all other risk models combined. Customers applying the optimizer to asset management have produced a broad spectrum of results, as would be expected with a system used so pervasively.

In 1997, the BARRA E-models will have enjoyed 20 years of application by the investment management community. In 1977, it was a rare investment management firm that even owned a computer, and most of those that did used punch cards and limited their usefulness to certain routine processing tasks. As technology has progressed light-years during the past score, so have the informational needs of money managers. But as those needs have evolved, BARRA's E-models have retained their importance in providing analytic solutions. For example, in this decade, a number of asset managers, most notably Dr. Robert Arnott and David Leinweber of First Quadrant, have enjoyed considerable success in applying the E-model to style-rotational and market-neutral strategies.

The Arbitrage Pricing Theory Model

In 1976, a finance professor at the Yale School of Organization and Management named Dr. Stephen Ross expounded an alternative to the CAPM that he called the Arbitrage Pricing Theory (APT). At first blush, the APT does not appear to be much of a radical departure from the CAPM. As with the CAPM, the APT supposes that asset returns are generated by a linear model. The APT model states that the total risk of an asset can be separated into two components. Again, as with the CAPM, one of the factors is alpha, the nonsystematic, idiosyncratic component of risk. And the other component, in the aggregate, again expresses the common risks that affect all asset returns—but with a key difference: Rather than trying to explain all market risk with one factor, Dr. Ross allows for systematic risk to be represented by *k* factors, where *k* may be any real, positive integer greater than one. Algebraically, the APT can be expressed as:

$$R_i - \rho = \alpha_i + \Sigma_{j=1,k} (\chi_{ij} * \phi_j)$$

where:

R_i = the holding period return for asset i
ϕ_j = the return of factor j
ρ = the risk-free rate of return
α_i = the nonmarket excess return on asset i
χ_{ij} = the exposure of asset i to factor j, for factors j=1,..., k
$R_i - \rho$ = the excess holding period return for asset i

Somewhat surprisingly, the APT actually requires weaker assumptions than the CAPM. The CAPM is explicit; we need beta and the excess market return to calculate the expected returns for each asset. The CAPM must be applied to the entire universe of available securities. The market portfolio should, in theory, include all assets. The APT is much more general. It does not say what these factors are, nor does it say how many factors exist. In contrast to the CAPM, the APT will work with any collection of assets. For example, APT's assumptions would still hold if it were applied to a collection of stocks whose company headquarters were domiciled in Arkansas. Nevertheless, the APT and CAPM are not only consistent with each other; they also help to explain each other.

Specifying an Arbitrage Pricing Theory Model

For seven years after Stephen Ross first proposed it in 1976, the Arbitrage Pricing Theory model gathered dust in its ivory tower as just another interesting but impractical market theory to kick around academic journals. One problem is that in its theoretical form, APT does not provide a straightforward prescription for implementation. The key issue that needed to be addressed was the identification of the factors. To find an answer, Dr. Ross joined forces with Dr. Richard Roll, professor of finance and insurance at the University of California at Los Angeles. Together they applied a statistical technique known as principal component factor analysis to the data in order to identify potential factors.

The purpose of factor analysis in this context is to uncover a set of factors that are both interpretable and contribute to understanding. It operates only on the independent variable side of the time series used in the regression equation. Principal-components factor analysis postulates a model of empirical interrelationships through geometric rotation. Rather than remaining stationary, the x- and y-axes are rotated at all linearly possible angles while preserving the right-angle, or orthogonal, construct to each other. As with other empirically derived models discussed earlier in this chapter, the potential pitfalls of data mining must be confronted rigorously when implementing such a solution.

Identifying the Factors

With this methodology, Drs. Roll and Ross identified five key economic factors that, in the aggregate, account for more than 95% of the systematic risk present in the U.S. stock market, according to research they published in 1983. An interesting point of debate is that these factors are macroeconomically driven, not fundamental or market-driven. Many find it more intuitively pleasing to use market-driven data to explain the systematic risk of the market. Drs. Roll and Ross asserted that they explored this avenue but could not find factors that explained as much systematic risk without accepting significantly more co-linearity.

The specific economic factors selected include unanticipated changes in: the term structure of interest rates; interest rate projections; the long-term rate of inflation; the business cycle as measured by the level of industrial production; and the market risk premium as measured by the spread between high-grade and low-grade corporate bonds. For U.S. stock market applications, the next stage of implementation requires identifying each equity's sensitivity, or factor beta, to each of these five factors. Once again, the multiple regression model plays a major role in explaining the sources of security returns. For each security, a time series of total returns (usually monthly or quarterly) is regressed against corresponding time series for the five factors in order to calculate its factor betas.

Asset Management Implementations

Drs. Roll and Ross applied this model to institutional asset management for the first time in late 1985 and formed Roll and Ross Asset Management in 1987. The most common asset management application they have implemented in the United States has been to duplicate index risk as designated by a client-specified benchmark while optimizing exposure to APT residual alphas.

This application is consistent with work done by Dr. Philip Dybvig of Washington University, who demonstrated in a 1986 *Journal of Portfolio Management* study that APT alphas tend to be both more consistent and more robust than CAPM alphas.

In the 10-year period of its existence, Roll and Ross Asset Management has recorded significantly above-average performance among index-based U.S. pension managers in the Russell Performance System Universe, despite being a below-average performer in the 1991-93 period. Two other asset managers utilizing APT models, albeit with some market factors in lieu of purely macroeconomic ones, Dr. Robert Jones of Goldman Sachs Asset Management and William Jacques of Martingale Asset Management, have also established noteworthy track records during the past 10 years. Jacques also utilizes his APT model to manage market-neutral accounts. However, it is important to be equally aware that virtually every such model utilized in asset management has suffered periods of underperformance as well. It seems to be a tautology that the efficacy of models built on observed relationships over any time period will always be time-period dependent.

Risk Analysis Systems

The APT factor solution implemented by Roll and Ross is by no means unique. The flexibility of the APT model structure allows that many such factor specifications are possible. The asset management applications by Jacques and Dr. Jones, referenced above, both employ somewhat different factor specifications than Roll and Ross. Both are proprietary risk analysis modules available only for internal asset management applications. In contrast, the Roll and Ross risk analysis model and optimizer is made available for purchase to asset managers and plan sponsors through an affiliated company, BIRR, Incorporated. Three notable rival implementations of Arbitrage Pricing Theory, which are similarly offered to these communities as stand-alone modules, include: a 20-factor APT model from Advanced Portfolio Technologies, Incorporated (APTI), an eight-factor model known as RAM (Risk Attribution Measurement) from Salomon Brothers, Inc., and a six-factor model developed by Quantec Systems, Ltd. The last two of these, albeit identifying different factors, use the same statistical methodology as Roll and Ross—applying principal component analysis to macroeconomic variables in order to identify the factors. The statistical construct for factor selection of the APTI model differs substantially and thus merits further discussion.

An Empirical Application

The APTI methodology is significantly more empirical in its factor specification and construction methodology than the Roll and Ross model. This model, developed by Dr. John Blin and Steven Bender, uses the purest possible form of factor analysis, employing a methodology called VARIMAX rotation, to let the data determine orthogonal, linearly independent factors. Moreover, in order to account for as much factor risk as possible, the APTI model uses not five factors, not six, not eight, not 13, but 20 factors.

It is important to note that the factors are not variables but newly created constructs created from linear combinations of several macroeconomic and market-driven time series. The factors are respecified at relatively frequent intervals, usually quarterly, in order to explain as much risk as possible from the most recent snapshot available of the market. This is the one multifactor model reviewed here whose factors are dynamic—i.e., the formulation of the factors changes regularly. For example, factor 17 this quarter was not necessarily factor 17 last quarter. By its very design, this model is not appropriate for cross-temporal applications such as monitoring a portfolio manager's "bets" over time—which are a major strength of the BARRA and traditional APT models. Moreover, the concept of factors constructed from orthogonal combinations of disparate variables is neither easily understood nor intuitively pleasing. However, the trade-off in the design is not without its appeal.

From a statistical standpoint, the APTI model combines the most degrees of freedom with the least co-linearity. The Blin-Bender philosophy is that the price history of every stock leaves an indelible risk signature, which has a lot of information to convey if allowed to do so. The approach can be thought of as a variation on the Latin phrase, "*Res ipso loquitor*": let the data speak for themselves.

The Dividend Discount Model

It would be remiss to conclude a chapter on multifactor equity models without touching upon one of the oldest of such models fitting our original definition of a multifactor-equity model: the Dividend Discount Model (DDM). The model was originally developed by John Burr Williams, a Harvard graduate student, in his 1937 book, *The Theory of Investment Value*. It calls for the investor to make a long-term projection of a company's future earnings stream and payout ratios, thus providing an estimate of a company's future payments. Then, the investor must quantify his or her own confidence in the accuracy of this prediction. In most DDM implementations, the accuracy of this forecast depends upon the economic sector of the security. The amount of the discount to be assigned is quantified by sector in a "decay matrix." By comparing the present value of the discounted cash flows with the current price of the stock, it is possible to calculate an internal rate of expected return for any stock. Therefore, the classical DDM is, like the models we discussed at the beginning of this chapter, a return-only model. But in the late 1960s, Dr. Merton Miller applied the CAPM to the DDM to create an expression that linked return to beta. The discount rate in Williams' equation is a linear function of the risk-free rate of return and the risk premium—the latter being a linear function of beta.

The marriage of fundamental valuation theory and Modern Portfolio Theory made the DDM an extremely popular asset management tool in the late 70s and early 80s. Although a number of organizations still use a DDM as part of the investment process, it is far less prevalent than it was 15 years ago. The marked decline in popularity of the DDM is directly attributable to disappointing results suffered by the majority of practitioners. Remember that for the DDM's assumptions to hold, the fundamental analysts supporting the model have to project the company's future earnings stream payout ratios and rate of decay in a reasonably accurate manner. For further information about the demise of the DDM, please refer to the subsection near the beginning of this chapter entitled, "Garbage In—Garbage Out."

Beyond Two-Dimensional Space

Although most optimizers are quadratic, and the internal rate of return portion of the DDM is nonlinear, the major statistical models we have discussed thus far—multiple regression and factor analysis—have been linear. Increasingly, expanding information-processing capabilities are expanding our horizons beyond two-dimensional space. As new techniques become available, innovators in the investment industry seem to be increasingly unafraid to apply them. In particular, three unconventional techniques have risen to the forefront during this decade: artificial intelligence, chaos theory, and fuzzy logic. All three of these procedures allow the computer the freedom to leave the linear and quadratic worlds in order to find the best potential solution by roaming through n-dimensional space. Thus far, fuzzy logic has been used primarily for interesting, graphical displays of historical time series without providing any application to risk analysis or asset management. Chaos theory, alternatively, is being used to analyze risk and manage money by Dr. Tonis Vaga, with some eye-catching results thus far.

Of the three new technologies, so-called artificial intelligence (AI) software and neural networks have garnered the most attention. Bradford Lewis of Fidelity Management and Research has been running two funds with an AI implementation that he designed himself, with mixed success. James O'Sullivan, founder of OBIL Capital Management, has also attracted attention by applying a neural network to hedge fund management, with rather impressive performance in the short period of time that the fund has been live. These new technologies are not without their potential pitfalls, however.

In their article, "Artificial Stupidity," Murphy, Kochler, and Fogler (*Journal of Portfolio Management*, Winter 1997) illustrate the potential dangers of overtraining the neural network and overfitting the data by allowing the software to utilize "hidden" nodes. The result can easily turn out to be n-dimensional data mining, where the user gets a great fit for the period on which the network was trained. However, the fit is too time-period specific and will fail to remain significant. The authors believe that artificial intelligence can be a useful tool for exploring new data interrelationships, but care must be taken to keep the model's specifications as general as possible. Artificial intelligence is an intriguing tool with interesting early results. However, insufficient evidence is available thus far to know whether its place in history will turn out to be elevated alongside the CAPM or consigned to the scrap heap alongside other innovations that once shone brightly with potential, then burned out quickly, such as portfolio insurance.

Summary

Multifactor equity models have been used in attempts to provide superior returns for a number of years. Multiple regression is the most widely used statistical framework for such models. Modelers must be aware of the assumptions of regression and common statistical errors that should be minimized to the greatest extent possible. The early models focused exclusively on the return side of the equation. The advent of Modern Portfolio Theory shifted this emphasis to developing a true understanding of the fundamental relationships between risk and return.

The BARRA E-models have been at the forefront of gaining acceptance for the importance and utility of multifactor equity models. ERISA requirements created a need that the BARRA factor models have filled for the majority of plan sponsors and their managers. For the first time, these investment professionals had a powerful and flexible tool for creating optimal multifactor models. Similarly, a number of Arbitrage Pricing Theory models have gained acceptance from the investment community during the past 10 years. Implementation has largely underscored the usefulness of these models. At this time, artificial intelligence software programs loom as potentially fertile ground for exploration, but conclusive evidence regarding their ultimate usefulness is probably still a few years away.

INDEX

A

Abate, James, 27
ABB, 41
Above-average return, 147
Active equity managers, 27
Active equity portfolio managers, 27, 42
Active equity portfolio manager, 39
Active fund management, 30
Active management:
  process, 4
  costs, 27
Active managers, 28, 42
Active portfolio managers, 30, 34, 37
Active U.S. equity managers, 42
Advanced Portfolio Technologies, Incorporated (APTI), 148, 156
  methodology, 156
  model, 156
Aggregate portfolio risk, 145
AI. *See* Artificial intelligence
AIMR. *See* Association for Investment Management & Research
A-location retail property leases, 45
Alphas, 125, 146, 153. *See also* Arbitrage Pricing Theory; Capital Asset Pricing Method; Portfolio Alpha
American Electric Power, 16
American equity market, 12
American In Home Products, 16
Amgen, 34, 35, 37
Amoco, 16
Amortization. *See* Cumulative goodwill amortization
Analytical Approaches to Stock Selection, 79
Annual decomposition, 12
APT. *See* Arbitrage Pricing Theory
APTI. *See* Advanced Portfolio Technologies, Incorporated
Arbitrage Pricing Theory (APT) model, 122, 153-157, 159. *See also* Roll Ross APT model alphas, 155
  empirical application, 156-157
  factors, identification, 154-155
  multifactor model, 127
  specificaion, 154
ARCH model, 127
Arnott, Dr, Robert, 153
Arthur, W. Brian, 32, 33
Artificial intelligence (AI), 27, 158
  software, 159
Asset management, implementations, 155
Asset managers, 156
Association for Investment Management & Research (AIMR), 140
AST Research, 41
Atchison, T.A., 132, 136
Atlantic Richfield Co., 88
Autocorrelationships, 127
Average E/P, 113
Axtell, Robert, 32

B

Balance sheet, 45
Barnevik, Percy, 41
Barr Rosenberg Associates, 150
BARRA E-moel, 149-154,156, 159
  change, 151
  criticism, 152
  customer applications, 152-153
  global applications, 151-152
  uses, 150-151
BARRA-model-based global research, 151
Bartlet, M.S., 132-136
Baysian estimate, 132
Beckers, 152
Benchmark-equivalent, 150
Bender, Steven, 156. *See also* Blin-Bender philosophy
Bernstein, Peter L., 144
Beta, 48, 146, 147
  linear function, 157
Beta model coefficients, 126
Bionomics, 32, 37
Bio-technology, 39, 42
Bio-technology companies, 30, 36, 37
Bio-technology industries, 34
Bio-technology sectors, 30, 33, 36, 42
BIRR, Incorporated, 156
Black, Fischer, 144
Blank, Herbert, 108, 139
Blin, Dr. John, 156
Blin-Bender philosophy, 157
Boeing, 16
Bogle, John, 147
Book Value to Market Value ratio (B/P), 120
Book Value per Share, 79, 120
Book-to-market ratio, 108
Book-to-market value, 107
Bottom-quintile returns, 55, 58, 62
Bottom-up qualitative analysis, 41
Bottom-up quantitative analysis, 41
Bowmar Brain, 139
B/P. *See* Book Value to Market Value ratio
BPS. *See* Book Value per Share
Brown, Melissa R., 53
Bruner, Ross Paul, 1, 27, 75
Business risk, 48

C

Capital appreciation, 1, 2, 10
Capital Asset Pricing Method (CAPM), 127, 139, 145, 147, 153, 154, 157, 159. *See also* Single-factor CAPM
  alphas, 155
  implementation, 147
  structure, 152
Capital employed, 45-46. *See also* Return on capital employed
Capital equipment, replacement cost, 35
Capital expenditures, 37
Capital Expenditure-to-Sales ratio, 37
Capital spending, 62, 74
Capital structure, 43
  effects, 47
Capital-appreciation stream, 10

Capitalization-weighted format, 127
Capitalization-weighted basis, 13, 25, 89
Capitalization-weighted version, 114
Capitalization-weighting, 11
  strategies, 11
CAPM. *See* Capital Asset Pricing Model
CAPM-indicated returns, 149
Cap-weighted approach, 118
Cap-weighted ranking, 119
Cap-weighted sets. *See* Industries
Cap-weighted version, 114, 116, 117, 119
Cash flow, 40
  analysis. *See* Pure cash flow analysis
Cash return, 45
Casti, John L., 32
CCH, 46
Chen, Ping, 32
Chevron Corp., 88
Chrysler Corp., 88
Cisco Systems, 28, 37
Client-specified benchmark, 155
Closet indexing, 151
Co-linear variables, 143
Co-linearity, 143, 152, 154, 157
Columine Investment System, 144
Company managers, 43
Compustat, 142
Computer-resident statistical programs, 142
Confidence limits, 126
Connor, 152
Consistent earnings growth. *See* Price-to-earnings/consistent earnings growth
Consistent-growth, 25
Consumer cyclical services, 55
Consumer services, 62, 74
Corporate bonds. *See* High-grade corporate bonds; Low-grade corporate bonds
Corporate earnings, 36
Cost of capital, 43, 48
Cost of capital employed, 44
Covariance estimates, matrix, 130
Covariance optimization. *See* Enhanced index portfolio construction
Credit institutions, 47
Cross-sectional correlationships, 127
Cross-temporal applications, 156
Cumulative exceptional gains/losses, 46
Cumulative goodwill amortization, 46
Cumulative return differential, 114
Curds, 152

D

Data mining, 154. *See also* N-dimensional data mining
  perils, 143
Data quality issues, 142-143
Day, Richard, 32
DCF, 44
DDM. *See* Divident Discount Model
Decay matrix, 157
Denning, Peter, 29

Disclosure, 142
Diversification, *See also* Global diversification
Diversifiers, comparison. *See* Small-cap stocks
Dividend Discount Model (DDM), 157-158
Dividend stream, 10
Dividend yield, 12, 109
Dividends, 13
  forecasting, 109
  importance, 10
Double-relative perspective, 109
Dow Chemical, 88
Downside protection, 134
Durable equipment spending, 29
Dutch accounting standards, 46
Dybvig, Dr. Philip, 155

E

E2 (model), 151
E-3 model, 152
Earnings
  forecasting, 109
  growth. *See* Price-to-earnings/consistent earnings growth
  streams, 157
Earnings per share (EPS), 4, 39, 75, 77, 79
  cycle, 9
  growth, 9
  rate, 9
Earnings time series, 140
Earnings/price (E/P). *See* Average E/P
  quintile, 114. *See also* Lowest E/P quintile
  ratio, 112, 122. *See also* Forwardlooking E/P rations
EBIT, 40, 47
EBITDA, 40, 47
Economic analysis, 32
Economic value added (EVA), 43-52
  introduction, 43-44
Ecosystems, 32
Edvinsson, Leif, 35
Efficient Market Hypothesis, 146
Efficient portfolios, construction. *See* Markowitz efficient portfolios
Efron, B., 132, 136
Eisenstadt, Sam, 139
Elderton, W.P., 132, 136
Emerson Electric, 16
EMI. *See* Salomon-Russell Extended Markets Indices
E-model. *See* BARRA E-model factors 149
Endnotes. *See* Sector rotation; Style rotation
Enhanced index portfolio construction, full covariance optimization usage, 125, 137
  references, 136-137
Enterprise value/sales, comparison, 53-74
  conclusion, 74
  results, 54-55

Enterprise value-to-replacement cost, 34, 35
ratios, 36
EPS. *See* Earnings per share
Epstein, Joshua, 32
Equal-weighted approach, 116, 118
Equal-weighted average, 113. *See also* Morgan Stanley Capital International
Equal-weighted basis, 13, 25, 89
Equal-weighted portfolios, 114
Equal-weighted version, 117
Equal-weighting
capitalization-weighting comparison, 1
discipline, 11
positions, 11
Equlibrium points, 33
Equity fund managers. *See* U.S. equity fund managers
Equity management, results. *See* Mathematical equity management
Equity modelling, 141
Equity models. *See* Multifactor equity models
Equity portfolio, 109, 110, 123
risk exposures, 144
Equity returns, 140
ERISA. 148
ERISA requirements, 159
Error risk. *See* Mean squared error risk
ESR, 53
comparison, 57-58
ESR model, 56-57
correlation, 58-59
functioning, 62-74
usage. *See* Sell side
EVA. *See* Economic value added
Exceptional gains/losses. *See* Cumulative exceptional gains/losses
Excess-returns. *See* Risk-adjusted excess returns
Exxon Corp., 88
Extra-market covariance, 149

F

Factor analysis, 156
Factor exposures, 148
Factor loading constraints, 131
Factor selection, 143
Factor sensitivities, 152
Factor signature, 151
Fama, E.F., 130, 136
Feedback. *See* positive feedback
Federal Nat'l Mortgage Assn., 88
Ferguson, 144
Fidelity Magellan, 28
Fidelity Management and Research, 158
Fifth Third Bancorp, 16
Financial reporting, 142
Financial services, 55, 60, 62, 74
Financial statement item, 53
First Quadrant, 153
Fogler, 158
Ford Motor Co., 88
Forward-looking E/P ratio, 112, 122
Fouse, William, 147

Fox, Dan, 107
Full covariance optimization, usage. *See* Enhanced index portfolio construction
Full-covariance approach, 125
Fund manager, 38
Fundamental analysis, 125
Fuzzy logic, 158

G

Gains/losses, 47. *See also* Cumulative exceptional gains/losses
Garbage In - Garbage Out, 142-143, 158
GARCH model, 127
GARP. *See* Growth-at-a-reasonable-price
Gates, Bill, 34, 35
GDP. *See* Gross Domestic Product; US nominal GDP
General Motors, 37, 88
Geometric mean input estimation/optimization, 131-133
Gibson, Steve, 27
Gilead Sciences, 34
Global diversification, 119
Global economy/economies, 28, 30, 37
Global equity managers, 42
Global equity markets, 107
Global equity portfolio, 122
Global healthcare sector, 36
Going-concern business activities, 45
Goldman Sachs Asset Management, 155
Goodwill amortization, 47. *See also* Cumulative goodwill amortization
Grand mean, 132
Grinold, 151
Gross Domestic Product (GDP). *See* US nominal GDP
growth, 122
Grove, Andy, 34, 35
Growth, *See* Gross Domestic Product
long-term underperformance, 1-4
rate, 9
stocks, 1, 4, 12
value discovery, 1
Growth flow
concept, 40
screen, 41
Growth versus Value style measurements, 108
Growth-at-a-reasonable-price, 1-17
composition, 13-24
conclusion, 17
construction, 11-12
contemporaneous selection, 11-12
methodology, 9-11
overview, 1-9, 75-78
performance, 13-24
results, 12-24
valuation, 13-24

H

Hagin, Robert, 146
Harrison, Jeff, 132, 137
Heineken, 49-52
Hidden nodes, 158
Higher-P/E stocks, 58

Highest-PSR quintile, 57
Highest-ranked quintile, 116
High-grade corporate bonds, 155
High-P/E-to-growth quintile, 4, 17
High-P/E-to-growth shares, 13
High-P/E-to-growth strategy, 16
Historical probability beliefs, 128-129
Holding period, 117, 131, 146. *See also* Investment holding period; Portfolio holding period
Holland, John H., 32
Holy Grail equation, 141
Hubbell, 16
Human capital, 34, 35
    importance, 32
    processing, 33
Human-capital-intensive companies, 35

I

I/B/E/S, 112
Idiosyncratic returns, 149
Increasing-returns world, 33, 34
Index funds, 147
Industrial Age, 31, 38
Industries, cap-weighted sets, 113
Industry affiliation, 122
Information Age, 30-32, 35, 38
Information-age companies
    techniques, search, 38-41
    today, 41-42
    valuation tools, 38-41
Information-age portfolio management, 29-30
Information technology, 29, 41
    global demand, 28
    sector, 28, 30, 36
Information-age firm, 36
Information-age stocks, 37
Information-technology 39, 42
Information-technology companies, 30, 36, 37
Information-technology industries, 34
Information-technology sectors, 30, 33, 36, 42
Information-technology stocks, 28
Input estimation. *See* Mathematical/statistical input estimation
    error, 127
    procedure, 126
Input estimation/optimization. *See* Geometric mean input estimation/optimization
Inputs, 128-129
Institutional investment, 140
Institutional investor, 112
Intel, 28, 34, 37
Intellectual capital, 34
Interest rate projections, 154
Internal asset management applications, 156
International data, 142
International portfolio management, 152
Internet, 29
Intraoptimization period, 134. *See also* Portfolio intraoptimization period
Intrinsic value, 48
Investing. *See* 21st-century investing

Investment characteristics, 109
Investment data, 141
Investment environment, 30
Investment holding period, 128
Investment management community, 152
Investment time horizon, 125
Investor. *See* 21st-century investor risk aversion, 130

J

Jacques, William, 155, 156
James, W., 132, 136
James-Stein estimators, 132, 133
James-Stein ex-anti estimates, 133
Jefferson Pilot, 16
Johnson, N.L., 132, 136
Jones, Dr. Robert, 155, 156

K

K factors, 153
Kalman filter models, 127
Kelm, Kathryn, 38
Kluwer, Wolters, 46
Knowledge, processing, 33
Kochler, 158

L

Lantane, H.A., 131, 136
Large-cap stocks, 122
    outperformance comparison. *See* Samll-cap stocks
Large-cap universe, 60
Leinweber, David, 153
Lewis, Bradford, 158
LIFO reserves, 47
Linear equality constraint, 130
Linear optimizers, 148
Long-run projection, 157
Long/short portfolios, 114, 116
Long-term underperformance. *See* Growth
Lowest E/P quintile, 114
Lowest-P/E companies, 58
Lowest-P/E quintile, 57
Low-grade corporate bonds, 155
Low-P/E-to-growth quintile, 13, 16, 25
Low-P/E-to-growth strategy, 3, 10,16

M

MacElwee, Elizabeth M., 123
Machine Age, 30, 31, 34, 35
Machine-age firms, 35-37
Machine-age metaphors, 31
Machine-age thinking, 31
Machine-age valuation tools, inadequacies, 34-38
Macroeconomic time series, 156
Mad regression, 143
Malone, Michael S., 35
Management methodology, 125
Market cap, 53
Market efficiency, 140
Market index, 151
Market inefficiencies, 28, 29
Market return, 130

Market risk, 146, 147, 151. *See also* Systematic market risk
Market value, 48, 113
Market-driven time series, 156
Market-neutral strategies, 153
Markowitz, Harry M., 126, 128, 131, 144, 145, 148
Markowitz efficient portfolios, construction, 129-131
Markowitz optimization methods, 128
Martingale Asset Management, 155
Martz, Jr., H.F., 132, 136
Master mean, 132, 133
Mathematical equity management, results, 133-136
Mathematical/statistical inputs, 128
estimation, 127
McDonalds, 16
McKinsey & Company, 44
McQuown, John, 147
Mean squared error risk, 132
Mean-covariance efficient portfolios, 145
Mean-variance approach. *See* Portfolio selecion
Mercantile Bankshares, 16
Merchant of Venice, 44
Metcalfe, Robert, 29
Microsoft, 28, 34, 37
Miller, Dr. Merton, 44, 144, 157
Milunovich, Steven, 28
Mobil, 16, 88
Model inputs, 126
Model quintiles, 62
Modelling method, 128
Models, applications, 148
Modern Portfolio Theory (MPT), 28, 147, 148, 157
revolution, 144-145
Modigliani, Franco, 44
Moffatt, 144
Money managers, 152
Morgan Stanley Capital International (MSCI), 112
universe, 112
Morris, C., 132,136
MPT. *See* Modern Portfolio Theory
MSCI. *See* Morgan Stanley Capital International
MULMAN, 151
Multifactor equity models, 108, 139-159
summary, 159
Multifactor models, 126, 139, 159
Multifactor regression framework, 108
Multifactor risk models, 147-148
Multiple regression, 122
Multivariate time series methods, 127
Murphy, 158
Murphy, Michael, 39, 40
Mutual fund companies, 38

N

Narayanan, V.K., 38
N-dimensional data mining, 158
N-dimensional space, 158
Network Wizards, 29
Newtonian framework, 31

Nodes. *See* Hidden nodes
Non-capitalized leases, 45
Nonlinear estimation formulations, 127
Nonmarket returns, 149
Nonstationary time-series phenomenon, 127
Nonsystematic risk, 146
Normalized Value, 75-106
  Conclusion, 106
  Construction, 84-85
  Methodology, 79-84
  Overview, 75-78
  Results, 85-89
Novartis, 45

O

OBIL Capital Management, 158
Occidental Petroleum, 16
OLS, 127
O'Neill, William, 140
Open-ended scale, 110
Operating capital, 46
Operating distortion, 47
Operating profit, 44
Optimization construction process, 131
Optimization method, 126
Optimization process, 127, 132
Optimizer. *See* User-friendly optimizer
Oracle, 34
Organizational learning, 37
O'Sullivan, James, 158
Overseas Shipbuilding, 16

P

Pass/fail tests, 139
Passive fund management, 30
Payout ratios, 157
P/B, 75, 77, 79, 122
PB/ROE valuation model, 109
P/E. *See* Price/earnings
Pearson's r, 141
P/E-to-consistent-EPS-growth, 9
P/E-to-consistent-growth, risk relationship, 25
P/E-to-growth, 1, 11, 12
  added value, 4-9
  basis, 10
  risk reflection, 17
  strategy, 16
Performance benchmark, 108
Performance cycle, 49
Philip Morris Co., 88
Physical assets, 34
Physical capital, 32
Pinches, George, 38
P&L., 44, 47
Plain PSR, 56
Portfolio alpha, 127
Portfolio analysis, 128
Portfolio characteristics, 108
Portfolio compilation algorithm, 126
Portfolio construction. *See* Enhanced index portfolio construction; Markowitz efficient portfolios
  process, 128
Portfolio holding period, 125, 129, 131
Portfolio intraoptimization period, 133

Portfolio management. *See*
Information-age portfolio management
process, 39
Portfolio managers, 31, 33, 34, 38, 39, 43, 62, 108, 156, *See also* Active equity portfolio managers; Active equity-portfolio manager; U.K portfolio managers
Portfolio optimization, 145
Portfolio returns, 11, 112, 125
Portfolio risk. *See* Aggregate portfolio risk
Portfolio risk. *See* Aggregate portfolio risk
Portfolio security, risk-equivalent substitute, 148
Portfolio selection, mean-variance approach, 129
Portfolio simulation, 12, 118
Portfolio size, 108
Portfolio turnover, 131
Portfolio weightings, 108
Portfolio-management process, 41
Positive feedback, 32, 33
Pre-tax earnings, 39
Price change, comparison. *See* Total return
Price directions, 127
Price-book, 148
Price/earnings (P/E), 57, 131
added value. *See* P/E-to-growth added value
growth. *See* P/E-to-consistent-EPS-growth
model, 58
quintile. *See* High-P/E-to-growth quintile
ratio, 12, 36, 37, 107, 112
strategy. *See* Low-P/E-to-growth strategy
Price/earnings (P/E) comparison, 53-74
conclusion, 74
results, 54-55
Price-performance-only oriented regression model, 140
Price/sales comparison, 53-74
conclusion, 74
results, 54-55
Price/sales model
comparison, 57-58
correlation, 58-59
test, 62
Price/sales ratio (PSR), 53. *See also* Plain PSR
comparison, 57-58
correlation, 58-59
model, 55, 58
quintiles, 54
strategy, 55-56
Price-to-book ratios, 2,35,77
Price-to-book value, 34
ratios, 37
stocks, 37
Price-to-book-ranking, 10
Price-to-earnings, 34
per share, 40
valuations, 37
Price-to-earnings/consistent earnings growth, 1

Price-to-growth flow, 39
ratio, 40
Price-to-sales ratio, 40
Principal-components factor analysis, 154
Probability beliefs, *See* Historical probability beliefs
Providian, 16
PSR. *See* Price/sales ratio
Pure cash flow analysis, 44

Q

Q.E.D., 134
Quadratic optimizers, 116
Qualitative analysis. *See* Bottom-up qualitative analysis; Top-down qualitative analysis
Quantitative analysis. *See* Bottom-up quantitative analysis; Top-down quantitative analysis
Qualitative screens, 41
Quantitative screening process, 41
Quantitative screens, 41

R

RAM. *See* Salomon Brothers Risk Attribution Measurement
Ranking System. *See* Value Line Timeliness Ranking System
Raytheon, 16
R&D. *See* Research & development
R&D-intensive companies, 39
R&D-to-Sales ratio, 37
RDS. *See* Research & development
Recomposition. *See* Annual recomposition
References. *See* Enhanced index portfolio construction; Small capitalization portfolio
Regression. *See* Mad regression; Multiple regression
Regression analysis, 144
Regression equations, 140
Regression models, 140-142. *See also* Price-performance-only oriented regression model
limitations, 141-142
Republic New York, 16
Research & development (R&D), 36, 37, 46
expenditures, 38
projects, 46
spending, 38-40
per share (RDS), 39
Reserves/provisions, 47
Resnick, Mitchel, 32
Return differential. *See* Cumulative return differential
Return on capital employed, 43, 46-48
Return on debt, 46
Return on equity (ROE), 39, 46, 75, 77, 79, 89
Returns. *See* Bottom-quintile returns; Market return; Portfolio returns; Risk-adjusted excess returns; Top-quintile returns; Total return
Revision intervals, 131
Risk, investor-selected level, 145
Risk analysis systems, 155-156

Risk models. *See* Multifactor risk models
Risk reflection. *See* P/E-to-growth
Risk relationship. *See* P/E-to-consistent-growth
Risk-adjusted excess returns, 27
Risk-averse investors, 130
Risk-free rate of return, 145, 157
Risk/return profile, 150, 151
Roche, 45
ROE. *See* Return on equity
ROE/P/B, 75, 89
Roll, Dr. Richard, 154-156
Roll and Ross Asset Management, 155
Rolling basis, 58
Roll-Ross APT model, 148
Rosenberg, Dr. Barr, 144, 149, 154
Rosenberg Capital Management, 151
Ross, Dr. Stephen, 144, 153-156
Rothschild, Michael, 32
R-squared, 141, 143
Rudd, 151
RUSSELL Performance System Universe, 155

S

Sales growth, 39
Saloman Brothers Risk Attribution Measurement (RAM), 148, 156
Sample bias, 142
Samsonite, 147
Samuelson, P.A., 129, 136
Santa Fe Institute, 32
Schering-Plough, 16
Seagate Technology, 40
Sector, composition, 60-62
Sector rotation, valuation approach, 107-123
  applications, 108
  conclusions, 119-120
  endnotes, 123
  example, 110-114
  findings, 114-119
  overview, 107
  summary, 122-123
  value.
    direct addition, 109-110
    indirect addition, 109-110
Secor weightings, 60
Sell side, 58
  ESR model usage, 56-57
Share price performance, 44
Shareholder value, 43, 44
Sharpe, William F., 126, 136, 144, 145, 149
Shrinkage factor, 132, 133
Single-factor CAPM, 147
  model, 149
Single-factor models, 109, 146
Small capitalization portfolio, 125-137
  references, 136-137
Small-cap equities, 122
Small-cap stock manager, 125
Small-cap stocks, 122. *See also* Capitalization-weighting, 11
Small-capitalization
  bias, 11
  effects, 11
S&P. *See* Standard & Poor's

S&P 500. *See* Standard & Poor's 500
Standard deviation, 9, 116, 132-133
Standard & Poor (S&P), 55, 56, 58
  Composite, 55, 56, 74, 75
Standard & Poor's 500 (S&P 500), 1, 2, 13, 30, 40, 41
  index, 27-30, 40
Stefek, 151
Stein, C., 132, 137. *See also* James Stein estimators
Stewart III, G. Bennett, 44
Stipp, David, 30
Stochastic price process, 127
Stock manager. *See* Small-cap stock manager
Stock portfolio, 125, 148
Stock price volatility, 48
Stock prices, 149
Stock screen, 40-
Stock selection, 74. *See also* Small-cap stocks
Stock-specific risk, 146
Structured contrarianism, 134
Style analysis, 107
Style measurements. *See* Growth versus Value style measurements
Style rotation, valuation approach, 107-123
  applications, 108
  endnotes, 123
  example, 110-114
  findings, 114-119
  overview, 107
  summary, 122-123
  value:
    direct addition, 109-110
    indirect addition, 109-110
Style-rotational strategies, 153
Subholding period, 131
Sun Microsystems, 40
Survivorship bias, 11, 84
Sweet spot, 13, 17, 89
Symmetric interdependence, 130
Systematic market risk, 147

T

21st-century investing, 27-42
21st-century investor, concepts, 31-34
Tax interest charges, 47
Technical analysis, 125
Technology services, 62
Tew, Bernard V., 125
Texaco Inc., 88
Time horizon. *See* Investment time horizon
Time period, 143
Time series. *See* Macroeconomic time series; Market-driven time series
  data, 142
  methods. *See* Multivariate time series methods
Time-dependent results, 117
Timeliness Ranking System. *See* Value Line Timelines Ranking System
Time-period dependency, 143-144, 155
Time-series phenomenon. *See* Nonstationary time-series phenomenon
Time-series processes, 128

Timing, 143-144
Tobin, 131
Top-down qualitative analysis, 41
Top-down quantitative analysis, 41
Top-quintile returns, 55, 58, 62
Top-to-bottom spreads, 62
Total return, price change comparison, 12
Tracking error, 131
Trading costs, 40, 117, 134
Trading pattern, 107
Transaction costs, 131, 134
Trent, R.H., 131, 137
TRW, 16
T-statistic, 107
Tsuei, Albert, 28
Turn-of-year effect, 109
Turnover, 12, 114. *See* Portfolio turnover
    control, 9-10
Tuttle, D.L., 131, 136
Two-dimensional space, 158-159

U

U.K. equities, 112
U.K. equity market 110
U.K. portfolio managers, 27
University of California at Los Angeles, 154
U.S. equity fund managers, 28
U.S. equity managers. *See* Active U.S. equity managers
US nominal GDP, 29
U.S. pension-fund industry, 149
U.S. stock market applications, 155
User-defined variable, 151
User-friendly optimizer, 149
User-selected tolerance, 151
User-specified benchmark, 148
User-specified criteria, 148
User-specified index, 148
USX-Marathon, 16
Utilities, 62, 74

V

Vaga, Dr. Tonis, 158
VAL. *See* Valuation Attractiveness Level
Valuation. *See* Growth-at-a-reasonable-price; Price-to-earnings
Valuation approach. *See* Sector rotation; Style rotation
Valuation Attractiveness Level (VAL), 110
    measure, 108
Valuation model. *See* PB/ROE valuation model
Valuation parameters, 34
Valuation techniques, 29, 42, 110
Valuation tools, 27, 29, 42. *See also* Information age companies
    inadequacies. *See* Machine-age valuation tools
Value, 48-49
Value Line, 142
Value Line Asset Management, 140
Value Line Investment Survey, 139

Value Line Timeless Ranking System, 139-140
Value Line universe, 140
Value orientation, 58
Value strategies, 10, 25
Value-creating industries, 28
Value/sales. *See* Enterprise value/sales
van Doorn, Vincent, 43
Vanguard Group, 147
Variance portfolio, 130
Variance-covariance, 127
  construction, 126
VARIMAX rotation, 156
Vector autoregressive approaches, 128
Vertin, James, 147

W

WACC. *See* Weighted average cost of capital
Waite, Stephen R., 27
Wall Street, 31
  analyst forecasts, 112
  analysts, 35
  strategists, 34
Weighted average cost of capital (WACC), 48
Wells Fargo Investment Advisors, 147
West, Mike, 132, 137
Wilcox, Jarrod, 109, 123
Wilcox, Michael F., 107, 123
Williams, John Burr, 157
World Wide Web, 29
Written-off assets, 46

X

Xerox, 40

Y

Yale School of Organization and Management, 153
Young, W.E., 131, 137

Z

Zero-sum games, 32
Zero-yield shares, 10

Profit in the Futures Markets!

Insights and Strategies for Futures and Futures Options Trading: Jake Bernstein

GREAT VALUE EDITION
80% LOWER THAN INTERNATIONAL PRICE

Filled with practical tools and techniques for understanding and prospering in the world of futures trading, *Profit in the Futures Markets!* shows how to use such information to your best advantage. In addition, you will discover how to improve your trading strategies by understanding and building upon your own style and developing a customized plan for success based on your individual needs and abilities.

Investors interested in expanding into the potentially lucrative world of futures need look no further than this easy-to-read, insight-filled guide.

"Jake Bernstein is one of the best at putting together the emotions and mechanics of trading"
Futures Magazine, USA

"One of the best books I've ever seen on the futures markets" *Rick Bensignor Chief Technical Strategist, Morgan Stanley*

"This exceptional book fast forwards the learning curve..."
Adrienne Laris Toghraie, Trader's Success Coach

Rs. 395/- **No.520-8**

Dictionary of Futures & Options

Over 1,500 Terms Defined and Explained

Alan Webber

The *Dictionary of Futures & Options* is a comprehensive reference source of essential information for any investor involved in futures and options. Both the complete beginner and the seasoned professional will find this book invaluable. It contains all the basic terminology used throughout the international derivatives arena, as well as substantial descriptions of options strategies, the "Greek" letters, position exposure to certain measures, and more.

In addition, the appendices include graphics which will enable interested readers to absorb the intricacies of various derivative trading scenarios in a quick, but thorough, manner.

"Reference book on futures & options" *The Hindu*

Rs. 395/- **No. 331-0**

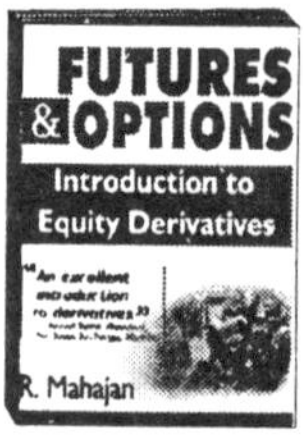

Futures and Options

Introduction to Equity Derivatives

R. Mahajan

BEST SELLER

Derivatives include futures and options and are an indispensa-ble part and parcel of developed financial markets. How deriva-tives work and how you can benefit from them to protect your stock market investment is the thrust of this book.

The book covers both futures and options and risk-proofing tools available to the Indian investor. The author explains both the underlying concepts and procedures in a straightforward manner.

Assuming no prior knowledge, both beginners and market operators will find this an easy-to-understand book to get started in futures and options.

"The book draws the reader into this esorteric subject with lucid writing style and simple examples, and tries to explain the *raison d'être* of futures and options" *Business India*

"An excellent introduction to derivatives for all market participants and investors" *Anand Rathi, President, The Stock Exchange, Mumbai.*

Rs. 280/- **No. 691-3**

New Insights on Writing Covered Call Options

The Powerful Technique that Enhances Return and Lowers Risk in Stock Investing

Richard Lehman and Lawrence G. McMillan

BEST SELLER

GREAT VALUE EDITION
80% LOWER THAN INTERNATIONAL PRICE

Writing covered call options is an investment strategy that bridges the gap between equity and fixed-income investments. It offers much of the upside potential of equities — but with less volatility. Thus, you can achieve long-term returns com-mensurate with stock market returns but with lower volatility and less downside risk.

This book shows how to use this powerful and accessible investment technique — giving you the edge to enhance your returns and lower your risk.

"This book makes a great case for basic reading and writ-ting --- reading stock charts and writing covered calls"
John Murphy

Rs. 395/- **No. 555-0**

TECHNICAL ANALYSIS

GREAT
VALUE
EDITION
80% LOWER THAN INTERNATIONAL PRICE

Technical Analysis of Stock Trends

BEST SELLER

Robert Edwards & John Magee

"This book is a classic — the standard of excellence against which everything in technical analysis is measured... learn from this wonderful book" *Prudential Securities, USA.*

Rs. 595/- No. 663-8

Technical Analysis from A-to-Z

BEST SELLER

Steven B. Achelis

"All aspects of technical analysis in one easily digestible book ... belongs on every technician's bookshelf" *Steven Nison*

"Can be used as a dictionary for technical analysis" *Business Investor's Daily, USA*

Rs. 395/- No. 312-4

The Technical Analysis Course

BEST SELLER

A Winning Program for Investors & Traders

Thomas A. Meyers

This book highlights when, where, and how you can employ the variety of technical analysis tools available.

"Mastery to this arcane but widely followed art" *The Wall Street Journal, USA*

Rs. 325/- No. 489-9

Technical Analysis of Stocks, Options & Futures

Advanced Trading Systems and Techniques

BEST SELLER

William F. Eng

This book provides detailed and practical information on fifteen of the most widely used trading systems.

"Encyclopedic in scope . . . should be in every trader's library" *Leslie Rosenthal, Former Chairman, Chicago Board of Trade.*

Rs. 495/- No. 531-3

Timing the Market

BEST SELLER

How to Profit in Bull & Bear Markets with Technical Analysis

Curtis M. Arnold

"For the savvy investor" *Business Today*

"The Bible of technical analysis !" *MBH Commodity Advisors, USA*

Rs. 280/- No 662-X

Using Technical Analysis: *The Basics*

Cliford Pistolese

"Enables investors to take profitable decisions" *Business India*

Rs. 190/- No. 391-4

International Encyclopedia of Technical Analysis

Joel G. Seigel, Jae K. Shim,
Anique Qureshi, Jeffrey Brauchier

A-to-Z of Technical Analysis for trading stocks, derivatives and Commodities

Rs. 495/- No. 648-4

The Psychology of Technical Analysis

Tony Plummer

"One of the most exciting and innovative books on technical analysis" *Market Technician, U.K.*

Rs. 395/- No. 492-9

Elliott Wave Explained

How to use the Elliott Wave System to Forecast Future Share Price Movements: Robert C. Beckman

A superb introduction to one of the best-performing forecasting methods ever devised. With real-life examples.

"Robert Beckman's forecasts of major market movements . . . have shifted huge sums of money as institutions have been jerked into action." *Investor's Review, USA*

Rs. 395/- No. 532-1

Martin Pring on Market Momentum

BEST SELLER

Martin J. Pring

The A-to-Z of market momentum by one of the world's foremost technical analysts.

"Definitive guide to momentum" *Trader's Press, USA*

"A Bible on momentum" *The Economic Times*

Rs. 395/- No. 570-4

Technical Analysis for Futures Traders

A Comprehensive Guide to Analytical Methods, Trading Systems and Technical Indicators

Darrel R. Jobman

Technical Analysis for Futures Traders is a definitive book on the application of technical analysis for trading.

Rs. 495/- No.577-1

Candlestick Charting Explained

BEST SELLER

Timeless Techniques for Trading Stocks and Futures

Gregory L. Morris

"Arguably the best book on candles, tying them together, with technical analysis ..." *Technical Trends, USA*

Rs. 395/- No. 240-3

Indian Mutual Funds Handbook

A Guide for Industry Professionals and Intelligent Investors

Sundar Sankaran

This comprehensive handbook by an expert lays out the working of Indian mutual funds, their operational and regulatory mechanisms, the advantages and limitations of investing in them along with suitable approaches to personal financial planning. The author's experience of handling hundreds of training programmes ensures an engaging and easy to understand approach to mastering the subject.

Highlights: Benefits of investing in mutual funds; how they compare with bank and company fixed deposits and other investment avenues ■ The different types of equity, debt, balanced and liquid scheme available for investment — and the rewards and risks each one entails ■ NAV — what it reveals, its calculation and finer nuances ■ The costs of investing in mutual funds — loads, expenses and management fee.

"I recommend this book to everyone who wants to make informed investment decisions"
Shekhar Sathe, Kotak Mahindra

"The best book for understanding (Indian) mutual funds"
M. Subramanian CEO India, Barclays Bank, plc.

"If you think you know everything about mutual funds, read the book to find out how much you don't know!"
Prof. G. Sethu, Dean, UTI Institute of Capital Markets

Rs. 190/- **No. 536-4**

SPECIAL LOW PRICE EDITION

The New Commonsense Guide to Mutual Funds: Mary Rowland

This book shows you how you can best use mutual funds to meet your financial goals.

This is a top-selling book, by one of America's pre-eminent financial journalists. It cuts through the hype and confusion surrounding mutual funds and tells you exactly what you need to know.

"Remarkable! A splendid combination of wisdom and simplicity" *John C. Bogle*

"Nuts and bolts of fund investing, plus an excellent section on measuring an investor's tolerance for risk"
The Wall Street Journal, USA

Rs. 280 **No. 479-1**

SPECIAL LOW PRICE EDITION

INTERNATIONAL BESTSELLER

The Winning Portfolio

How to Choose the Best Mutual Funds: Paul B. Farrell

Farrell's strategy is easy-to-follow and will help you diversify your portfolio while shielding your investment in mutual funds from market downturns.

'An easy-to-follow roadmap for maximizing your mutual fundε profitε ... both rational and intuitive" *Brian Murray*

"Eminently practical advice for selecting mutual funds"
John C. Bogle

Rs. 190/- **No. 481-3**

POINT AND FIGURE CHARTING

The Complete Guide to Point and Figure Charting

A Manual of Charting and Trading Techniques

Heinrich Weber and Kermit Zieg

"Point-and-figure is the best of all technical analysis methods," assert the expert authors and demonstrate in this book how this method produces consistent and reliable trading profits.

"A natural 'primer' for new users, (with) plenty for the more experienced." *Dave Baker, PFscan Charting Software*

""A masterpiece of clarity ... puts most treatments of technical analysis to shade" *Alexander Davidson*

Rs. 595/- **No. 670-0**

ASSET ALLOCATION

Asset Allocation and Portfolio Optimization

Warren E. Bitters

A study of the late 1980s suggested that asset allocation policy alone explained as much as 93.6% of investment return. It implied that market timing and security selection are far less influential factors in determining total return. The startling conclusion led to tremendous focus on the importance of asset allocation in the investment management process. This book provides a comprehensive survey of the increasingly sophisticated methods which have since been developed and applied in this area.

Rs. 395/- **No. 571-2**

INVESTMENT BASICS

Investing for Beginners

Kathy Kristof

This book is simple. It's straightforward. It skilfully guides you step-by-step to investment success. Highlights: ■ Investment Risks and Rewards ■ Your Starting Point ■ How to pick stocks ■ Investing in Bonds ■ Mutual Funds Primer.

"Smart, sensible advice . . . a road map to financial success without gimmicks or secret formulas."

Los Angeles Times, USA

Order No. 482-1
Price: Rs. 190/-

How to Manage Your Investment Risks & Returns

An Essential Self-teaching Guide for Every Investor

David L. Scott

The secret of successful investing lies rather in understanding and controlling the risk involved in any investment. Step-by-step this book shows you how to control your investment risks.

"An object lesson." *The Economic Times*

Order No. 394-9
Price: Rs. 145/-

INVESTMENT OPTIONS

Profitable investment in shares : *A Beginner's Guide*

S. S. Grewal & Navjot Grewal

This hugely popular book tells you the basic principles and guidelines of profitable investment in shares. It also highlights the basic rules to follow in order to ensure reasonable safety of your capital. And it does all this in simple, clear language without resorting to jargon or technicalities. So, if are you one of those who wants to invest in shares but doesn't know quite how to go about it, then you can't do much better than starting with this book.

"Positively rewarding." *Financial Express*

Order No. 573-9
Price: Rs. 145

The Basics of Investing

Gerald Krefetz

The rapidly growing number of investment avenues often lead to confusion. In this book, an investment expert offers you the must-know principles, expert guidance and sensible solutions to invest your money profitably.

Order No. 446-5
Price: Rs. 190

The Basics of Stocks

Gerald Krefetz

You probably need to invest in shares to achieve long-term capital appreciation. What you also need to do is to do it right. In simple, easy-to-follow steps, a Wall Street expert offers you solutions for making the most out of investing in shares.

Order No. 448-1
Price: Rs. 190

The Basics of Bonds

Profitable Fixed-Income Investing

Gerald Krefetz

The lure: bonds and other fixed income investment avenues offer relatively greater safety of capital with predict-able returns.

This book by a U.S. investment expert will assist you in making intelligent decisions about your fixed-income investing.

Order No. 447-3
Price: Rs. 190

The Basics of Speculating

How to Speculate Most Profitably with Your Hard-Earned Money

Gerald Krefetz

This book tackles in detail the most popular financial instruments used for speculation: stocks, bonds, options, futures, commodities, precious metals and foreign exchange, etc.,

Order No. 449-X
Price: Rs. 190

INVESTMENT

Vision PROFESSIONAL INVESTING Series

GREAT VALUE EDITION 80% LOWER THAN INTERNATIONAL PRICE

The Financial Analyst's Handbook: *What Practitioners Need to Know:* Mark Kritzman

Mark Kritzman shows financial analysts and serious investors how to employ both sophiscated tools as well as common sense when evaluating past results and projecting future performance. Objective, practical and essential, the book covers the key concepts, methodology, and strategies inherent to thorough and rigorous investment analysis.

"Covers the key tools of modern investment practice . . . valuable volume"
William F. Sharpe, Nobel Prize Winner

"Kritzman explains the tools in the financial analyst's toolbox with astounding clarity" *Gary L. Gastineau*

Rs. 395/- **No. 563-1**

Vision PROFESSIONAL INVESTING Series

GREAT VALUE EDITION 80% LOWER THAN INTERNATIONAL PRICE

Advanced Approaches to Stock Selection

Ross Paul Bruner, editor

This book explores contemporary investment concepts and tools for improving the stock selection process. The expert contributors examine various investment strategies organized around growth, value, size and sector rotation from a number of different perspectives. Price-momentum strategies, such as covariance and factor analysis, are also explored.

Rs. 395/- **No. 572-0**

Stock Market Logic

Norman G. Fosback

Some investors, utilizing more sophisticated approaches than the public at large, can earn above-average returns, year in and year out." This book will show you how.

"A brilliant book ... should be read by everyone interested in the market" *The Bull & Bear Magazine, USA*

"Amcng the modern classics in stock market literature. A veritable bible" *Miami Herald, USA*

Rs. 280/ **No. 440-6**

GREAT VALUE EDITION 80% LOWER THAN INTERNATIONAL PRICE

Investing Under Fire

Winning Investment Strategies from the Masters for Bulls, Bears, and Bewildered Investors

Alan R. Ackerman, editor

The initial years of the 21st century have thrown up for investors a most complex cycle of uncertainty with the additional risks posed by terrorism and political turbulence added to normal market volatility.

In *Investing Under Fire* a most distinguished assembly of world's leading investment managers review the issues contemporary investors need to consider for investment success. They offer invaluable topical and timeless lessons on controlling risk and selecting profitable investment opportunities:

■ James Awad on small-cap stocks; ■ Vanguard Group founder John Bogle on mutual funds; ■ American Express Financial Advisors' Craig Brimhall on wealth strategies ■ Value Line's Jean Bernhard Buttner on equity research ■ Oakmark Funds' Bill Nyger on the search for value.

"Artfully conceived collection . . . combines perceptive commentary on issues of the day with enduring insights on the nature of investing, markets, and human affairs. A valuable resource for investors seeking to understand the forces at play today" *Lynn Sharp Paine, Professor, Harvard Business School.*

Rs. 395/- **No. 567-4**

Stock Market Probability

How to Predict Future Events and Improve Your Stock Market Returns using Statistical Techniques

Joseph E. Murphy

This book presents a unique and innovative approach that combines investment analysis the market's probably future. The ability to estimate the various investment outcomes in advance will lead to better-informed decision.

"Brilliant . . . refines your decision-making" Business Today

"Clear, concise and informative . . . a non-traditional approach to stock market investing" Managing Director, Mitchell Hutchins, USA

Rs. 280/- **No. 200-4**

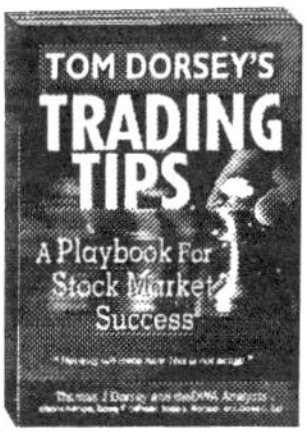

SPECIAL LOW PRICE EDITION
INTERNATIONAL BESTSELLER

Tom Dorsey's Trading Tips

Thomas J. Dorsey and the DWA Analysts

BEST SELLER!

Tom Dorsey's Trading Tips shows you how to invest confidently using point and figure charting, a proven, objective plan. You will learn: the essentials of stock selection, including a four-step chekclist for starting new positions, how to evaluate technical pros and cons, and how to accurately compare your stocks to market leaders.

"Reading Dorsey's recipe for success is a must" *Frank Capiello, President, McCullough, Andres, & Capiello, USA*

"A must-read for both the individual investor and the investment advisor" *Gino Toretta, Prudential Securities. Inc. USA*

Rs. 395/- **No. 480-5**

SPECIAL LOW PRICE EDITION
INTERNATIONAL BESTSELLER

Market Neutral Investing

Long/Short Hedging Strategies for Risk Reduction and Return Enhancement

Joseph G. Nicholas

In this book, U.S. investment expert Joseph G. Nicholas explores important new market-neutral approaches to return enhancement and risk reduction.

"A comprehensive road map to market-neutral investing" *Gene T. Pretti, Zazove Associates LLC, USA*

"A milestone publication, which broadens our knowledge and investment horizons — an invaluable reference tool for portfolio managers . . . and the investor community" *Sohail Jaffer,*

Rs. 395/- **No. 538-0**

SPECIAL LOW PRICE EDITION
INTERNATIONAL BESTSELLER

Stock Market Trading Rules

Fifty Golden Strategies

William F. Eng

BEST SELLER!

Stock Market Trading Rules will help you listen to the market. Fifty "Rules," each one a strategic gem, show you how to survive and succeed in the marketplace.

Each of the 50 rules is clearly explained and illustrated with examples of what works, what doesn't and why.

"A great collection of trading rules, and how to apply them to varying market conditions" *CompuTrac, Inc., USA*

Rs. 225/- **No. 343-4**

SPECIAL LOW PRICE EDITION
INTERNATIONAL BESTSELLER

Swing Trading

A Guide to Profitable Short-Term Investing

Marc Rivalland

Swing trading is a method of profiting from the stock market's short-term upswings and downswings. And since such short-term swings are an ever-present phenomenon, knowledgeable swing traders can make money all the time, whether the market is going up or down — or, even, sideways.

Based on the author's two-decade trading experience, this book is packed with expert guidance on a disciplined approach to profitable short-term trading — and one by which you can make money both during the market's upswings and downswings.

"Marc Rivalland offers amazing new insight, clarity and refinement to Gann swing charts" *Ashwani Gujral, Author of the bestseller book* How to Make Money Trading Derivatives

"You can make far greater profits (by trading) swings than in any other way" *W. D. Gann, Legendary Trader*

Rs. 495/- **No. 666-2**

SPECIAL LOW PRICE EDITION
INTERNATIONAL BESTSELLER

Market Masters

How Successful Traders Think, Trade and Invest & How You can Too!

Jake Bernstein

■ Play your own game. ■ Don't expect immediate results. ■ Do your homework. ■ Don't force trades. ■ Develop discipline, perseverance and willingness to accept losses.

These are just a *few* of the dozens of winning tips you'll find in *Market Masters.* What does it take to succeed? What do winners have in common? How can their experiences help you succeed?

According to Jake Bernstein, great traders are created, not born. Those who lack discipline, persistence and self-confidence lose the never ending challenge of trading profits. But those who survive the battle by using the tools of the masters enjoy the fruits of consistent success.

***"Bernstein has done it again! Market Masters* ranks among the greatest trading books ever"** *Commodities Educational Institute, USA*

Rs. 395/- **No. 411-2**